WHEN GENERALS FAILED
The Chinese Invasion
(Abdication from Battle: Tawang, Sela and Bomdila - 1962)

This book is published under the auspices of
the General Palit Military Studies Trust

Attention Authors

'We Convert Fighters into Writers'. That's the motto of Manas Publications since more than four decades. Our message to the world is that India can win the battle not only by the bullet but also by the pen. There is no dearth of intellectuals in our country, but their knowledge is confined to them only. No sincere effort has been made by any other publisher to channelise their knowledge in national interest. That is why the talent of a large number of intellectuals remains latent. An author transforms his knowledge into a manuscript, and it is our job to spread his/her knowledge by converting it into a beautiful book. For over four decades, Manas has been motivating the intellectuals by publishing their manuscripts and would like to publish your manuscript too. If you or your colleagues have any manuscript ready for publication or are working on it, kindly contact us with detailed synopsis and list of contents. We will transform your work into a valuable publication. If you wish, we can also suggest you the suitable subjects for writing the books related to your area of expertise. Manas is known for its publishing quality and commitments. We take utmost care in production and give wide publicity to the book as well as its author through our national and international distribution network.

WHEN GENERALS FAILED

The Chinese Invasion

(Abdication from Battle:
Tawang, Sela and Bomdila - 1962)

Brig. Darshan Khullar (Retd.)

Foreword by

Field Marshal Sir John Chapple, GCB CBEDL

Formerly 2nd K.E.O. Gorkhas and
Chief of the General Staff, 1988-1992

Manas Publications
New Delhi - 110002

MANAS PUBLICATIONS
(We Convert Fighters into Writers)
(Publishers, Library Suppliers, Importers & Exporters)
4402/5-A, Ansari Road (Opp HDFC Bank)
Darya Ganj, New Delhi-110 002 (India)
Off. (23260783, 23265523, Fax: 011-23272766
E-mail: manaspublications@gmail.com
manaspublications@yahoo.com

Third Impression 2013 (FP 1999)

Due to non-availability of good quality photographs/diagrams, which are old and have great historical importance, the publisher does not take any responsibility of their good quality reproduction in spite of best efforts.

ISBN 81-7049-098-7
₹ 495/-

Designed at
Manas Publications

Printed in India at
RK Offset, Delhi
and published by Mrs Suman Lata for
Manas Publications, 4402/5-A,
Ansari Road (Opp HDFC Bank),
Darya Ganj, New Delhi-110002 (INDIA)

This book is dedicated to the memory of
Colonel Bhupinder Singh, our lion-hearted
Commanding Officer, under whom I overcame the
fear of committing mistakes

Foreword

The actions of military forces in the North-Eastern Frontier regions of India in 1962 are still neither well known nor well understood. A good deal has been written but much of it has been motivated by concern about reputations and responsibilities - the reputation often being that of the author; the responsibility being some one else's.

The topography of the area Tawang-Sela-Bomdila is now easy to understand. Clearly it was not well known to the defence planners of India at the time. Thus the actual course of events in this sector during a comparatively short period of time has always been difficult to unravel. This book makes it much easier to understand and also makes the story of the precipitous withdrawal of the Indian Army formations more coherent, that is to say which cause had what effect, than it probably was to the participants.

Therefore a much fuller story emerges. It traces the main events, interspersed with illuminating excerpts from the highest level of Chinese military and political thinking. It also uses to dramatic effect the personal interludes of the author. These not only add great colour and authenticity to the narrative but they do not avoid comment on the less praiseworthy action both of the author himself and those in his immediate vicinity. His own actions are therefore recounted with both honesty and objectivity. This enhances the value of his comments on the actions and motives of others.

The author was a very junior officer at the time. He knows that he could not have seen everything or known much of the higher directions of affairs. However his observations about the conduct of a famous fighting formation are dramatic, vivid and rather saddening.

At the time this debacle took place, my own battalion in the British Army had just finished serving in 48 Infantry Brigade, and moved to 63 Infantry Brigade. It had fought before my time during World War II in 4th Indian Division, as part of 7 Infantry Brigade. There is a special poignancy therefore for me about this account since we retained some of these Brigade titles by directly recreating them in our Army. When I was Adjutant to my own battalion in 48 Brigade we were facing China across the Hong Kong border. I do not know how we would have fared if put to the test, but I do know that I am glad we were not.

Field Marshal Sir John Chapple, GCB CBE DL
formerly 2nd K.E.O. Gorkhas
and Chief of the General Staff 1988-1992

Preface

One of my desires in life had been to write on the 1962 Sino-Indian war in Kameng sector, the scene of battle where I was one of the many minor participants. Odd as it may seem, I have some very happy memories of that period.

I had a threefold aim in writing this book. The first was to demolish the impression that the Indian Army in 1962 was in any way an inferior force. I do not say that we could have won the war. There is no way that the outcome in Ladakh and Walong sectors, where the showing of Indian troops was plucky to say the least, could have been different; but it was in Kameng sector, where the Chinese had gambled and stuck their neck out once they decided to cross the Tawang Chu, that we could have foiled their plans. If only there had been a great general and a few good brigadiers on the Indian side to seize the opportunity, or say if the Vietnamese had been in our place, the tables could well have been turned on the Chinese. I am aware I am writing this with the benefit of a fair amount of hindsight and many analysts will scoff at this assertion, but I hope to prove my point in the course of this book. The tragedy is that Kameng was the one sector where Indians could have defeated the enemy, or at least given him a bloody nose; and yet it is here that we suffered our most humiliating defeat. It was a very costly failure of the high command.

My second aim was to analyse the Indian psyche and the failure of the high command, by focusing on the 1962 war in the overall historical context. For some reason the Henderson Brooks Report continues to be kept under wraps, which is unfortunate because there is a danger of it being confined into the dustbin of history after a few years and who knows that may precisely be the motive. Haven't we heard the of repeated pontification in the Indian Army that 1962 will never be repeated ? The lessons this short war has given us are too valuable to be forgotten or wished away simply because they may be embarrassing, and unpleasant. Fifty years of independence ought to have given us the self-assurance to face certain hard facts about ourselves in an objective and positive manner.

My third and final aim was to recount my own personal experience of the 1962 war because there is tremendous nostalgia. There was great human drama -- poignant moments, heroism of junior leaders as also cowardice of some (mostly the seniors), pathos, touches of irony, wit and humor. There was also great suffering, which I did not witness or undergo, not because I was able to run faster to the rear than others but because I was plain lucky. I do dare to say that I enjoyed this war. So far fifty per cent of the books have been written in self-justification propelled by guilty consciences, and the others are chiefly of academic interest. As for me, I was just a happy subaltern at the time and in tremendous love with the army. Accordingly the postcript of the book has been devoted to the 'lessons' from the 1962 War. It takes a wider historical view and alludes to actions before and after 1962. Their inclusion is relevant to give the book its proper perspective and weightage.

Every book has a starting point. In this case it was the 'General Palit Military History Trust'. I had served as a Platoon Commander at the Indian Military Academy, Dehradun, when General Palit was the Commandant. I began my mountaineering career under him and it was a most timely break. In many other ways he has been my mentor. So, when *War in High Himalaya* came out in 1992, I wrote to compliment him for writing a masterpiece. When I mentioned to him that I was one of the participants of the 1962 war in the Kameng Division, he asked me whether I would like to do some research work on the operations fought there. I found the offer irresistible.

This book, accordingly, has been written as a mix of purely professional aspects laced with a subaltern's memoirs. On the face of it, they may seem quite unrelated but this is not so. While objectivity demands that one keeps the personal angle out of the text when dealing with hard-headed analysis of historical events, the human touch can only contribute to the theme's subjectivity. The risk of distraction is yet another hazard I wished to avoid and I hope, I have at the end been able to produce an account, which is balanced and interesting. My personal interpolations are also given. I hope they will be of sufficient interest to the reader to make recompense for the obtrusions.

Brig. Darshan Khullar (Retd.)

Acknowledgements

I am indebted to Major General D.K. Palit VrC, for his encouragement and editorial guidance and improving the quality of the text while ensuring that my views and perceptions remained intact, and for guiding me in my uninhibited approach to a delicate subject.

I thank my erstwhile seniors, colleagues and others as mentioned in the Bibliography for sharing their memories of '62 War with me. That I have not been able to recount certain events strictly as narrated by some of them has been an occupational hazard, as I had to reconcile conflicting versions; then there is my own recollection of the war in question. I make no pretensions to have written the absolute truth. I have followed a theme and accordingly recorded events as dispassionately and truthfully as possible. If there have been any inadvertent errors, the responsibility is entirely mine. I am aware that this book is bound to hurt some individuals, even a few that I interviewed. It has been a painful and an unpleasant task undertaken for the benefit of posterity.

I am grateful to Sun Xia and Chen Zhibin, the authors of *The Snows of the Himalaya: The True History of China India War'* for having taken the liberty to insert a few excerpts of their book in order to show the other side of the hill. I must thank Major General C.S. Nugiyal, UYSM, for making available the English translation of the said book.

I also express my gratude to Lieutenant Generals Baldev Singh and R K Sawhney, the erstwhile GOCs 4 Corps, and their lower formation Commanders and staff, specially Major General DP Singh, Brigadiers Pawan Langar, Jaisinghani, Jambusarwalla, Virender Sehgal, Colonel J. K. Khan and Major S Vijayan for their hospitality and help during my visits to Kameng district in April 1995 and September 1997. Mr PP Khrimey and DP Thongdok of Rupa were my companions during my journey to Morshing village. I wish to thank them also for helping me to glean first-hand accounts of the heroic sacrifice made by Lt.Col B Avasthy and his men at Lagyala Gompa which accounted for a few hundred dead of the Chinese.

My appreciation also goes to Brig Charanjit Singh, Additional Chief Engineer, HQ Western Command, and his staff for making fair copies of the maps. Any inaccuracies or errors if any are entirely the author's responsibility.

Finally I thank my niece Sangita for assistance in preparation of the various maps and my younger son Ajay for suggesting the title of the book.

Brig. Darshan Khullar (Retd.)

Contents

Foreword

Preface 17

Acknowledgements 21

1. State Of The Army In 1962 27
2. The India-Tibet Border: A Historical Background 36
3. India Inherits A Legacy and Makes A Hash of It 41
4. Chinese Interlude-I 53
5. Topography of NEFA 66
6. The Hunter Becomes the Hunted : The Debacle at Nam ka Chu 74
7. Personal Interlude: Marching with Mules to Tawang 81
8. The Fall of Tawang 92
9. Personal Interlude : A Gunner's Shame 103
10. The Build-Up: Operations South of Tawang Chu 118
11. The Imperatives of Deployment 126
12. The Deployment of 4 Division 132

13.	Assessment of Chinese Strength And Offensive Pattern	140
14.	Chinese Interlude II: Snows of the Himalayas	146
15.	Personal Interlude: Honour Lost and Regained	152
16.	Conduct of Operations	158
17.	Activities upto 16 November 1962	168
18.	The Denouement : Sela Abandoned	181
19.	Headquarters Do a Bunk	201
20.	The Fall of Bomdila	211
21.	The Unilateral Ceasefire	232
22.	Postscript	234
	Glossary: Abbreviations and Indian and Tibetan Terms and Words	*248*
	Bibliography	*254*
	Index	*259*

Maps

1. India : Himalayan States And Sino-Indian Border
2. Ladakh : The Disputed Area
3. NEFA : September 1962
4. Battle of Nam Ka Chu: 20 October 1962
5. Battle of Bumla : 23 October 1962
6. Sela Sector: 16 November, 1962
7. Dirang Sector : 16 November 1962
8. Bomdila Sector 16-19 November 1962
9. Battle Of Nuranong --- The Chinese Suffer A Reverse
10. How The Withdrawal got Precipitated At Sela : 17/18 November 1962
11. Nyukmadung Ambush : 18 November 1962
12. 4 Rajputs' Action at Lagiyala Gompa 23 November 1962
13 Battle Of Thembang : 17 November 1962
14 Chinese Offensive South Of Tawang Chu: 16 - 20 November 1962

Some of our Learned Authors/Contributors

General S Padmanabhan; General VP Malik; Air Chief Marshal Fali Homi Major; Admiral Vishnu Bhagwat; Admiral Nirmal Verma; Admiral Arun Prakash; Vice Admiral Vijay Shankar; Lt Gen Arjun Ray; Dr A Sivathanu Pillai DRDO; Parvez Dewan IAS; Dhirendra Singh IAS; Kalyan Ray IAS; Sangeeta Goel IAS; HN Das IAS; Dr Surender Ghonkrokta IAS; Falguni Rajkumar IAS; G Sundaram IAS; PS Bhatnagar IAS; N Vittal IAS; PK Agrawal IAS; Sudhir S Baloeria IAS; NS Sisodia IAS; Dhirendra Singh IAS; Dr Yogendra Narain IPS; JK Bagchi IAS; TSR Subramanian IAS; Prakash Singh IPS; DC Nath IPS; Arun Prosad Mukherjee, IPS; Ajit Doval IPS; SP Mathur IPS; MK Dhar IPS; SK Datta IPS; HS Swan IPS; BR Lall IPS; PC Dogra IPS; DC Pathak IPS; ML Kumawat IPS; Dr. S Subramanian IPS; RK Ohri IPS; RB Sreekumar IPS; Kalyan K Mitra IPS; RS Gupta IPS; K Koshy IPS; Kuldeep Khoda IPS; Ajay Kashyap IPS; Dr N Dilip Kumar IPS; Dr Nazrul Islam IPS; Dr DV Guruprasad IPS; AP Maheshwari IPS; Loknath Behera IPS; Dr NC Asthana IPS; PM Nair IPS; Dr Sundari Nanda IPS; Keshav Kumar IPS; Dr Prateep V Philip IPS; Muktesh Chander IPS; Dr PS Pasricha IPS; K Ragothaman - CBI; M Narayanan – CBI; VK Agarwal IRS; Virendra Gupta IFS; Lt Gen SK Sinha; Lt Gen Raj Kadyan; Lt Gen Mukesh Sabharwal; Lt Gen HB Kala; Lt Gen PC Katoch; Lt Gen Gautam Banerjee; Lt Gen Ashok Kapur; Vice Admiral Suresh Bangara; Lt Gen CK Kapur; Lt Gen NS Narahari; Lt Gen Chandra Shekhar; Lt Gen ML Chibber; Lt Gen Ashok Joshi; Lt Gen DB Shekatkar; Lt Gen SRR Aiyengar; Lt Gen Utpal Bhattacharyya; Lt Gen Kamal Davar; Lt Gen Amitav Mukherji; Maj Gen Nilendra Kumar; Maj Gen Vinod Saighal; Maj Gen VK Singh; Maj Gen Anjan Mukherjee; Maj Gen Raj Mehta; Maj Gen Samay Ram; Maj Gen Y Behl; Maj Gen GD Bakshi; Gen Deepak Kapoor; Air Marshal SR Deshpande; Air Marshal RC Bajpai; Air Chief Marshal PV Naik; Air Vice Marshal AK Tiwary; Air Cmde (Dr) CN Ghosh; Ambassador Kishan S Rana IFS; Cmde Ranjit B Rai; Capt (IN) Alok Bansal; VK Singal IRS; Sudha Raman; Brig Yash Mohan; Brig Trigunesh Mukherjee; Brig. MS Patial; Col PK Gautam; Col MS Jaswal; Col Anil Shorey; Lt Col Anil Bhatt; Lt Col SS Parihar; Lt Col Arun Jha; Dr Harsh Vardhan; Ratan Sharda, Sudhakar Raje; Dr RK Tiwari; Anuj Dhar, Journalist; Ranjit Kumar, Journalist; Rajeev Bhattacharya, Journalist; SK Vikram; Gopal Chowdhuri; Dr Pramod Sharma; Swati Sharma, etc.

1

State of the Army in 1962

It has become fashionable to dismiss the Indian Army of those days as unprofessional. My premise and perception are quite different. I believe our constant poor showing in warfare has got a lot to do with our Indian psyche, which hasn't really changed over the last two thousand years. We may say that the NEFA debacle was caused by political failure and interference, and by a bunch of bumptious generals who were novices in the art of warfare and higher direction of war. But then hasn't it always been so since the days of Alexander's invasion of India in 326 BC? Except for the defeat of Seleukus at the hands of Chandragupta Maurya in 305 BC, we have continuously suffered humiliating defeats at the hands of invaders. The cause has always been poor leadership of military commanders, treachery and self-destructive valour of the Kshatriyas and Rajput rulers. We can take stock of all our battles and we will end up drawing the same causes and the same lessons, whether it be any of the three battles of Panipat or that of Plassey or the 1962 Sino-Indian war. Some scholars have described this phenomenon as the Panipat syndrome and in a more general term it could be attributed to our Hindu ethos. Whether we like it or not, barring a few exceptions, our leadership calibre has been negative or self-destructive. I am discounting the 1971 Indo-

Pak war because technically speaking it was a war between the same people of one subcontinent and one origin. If there is an exception it is of Shivaji against the Moghuls. That was something refreshingly different; he prevailed by displaying mobility of mind and body, indigenous innovations of a maverick, ruses, cunning and audacity. He was Asia's first guerrilla leader. It's a pity he died prematurely and was never able to record his doctrines for the benefit of posterity. The other is Zorawar Singh of Maharaja Gulab Singh's army. In China they have Suntzu and Mao Tse-tung; the West has the Duke of Marlborough, Fredrick the Great, Napoleon, Clausewitz and, later, Liddel Hart and Fuller whose doctrines on warfare have been successfully applied by their people. The nearest we have come to all this is Kautilaya's treatise on 'State craft' and no wonder it was he who was the master brain behind Chandragupta Maurya's victory over Seleukus. Yes, there is the *Panchtantra*, a great treasure-trove of worldly wisdom which can be suitably applied by the military, but on warfare as such there has been almost a total blank. What a pity, because there has been no indigenous development of India's military thought which could adequately match the tactical and strategic skills of our successive invaders; and China has been the last of them. Grandeur and mindless bravery do not help win a war. In fact they become liabilities against a ruthless and cunning enemy. King Porus had arraigned a grand army. His vanguard comprised hundreds of elephants who he thought would trample all over the Greeks, but he ended up being routed because Alexander's cavalry was able to spear the elephants' feet. Writhing with pain, these mighty beasts turned about and fled from the battle causing havoc in their own army. One would have thought that later generations would have learnt the lesson, but right till the demise of the Moghul empire, elephants continued to dominate our military thinking, with disastrous results.

We are all regaled with the personal bravery and stupendous deeds of Prithvi Raj Chauhan, Rana Sangha, Rana Pratap and Tippu Sultan; by studying their battles and campaigns, you will find that they were doomed to failure, because basically, as far as tactics are concerned, they were no match for their adversaries. Add to this the mumbo jumbo of the *Ramayana* and the *Mahabharata*, an escapist Indian's fantasy world, where gods and goddesses perform superlative feats and provide a surfeit of substitute victories and much vicarious pleasure. The grand illusion has carried on over the centuries.

It is to the credit of the British that having discovered the finest soldierly attributes of the Indian warrior classes, they were able to mould the British Indian Army to become one of the finest fighting organisations in the world. We may fault them for being cunning, keeping our society divided, and for creating the myth of martial and nonmartial races, but there is little doubt that they were the best leaders we Indians have ever had. After the Second World War the ideal or the dream army was described as the one which would have Indian soldiers, British commanders and the German General Staff. In 1947, India inherited a great asset and a legacy in the form of the Indian Army. Its only handicap was that when the British left, whereas junior officers had gained valuable operational experience in World War II battles, there was a void in the senior ranks, in the higher direction of war, because they had been side-tracked. What had kept the Army going were the solid foundation and the traditions laid down by the British. A dynamic leadership would have adapted itself to the emerging security threats in terms of training, planning and preparations. Unfortunately most of our senior officers simply stagnated and, to top it all, we had a pseudo pacifier as our Prime Minister. In the Kashmir operations we had overjudged ourselves and drawn the wrong lessons. In any case, they were wars fought in the sub-continental culture -- a vastly different matter from fighting a sophisticated People's Liberation Army (PLA) with its own theory of warfare -- and probably the world's most motivated army in 1962.

The country had, just before the 1962 war, one of its ablest Army Chiefs, General KS Thimayya, D.S.O. Professionally experienced and hugely popular, he had warned the government of Chinese threat in the crucial period from 1957 onwards when tension between India and China was building up, but his advice was disregarded. When General Thimayya's popularity was at its highest, a book with the presumptuous title *Thimayya of India*, by Humphrey Evans, an American author, was published. Inspite of Thimayya having absolutely no political ambitions, it was only natural that politicians, given their inherent suspicion of the military, saw the book as a CIA-sponsored plant for propping up a military leader in India (General Ayub Khan having taken over power in Pakistan at that time). Nehru started intrigues within the top brass of the Army, and thus began the phenomenal, brief and tragic rise and fall of Lieutenant General BM Kaul, who was not only a fellow Kashmiri Brahmin but had many of the attributes of Nehru. He was in fact a Nehru acolyte in uniform, who would have been most suitable in any other profession than the army. But with his dynamism, personality and burning ambition, he became the lone shining star on the Indian Army's horizon. He wanted to change the role of a peace-time army from training for war to one engaged in the economic uplift of the country. He could well have also replaced Nehru in course of time and probably overthrown him in a military coup; but destiny is a great leveller. What is pertinent however is that Kaul had no war experience and was too emotional, erratic and wavering during crisis situations, like his patron Nehru; and hence most unsuitable to lead in war. But such is the irony of nature that often personal relationships, myths that get perpetuated, and misplaced values make competence an irrelevant issue. That is what was happening in India. Kaul acquired prestige and influence beyond his rank generating a good deal of jealousy and, as a result, certain cliques arose within the officer cadre. Things became worse in June 1959 when the government promoted Kaul to the rank of Lieutenant General against the recommendations of General Thimayya.

Mr. V.K Krishna Menon, a restless character, controversial, Nehru's chief adviser on foreign affairs and a close friend, had become India's high profile defence minister in 1955. Menon was a brilliant thinker, innovative but also overbearing and sarcastic. After an initial rapport, he antagonised the three Chiefs of Defence Services. However, he became close to General Kaul. This was a matter of convenience because Menon must have known of Kaul's unofficial direct access to Nehru on matters of defence. Between them they bred a fetid atmosphere in the higher ranks. Thimayya, finding himself increasingly humiliated, submitted his resignation on 31 August, 1959, but was prevailed upon by Nehru to withdraw it and, adding insult to injury, the latter after a few days roundly condemned Thimayya in Parliament. The prestige of the Army suffered greatly. Thimayya should have known better than to trust a politician. His own high stature and standing in the Army also went down and he never recovered it in his life-time. He then became a mere passenger. He was outwardly his good old jolly self, enjoyed his leisure and his shikar trips, and no doubt still gave frank advice to the government on military matters including the Chinese threat, which because of Nehru's perceptions came to be disregarded. But Thimayya must take his share of the blame, indeed in no small measure. Warning the government was one matter, but his responsibility didn't end there. It must be realized that he had tendered his resignation on purely personal grounds and not on the issue of government's neglect of defence preparedness.

Being a practical, realistic and experienced soldier, General Thimayya had also advised against military confrontation with China owing to the sheer one-sidedness of the contest, under the then prevailing conditions. He was adhering to the well-known maxim, 'Fight no unprepared engagements. Fight no engagement in which there is no assurance of victory'. But merely warning the government did not absolve the Army Chief of not preparing the Army to make the best use of the prevailing resources, which were far from scanty. Nothing should have prevented Thimayya from reorientating the Army's training, at least its staff and commanders, to gain enough knowledge about India's potential enemy, the PLA, its tactics and doctrines, and the difficulties likely to be faced by the Indian Army. He didn't need the government's permission for all this. You can't wish away a threat by saying that it is best avoided. Sane advice no doubt, but that was no excuse for perpetuating ignorance and unpreparedness. The fact is that as far as the Chinese threat was concerned, under Thimayya, the Indian Army by and large trundled along unconcernedly. It is axiomatic that his own demoralisation would affect the Indian Army's preparedness against the Chinese. It was the ancient streak of the Indian character manifesting itself -- it must be stated that even a man of Thimayya's character had turned negative at a crucial phase of Sino-Indian relations, however much as one hates to sully the reputation of India's finest Chief ever.

Thimayya's decline strengthened Kaul's position, and at the former's retirement in May 1961, Kaul was made the Chief of the General Staff, a post second only in importance to that of the Army Chief. But he went far beyond that; he became virtually the de facto Chief. He came to be admired by his supporters, whom he had nourished over the years, feared by the diehard brown sahibs, and held in awe by the others including the non-exerting Thapar who succeeded General Thimayya.

Nevertheless the young officers were keen and professional; and the men were the best disciplined and the hardiest of any other ranks in the world. It was basically a good army we had in 1962 -- which had won laurels in South Korea, Congo, Gaza and Indo-China. Its stock in international circles was high. The training in the academies, schools of instruction and the many regimental training centers, was excellent though conspicuous by a total omission of mention of Chinese tactics or threat in the curricula. It remained sub-continental in culture and outlook.

There were marksmen in every battalion who, using 303 bolt action rifles, could get all their shots into the bull's eye at 300 yards. The young officers were energetic and highly motivated. Inspite of the Army Chief having been brought down a few pegs in the order of precedence, there was great izzat in civvy street for military personnel. A career in the armed forces was by far the first choice of many youngsters. We had elitist schools, like Doon School, Lawrence School Sanawar, Mayo College in Ajmer and Bishop Cotton School, Shimla and many others, subscribing in substantial numbers to each course at the National Defence Academy, Khadakvasala, besides RIMC Dehradun and the four Military Schools at Chail, Ajmer, Belgaum and Bangalore, where it was almost mandatory to join the NDA. From the vibrant middle-class dominated towns of North India like Dehradun, Ludhiana and Jullundhar, the cream of the youth vied with each other for a place at Khadakvasala. During the Republic Day parades those days, the members of the marching column of the NDA were the toast of Delhi girls. In a way it would not be a wrong to say that the status of armed forces officers was akin to what is presently enjoyed by our test cricketers. Nutan, a top film star of the fifties, married Lieutenant Behal of the Navy. Captain Malhotra bagged the Princess Holkar of Indore and a few years later one of my friends, Captain Biloo Bath of the Guards swept a Nalagarh princess off her feet after a torrid love affair in Dehradun. There might have not been much money in the Army but there was much glamour. The businessmen were yet nowhere near attaining respectability in Delhi society's elite gatherings. The scene was no different in Bombay, Poona and other towns, which had a reasonable military presence. Defence services definitely formed the Beau Ideals of Indian society in the fifties and sixties.

Rehabilitation of retired officers was also more assured. Look around any major North Indian town and you will find the older generation of officers owning sprawling bungalows, allotted at very differential rates by the government. Things have changed only in the last two decades owing mainly to the population explosion, the socio-economic upsurge, the "mandalisation" of society, money power and corruption. In short there are too many others wanting a share of the cake. A lot more money has come into the hands of bureaucrats, politicians, businessmen, the petty officials and traders, and the Army man has become the odd man out. But that's a different story and not indeed a concern of this book. I merely bring it in to show that I joined the Army at a time when we subalterns lived on top of the heap. And the point I particularly wish to make is to dispel the misinformation about the poor state of the Army then, spread by people looking for alibis to cover up their shortcomings. Things are never perfect and as we shall see, the Chinese too had their problems; and they genuinely believed that the Indian Army was better equipped and trained. Nay ! Our good old destiny brought together at that particular period a group of generals who were most unsuited in matters of warfare, specially against the Chinese. But then it often seems to happen to us that way -- going by Operation 'Blue Star', Exercise 'Brasstacks' and the events in Sri Lanka in 1987-90. There is strong evidence that our leadership, where it counted, remained a suspect lot.

It is wrong to say that it was only Nehru's political bungling and Krishna Menon's interference that brought about the debacle in 1962. Politicians will always tend to confuse matters. It is the business of the generals, especially the COAS, to give correct advice and stand up against any stupid or unrealistic political instruction and, if overruled, to tender their resignation in a dignified manner. How many have done that except General K.S Thimayya -- and he also did only half-heartedly.

Reverting to the good old theme of unprofessionalism of the Indian Army in 1962, this is quite pertinent if you consider that there was a total absence of preparations to counter the Chinese threat. But what about the current charge that the present Army has become very careerist? Frankly, there is a thin line dividing the unprofessional and the careerist, but in both there is a failure to stand up against professional incompetence and high-handedness, the saving grace being that the public and the media are now better informed and they can't be fooled easily. If our generals are timid, and there is the zero error syndrome that careerism and stiff competition help nourish and which encourage play-safe attitudes, yes-manship, and eliminate dissent and initiative, and when the forthright and also mavericks seldom rise beyond middle ranks, there is the risk that the flawed leadership will come to wield real power again and the country will be let down by it. There was a happy departure in the decade following the 1962 debacle, when strong characters did gain a brief ascendancy in the Army, and self-assured leaders like Kumaramanglam, Sam Manekshaw, Candeth, Prem Bhagat, Sagat Singh, Sartaj Singh, Inder Gill, Jacob and Eric Vas came on the scene and produced a happy outcome in 1971. We indeed need to thank the Chinese for the shaking they gave us. Prolonged peace can be quite hazardous for any army -- specially for us, given our national psyche, or call it the fatal streak in our character.

2

The India -Tibet Border

A Historical Background

Delineation of a nation's borders is only a century old concept in Asia. Earlier, it was a matter of sovereignty of rulers that shaded off into no-man's lands, providing 'a frontier' of separation rather than contact. India's Himalayan frontiers were marked by numerous zones of such no-man's lands which were either uninhabited, remote, inaccessible barren high altitude plateaus as in Ladakh, or thickly forested zones reaching upto snow-clad craggy peaks as in Eastern Himalaya. India's northern borders had remained peaceful for centuries. Trade, tolerance, religion, history, traditions and a modicum of autonomy enjoyed by buffer zones, and undisturbed tribal areas had helped to define the frontier, on both sides. Things changed after the British came on the scene.

During the nineteenth century, after Kashmir was added to the Empire, the British began consolidating and expanding their Indian empire and it was inevitable that they would head for a possible collision with two other powers -- Russia and China — vying for supremacy in Central Asia. In order to avoid the above, specially the Russian threat which was considered more menacing, the British began looking for buffer zones and thus began the phase of the 'Great Game', and adventurers and surveyors were sent out into the high regions to pre-empt Russia (and also China). It was a plucky but devious game, dictated at times by the perceptions of individual Viceroys and their advisers, and quite often the outcome was decided by the adventurers on the ground -- at their initiative and greed. During this period China's power waxed and waned with telling effect on the fate of Tibet, which was undoubtedly the most important buffer state with a 3520-kilometer common border with India.

China had always laid claim to a vague and disputable suzerainty over Tibet. However, as far as modern history is concerned, it was in 1720 when China, after driving out Mongol invaders from Tibet, claimed the suzerainty. But because of China's own turmoil on its mainland, for all practical purposes Tibet remained an independent theocracy under the Dalai Lama. In 1903, to thwart Russian influence in Tibet, the British dispatched a mission to Lhasa under Sir Francis Younghusband. Though the Dalai Lama himself had fled to Mongolia, a convention was signed with the principal officials of Tibet, whereby the Tibetans agreed to the opening of trading posts at Gyantse, Gartok and Yatung, and the stationing of a small British-Indian protection force in Tibet, as also pledging Chumbi valley for three years against an indemnity of Rupees twenty five lakhs. If the British had wanted they could well have annexed Tibet at this juncture but this would have been a highly uneconomical proposition. In 1906, they went a step further and signed a treaty with China under which they agreed not to annex Tibet or interfere in its internal affairs and in return they were given the right to set up telegraph lines connecting their trading posts with India. China also confirmed the trading rights conferred by Tibetan officials in 1903. In 1907, Great Britain entered into a treaty with Russia. Chinese suzerainty over

Tibet came to be recognized and they also agreed not to enter into any direct negotiations with that country i.e Tibet.

In 1910, with the Manchu government beginning to assert its rights over Tibet, General Chao Erhfing, known for his ruthless military measures, occupied Lhasa and for a time established Chinese rule there forcing the harassed Dalai Lama to flee, this time to India. The pressure of the Chinese challenge came to be felt along the whole length of the Tibetan frontier from Gartok in the west to Rima in the east, and a Chinese threat from the North East became discernible. Government of India promptly ordered a survey of the borders between Tibet and North-East Frontier Agency area (the present Arunachal Pradesh) to bring about a more effective control and to thwart the Chinese designs. Hitherto the British had found it prudent to leave the tribes inhabiting these areas undisturbed and free. The new policy led to a series of clandestine explorations for determining tribal territories and Chinese encroachments. The most famous of these was by Captain FM Bailey of the Royal Engineers described in his book *No Passport to Tibet*. It was based upon his report that the British established a post at Walong to preempt the Chinese attempt to move down into Lohit Valley to try and force Mishmi tribals into submission. However, the main British interest lay in their tea gardens in rich Brahmaputra Valley south of the foothills. They established a convenient administrative responsibility by laying down the outer and inner lines. The inner line generally ran along the foothills and British subjects were prohibited to proceed beyond without a permit.

The Tibetans staged a revolt in 1911 and drove the Chinese out of their country. The Dalai Lama returned from India in June 1912, re-assumed full powers and by a declaration annulled the vassal-suzerain relationship between Tibet and China. This gave the British a grand opportunity to settle matters for good but Europe was at the brink of war and time was short. It was clear that China was bound to reassert her rights over Tibet once she regained her strength. They, therefore, called a tripartite conference at Simla in 1913, and invited the representatives of the governments of China and Tibet under the chairmanship of its Foreign Secretary, Sir Henry McMahon. The aim was to assure Tibet its requisite autonomy with the trade-off that it accept Chinese suzerainty. The conference carried on in periodic sessions till July 1914. Tibet was to be divided into two zones -- Outer and Inner Tibet -- with China enjoying suzerainty but with the proviso that Outer Tibet, comprising areas that included Lhasa, Shigatse, Chamdo and skirting the Indian frontier, would enjoy complete autonomy. China was also to abstain from sending troops, stationing civil or military officers or establishing Chinese colonies there. The 1360-Km long frontier across NEFA was also fixed during this conference along a boundary that came to be known as the McMahon line which as well as the limits of Outer and Inner Tibet were attached to the convention papers. The representatives of all three countries initialled it.

However, problems cropped up when the new KMT Chinese government refused to ratify the agreement. Their objections were confined to the boundary between Inner and Outer Tibet; and since no objection was raised on the McMahon line, by implication this was taken as Chinese acceptance of the same. For the Tibetans, it meant that the Chinese had lost an opportunity to become their acknowledged suzerain and they were therefore now free to come to any mutual agreement with the Indian government. Consequently the agreement signed by the representatives of India and Tibet went further by barring the Chinese Government from enjoying any rights under the convention so long as its signature to the document was withheld. Ivan Chen, the Chinese representative, had some hard explaining to do to his authorities for the snafu i.e his initialling the convention maps.

Once World War I broke out, the Simla convention receded from the British-Indian Government's attention. A decade later they tried to revive it but China in her characteristics manner remained intractable. The convention therefore remained secret and was not published till 1929. From 1937 onwards, official maps depicting the McMahon line came to be widely circulated. At no stage then, and for nearly two decades thereafter, was any objection raised by the Chinese.

In 1944 the Japanese forces invaded Nagaland and Manipur in North-East India and a threat was perceived to the adjoining areas. Till then, the British had taken very few steps to extend effective control over NEFA. Assam Rifles posts now came to be established at Dirang, Walong and a few other places.

3

India Inherits A Legacy and Makes a Hash of It

The Sino-Indian border dispute is a legacy the British left to India. It was not at all a happy situation for a poor country to be saddled with. It was all very well for the British, then a global power, to carry on with their grand strategic designs and machinations, but for a weak and inexperienced India the task was far from easy. Yet a resolute and pragmatic political leadership could have done a reasonably good job; but this was not be once Jawahar Lal Nehru with his confused thinking entered the scene. With him around, China didn't really need to worry. Inspite of all his intellect and international fame, or possibly because of these, he continuously succumbed to the ruses the Chinese set up and in the end he became his own victim of deception and rushed an unprepared India into a humiliating war, the worst debacle suffered by India since the battle of Plassey in 1757.

Geographically the India-Tibet border can be divided into three sectors; the eastern consisting of the erstwhile NEFA and the present day Arunachal Pradesh, the central comprising Uttar Pradesh and Himachal Pradesh, and the western or the Ladakh sector from Demchok to the

Karakoram pass. Of the three, the central sector posed the least problems barring a few minor pockets viz Barahoti and Kaurik area. Geographically the Greater Himalaya crestline made for a very convenient border. Politically, the Indian hill rajas had established traditional borders with Tibet with which they had close trade and cultural ties.

There was much confusion as far as the boundary in Ladakh was concerned. The Dogra conquest of Ladakh under Zorawar Singh had many ramifications, compounded further by the surveys and exploits of the 'Great Game' adventurers which resulted in various claim lines drawn from time to time more or less in an arbitrary manner. Of these, the line drawn by a survey of India minor official named W H Johnson based upon his clandestine survey was to prove very contentious as this placed the Aksai Chin, an uninhabited and godforsaken barren plateau at 17000 feet, within India. It was inevitable that a strong China, knowing its strategic value as their only link between Sinkiang and West Tibet, would disregard the Indian claim. On the other hand China had no historical claim on it either. The Aksai Chin is highly inaccessible from the Indian side, it had absolutely no strategic value for Britain, who were obsessed with the Russian motives in Tibet. Nor was Aksai Chin ever known to ancient historians of India or mentioned in the Vedas and the Purans.

The eastern sector was the remotest of the three, but here the McMahon line should have obviated any dispute. However, in the event the border here flared up once the heat came to be felt in Ladakh. Nehru's reluctance to trade off Aksai Chin with China's acceptance of the McMahon line was to prove costly.

In the autumn of 1949, Mao Tse-tung's communist forces defeated the Kuomintang forces of Chiang Kai-shek and he proclaimed a People's Republic of China. India was the second country to accord recognition, Burma being the first.

China immediately began reasserting her authority over her outlying provinces. In October 1950, the Chinese People's Army entered Tibet at several points along its eastern border. They quickly routed the primitive Tibetan army and seized major eastern passes. In the north-west, they penetrated even deeper and captured the major Tibetan garrisons of Rudok and Gartok by surprise. On 23 May, 1951, they signed an agreement with Tibet establishing Chinese suzerainty over it and guaranteeing its regional autonomy. The Chinese army entered Lhasa on 19 November, 1951.

The Chinese thrust into Tibet in October 1950, sent alarm bells ringing in India. Sardar Vallabhbhai Patel, Deputy Prime Minister in Nehru's cabinet, wrote a detailed letter to Nehru on November 7, 1950, about a month before his death, warning him of the threat from Lhasa once the Chinese occupied Tibet.

There are two opposing schools of thought: one holds the view that given China's military power, which was vastly superior to India's, there was very little India could have done other than live with the realities and adopt a pragmatic attitude towards the Chinese presence in Tibet. The second (moral) school of thought rejects this defeatist and passive attitude. After all there was the 1914 Simla convention binding India and Tibet, which barred China from meddling in Tibet's affairs. If India could go to the UN over Kashmir, which it need never have done, what was stopping it from doing so now over Tibet? Truman and other western leaders would surely have acted very favourably in India's favour. It at least would have imposed a fair amount of caution on China, who had to reckon with the Kuomintang in Formosa besides her major occupation in Korea.

As a follow up of Sardar Patel's letter, a committee was set up under the Deputy Minister of Defence, Major General Himmatsinji, the Army being represented by its Chief of

General Staff, Lieutenant General Kulwant Singh. The committee's recommendations formed the basis for the development and administration of the border regions and their defence. These were approved by the cabinet and the departments concerned were asked to ensure implementation. But it was easier said than done, given the difficulties the Himalayan terrain presented.

Jawahar Lal Nehru was a man of many delusions. Howsoever great might have been his personality and stature in the world, there is little doubt that he was not well up in matters of strategy. He should have known that once Tibet was lost as a buffer state, India's security problems would increase a hundred fold. The Himalayas, which had been India's natural guardians in the north, far from remaining impregnable would pose grave logistical problems if and when the need arose to defend them. The Arab and the Camel parable aptly describes the situation as it unraveled in Tibet.

Nehru had been a great admirer of China and its ancient culture. A closer look at history will reveal that this so-called ancient cultural relations perception is a myth. Nehru invented (or deluded himself that there was) an ancient friendship between the two countries. In fact hardly any Chinese (except for a handful of Han Buddhists) ever visited the land of the Buddha in the first millenium. No Indian ever went to China - he wouldn't have been allowed in by the Son of Heaven's court of the Celestial empire. The Manchus, after they conquered the Han people, also persisted with this racial prejudice. Things are about the same even now. Nehru was keen that the so-called ancient cultural relations between the two countries be revived; but at what cost? A study of the modern history of China and a few other of Mao's works would have revealed that besides Tibet, China claimed large parts of Ladakh, pockets across central sector, the entire NEFA as also Sikkim and Bhutan. In Mao's words,

"China was a wounded civilisation which had suffered numerous humiliations in the past at the hands of the imperialists. That period had ended and now China was determined to correct the wrongs including restore its legitimate borders." There was a rider. China would wait for the ripe time to make its various moves. Anyone who is familiar with the Chinese psyche could tell you of their secretive and inscrutable character and their inherent patience. Mao believed in the maxim that power flowed from barrel of a gun. He had earlier ridiculed Nehru as a lackey of the imperialist powers and poured scorn on the policy of nonalignment so championed by India. Did Nehru believe that he would ever convert China to his pacifist ways by the force of his personality, his championing of China's cause in UNO and lastly turning a blind eye on Chinese consolidation of its control in Tibet? He was banking on non-existent Chinese goodwill and sense of gratitude. Unwisely he had made it a personal and an emotional issue and was certain that when it came to the delineation of the border, the Chinese would accept the Indian claims. He was being naive. It needed no genius to appreciate the importance of the Aksai Chin to China, but military science was a closed book to Nehru.

Questioned in parliament about the India-Tibet boundary in November 1950, Nehru had stated that the McMahon line was not negotiable, irrespective of what was shown on the Chinese maps. As far as China was concerned whenever questioned on the border problem, Peking kept giving evasive answers, to the temporary but false relief of Nehru, as it helped him to avoid face the hard reality.

The early fifties marked a period of great cordiality between India and China. Wide publicity was given to it. Known as the 'Hindi-Chini Bhai Bhai' phase, it caused much euphoria among the Indians. It was a one way traffic with India being at the giving end. On 29 April, 1954, India and

China signed an agreement over Tibet on matters of trade, pilgrimage to Mount Kailas and Indian missions in Tibet. Boundaries were not discussed other than an indirect reference to the portion that lay along Uttar Pradesh and Himachal Pradesh. At the same time, India chose to gift away her extra-territorial rights in Tibet without a quid pro quo. She surrendered her postal, telegraph, telephone and rest house facilities and recognised China's sovereignty (not merely suzerainty) over Tibet -- the agreement clearly referring to Tibet as a region of China.

The Indian government was surely well aware that China had refused to ratify the 1914 Simla convention. India had a strong bargaining position. The least it could have done was to obtain Chinese recognition of India-Tibet boundary. If not that then the boundary issue should have been discussed in a straight-forward manner so that China would have been made to express her views in unambiguous terms. India's was an escapist's attitude. It helped the Indian government to project the Chinese silence on the subject as an acceptance of India's stand. The Chinese on the other hand were in no hurry to open the border question. They had learnt from experience that such matters should be negotiated from a position of strength. (Much later when Chou En-lai was queried on their silence on the border issue, he quipped, 'The time was not right.')

All that India got in return for her mild proddings were the five principles of coexistence (Panchsheel) contained in the preamble to the (much flaunted) agreement, with the result that the real contents (India's meek surrender) became obscured and the Indian public's attention was side-tracked.

It has been said that by then Nehru's suspicions had been aroused about Chinese intentions. Yet he acted most deviously. On the one hand he strongly defended the April 1954 agreement, and on the other gave instructions to set up frontier posts to oversee India's northern borders. He thereby sent wrong signals to both sides. He kept the Indian public in the dark and at the same time warned the Chinese of future Indian intentions. Nehru's apologists hold the view that he was trying to buy time and was keen to avoid any armed confrontation with China for at least twenty years, to enable an impoverished India to build up its economy. If so, that motive was unexceptionable; but why did he keep parliament and the Indian people in the dark about the Chinese intrusions, which were increasing by the year? With his airy-fairy talks (mostly off the cuff) he kept leading India deeper and deeper into a trap, more of his creation than of the Chinese.

Within months of signing the 1954 agreement, the Chinese laid claim to Barahoti (near Niti Pass in the central sector) five km inside India, since Tibetans used to come to graze their yaks in its meadows in the summer. The fact is that the Chinese were moving much faster than the Indians in bringing the border areas under military control. By 1956, they had established checkposts on the entire boundary from NEFA to Ladakh and garrisoned troops in the rear. The two countries were moving inexorably on a course of confrontation under a facade of friendship.

It was the Aksai Chin that sparked off the trouble. In 1957, the Government of India was informed by its ambassador in Peking about the Chinese having completed the construction of a motorable road through this area, which as we have seen was claimed by both the countries (though never occupied by either). Nehru withheld this information from parliament and public, but the Director, Intelligence Bureau, on Nehru's instructions sent out two patrols to the Aksai Chin to investigate the circumstances in the summer of 1958, the rigours of winter having prevented any earlier action. One of them was captured and later deported by the Chinese. The other patrol after a successful mission confirmed the existence of the road. Protests and counter-protests followed. China at last let the cat out of the bag. While it agreed that their current maps were based upon the pre-liberation data, consultations they felt were needed between the two countries as the Sino-Indian boundary had never been delineated formally. China suggested maintenance of the status quo to avoid untoward clashes and incidents till discrepancies on both sides could be sorted out by mutual consultations. It was an alarming refutation of India's stand that the boundaries drawn on her maps were firm and not open to discussion. Nehru now resorted to a series of personal correspondence with Chou En-lai, which soon lost some of its cordiality and remained unproductive. China stressed on the status quo while India stuck to the status quo ante implying that China should first vacate the Aksai Chin, a precondition totally unacceptable to the Chinese.

Trouble was meanwhile brewing up in Tibet. The Khampa revolt spread to Central and Southern Tibet during the first half of 1959 inviting Chinese retaliation. Thousands of refugees crossed into India. On March 31, the Dalai Lama made good his escape and entered India via Tawang. He was warmly received and granted asylum by India. Nehru personally called on him in his temporary residence at Mussourie in the UP hills. There was great sympathy expressed by the Indian media for the Tibetan cause, greatly irking the Chinese. The Indian Government however, declared that the happenings in Tibet were an internal matter of China and hoped for a peaceful solution -- insufficient, however, to assuage Chinese feelings in the matter.

As a fall-out of the Khampa revolt on 25 August, 1959, the Chinese attacked an Indian post at Longju in the Subansiri Division of NEFA and overwhelmed it, causing some casualties. Both countries had their respective versions and accused the other of provocation. The Indian media reported the incident on 28 August. Nehru faced an angry and agitated Lok Sabha (Lower House of Parliament) that day. Caught in a bind, he now took the Lok Sabha into confidence and for the first time the House learnt about the boundary dispute and the Chinese road through the Aksai Chin. Gone was the pacifist Nehru. Just when the situation called for realism, caution and the blunting of jingoism of India's right wing, he began stealing its thunder. There is surely a psychological explanation for all this. Nehru had lost his convictions.

Soon after the Longju incident, the defence of NEFA was made the Army's responsibility, which was earlier the responsibility of a local force, the Assam Rifles, who were nevertheless to continue to man the border posts.

On 20 October, 1959, the Chinese ambushed a routine Indian patrol south of Kongka pass in Ladakh killing nine and capturing ten men. As in the past, China claimed that the Indians had intruded into their territory. A wave of anger swept across India. The defence of Ladakh, previously under the Intelligence Bureau, was now also handed over to the Army.

The attitudes on both sides hardened, yet neither side wanted a war. India was thoroughly unprepared, and as for China, the time was not yet ripe. They were prepared for a settlement but not on India's terms which denied them the Aksai Chin and other strategic areas in Ladakh like Chip Chap and Galwan Valleys.

In April 1960, Chou En-lai paid a week-long visit to India, his last. Enroute at Rangoon, he signed a boundary agreement with Burma that recognized the McMahon line as Burma's northern border. This was a broad enough hint, if Nehru needed any, about China's willingness to compromise. But Nehru who had got away with gifting away of Tibet to China in 1954 and for nearly a decade keeping his own people in the dark about there being a border dispute with China, had lost confidence in himself and failed to seize the initiative. Surely he could have convinced parliament and the public about the merits of give and take, specially when he should have been quite convinced of the Aksai Chin holding hardly any strategic importance for India. He had dished out many a fait accompli in the past and got away with them. Why then this hesitation at this critical juncture? The only explanation is that Nehru had now been driven into an inverted delusion. Prior to Chou En-lai's visit, Nehru had made an advance commitment to the Indian public not to compromise on any issue.

The only worthwhile result of Chou En-lai's visit was that both countries agreed to avoid border clashes. Both sides however, carried on with military preparations though the borders remained quiet and peaceful for more than a year i.e till the summer of 1961.

Nehru embarked on a "forward policy" in 1961. The idea was to push forward and site a string of border posts in Ladakh and NEFA to establish Indian claims on the ground, with instructions not to open fire unless fired upon by the Chinese. In Ladakh sector the Indian posts were to be interspersed between the ones established by the Chinese, including a few even to their rear. As far as NEFA was concerned, the aim was to establish presence all along the McMahon line. Unfortunately Indian maps were far from accurate and therefore map-reading was to prove problematic. China made it amply clear that she would retaliate in the east i.e along the McMahon line in case India pressed on with its designs in Ladakh sector. India ignored the warning, its leaders some-how convinced that China would never attack Indian posts, grossly miscalculating Chinese strength and intentions. It was a kind of military Satyagraha or a chess game of sorts without resorting to actual war, hoping that the other side would also play the game, with the border posts acting as pawns. Chinese patience was bound to run out in the end.

In the east, the "forward policy," code named Op 'Onkar' which could only begin in April 1962, owing to logistics problems, was to prove fatal. The western-most post (very near where the McMahon line joins the Bhutan border) was Che Dong in Namka Chu valley on the southern bank of a stream by that name. The commander of a patrol sent there was Captain Mahabir Prasad, of 1 Sikh, on loan to Assam Rifles. Accompanying him was an Intelligence representative (policeman). It must be understood that Che Dong, where the post was sited, was a good five kms north of the McMahon line whereas the post was to be actually sited at Dhola pass which was well south of the McMahon line. What prompted Captain Mahavir Prasad to cross the McMahon line and site the post at Che Dong was probably the availability of water, absence of snow and easier accessibility and the assertion of the Intelligence representative, who was emphatic that even the Thagla ridge, which was further north and dominated Nam Ka Chu valley and as yet not occupied by the Chinese, was Indian territory. The name of Dhola stuck, though it was a misnomer.

It was a tragedy of errors and it set in motion a chain reaction of events that were to end in disaster. One wonders what would have happened had Captain Mahabir Prasad stuck to the original instructions and occupied the actual Dhola post after clearing the snow or stamping it into a firm surface. Snow can always be melted to make water. Mountaineers are always doing it on their expeditions. One would think that Prasad's greater concern was the comfort of his men and may be the overbearing pronouncement of the Intelligence representative had further forced his hand. Tactical unsoundness of the post didn't seem to bother Prasad or any one higher up at this juncture because the Indian oracle (Mr Mullick, Director of the Intelligence Bureau) had given out that there was little likelihood of China going to war over a border problem.

General Niranjan Prasad, the GOC of 4 Infantry Division to whom the patrol commander made a personal report, was not happy with the erroneous siting of the post. He took no decision to rectify the mistake (IB's pronouncement must have been too daunting) and in typical play-safe fashion referred the matter to his superiors at Delhi who referred it to the government who ruled that the post must remain where it was . The Army brass showed its impotence. Indeed, it showed how a slip-up or over-zealousness on the part of some lowly officials can have disastrous consequences.

The Chinese were very sensitive about the Thagla ridge as it dominated their advance base at Le (their road-head) on the Tibetan side. In view of the earlier trouble at Khinzemane, it would have been prudent not to disturb the status quo. On 8 September, some 60 Chinese suddenly advanced down the Thagla ridge, took up positions dominating the Dhola post and cut it off by denying the log bridge on its supply route. The JCO incharge lost his nerve. He sent a frantic message for help and exaggerated the Chinese figures to 600. Someone could have flown by helicopter to see things on the ground. Instead, the very people who had pontificated till then the Chinese would never attack, took great affront at the Chinese insolence and decided to teach them a lesson.

4

Chinese Interlude-I

The following account is a selected excerpt, a rough translation from the book *The Snows of the Himalayas: The True History of China India War* by Sun Xiao and Chen Zhibin. Both the authors served in the PLA in the late 1960s where they heard accounts of the 1962 war from the senior field commanders. The authors traveled widely over China to interview other participants. They visited combat units, veterans' hospitals and also met Divisonal Commander Zhang Pengrian who had led the main attack. It carries a preface by General Yang Chengwu, the erstwhile Deputy Chief of General Staff of the PLA.

Peking: (Sometime in 1960) : Chou En-lai comes to see Mao. Mao has not been sleeping well. He has left instructions to say that he should be woken up as soon as Chou arrives. Mao has been troubled by the famine in China; says it's his fault. So he has given up eating meat and eggs and is growing his own food.

Mao : En-lai, What is the situation as regards India?

Chou: My visit to India has apparently not solved the problem. At present, the public opinion in India is highly charged. Mr Menon, the Defence Minister, is asking for a limited war with us. In this atmosphere, Nehru's stance is getting hard day by day. I have written to him several letters saying that we should have high level discussions, but he adamantly refuses. What he insists on is the precondition that we should totally withdraw all our troops from the disputed territory.

Mao : That will not do. If we totally withdraw and yield to him, what then is therefore totalk about? China has a territory of 9,600,000 sq kms. We know this from primary school text books. If, when it comes to my turn, the territory shrinks to 9,500,000 or 9,300,000 sq kms, how can I face 600 million Chinese people. If India is so adamant, there must be a back stage actor involved.

Chou: Needless to say that Britain and USA support them. According to reliable information the Soviet Union is also supporting India and is prepared to give 40 AN12 transport aircraft.

Some Pakistani papers have said that India has created the trouble with China, ostensibly for disputing territory but it is for getting more military aid.

Mao : That makes sense... it does make sense . The KMT was like that. They would fire a gun and then look at the face of their master. If they got a couple of silver pieces as a reward, they would fire again. If there was no reward, they lost the will to fight.

Mao, chain smoker that he was, lights up another cigarette, gets up and taking a few steps tells his friend Chou En-lai.

" Nehru is an old friend of ours. His country was the second one to establish diplomatic relations with us. We cannot embarrass him; he exerted himself to raise the world status of New China. If he does not want to negotiate, not to worry. We can wait. We should not shut the door on negotiation from our side. Send telegrams to Generals Zhang Guohua of Tibet and Jia Chen of Sinkiang saying that in this conflict we are determined not to harm even one person. We would do our utmost to avoid a bloody incident. We must be prepared for armed coexistence for a long time. In short, we do not want to make war. Let us make a last attempt to make Nehru come to the negotiating table."

7 October (1962), Chen Yi's (Chinese Foreign Minister) last meeting before the war with Indian Ambassador Banerjee. The atmosphere is tense and explosive.

Chen Yi : Mr Banerjee, your government, having completely ignored our government's repeated calls for resolving the border problem through negotiations and consultations has now crossed the traditional boundary between India and China and has amassed troops in the area of Ke-jie-lang (Namka Chu) river around the McMahon line. What exactly do you have in mind? Do you want to fight a war?

Banerjee: (mildly) No. It is not that we are unwilling to negotiate. It is you who are unwilling. Our government has already replied to your government's diplomatic note of 25 September, saying that it is willing to hold bilateral talks on 15 October. But we cannot accept the preconditions of your government.

Chen Yi: (laughing) Who, after all, has put preconditions ? It is not that you do not know my government's attitudes. The McMahon line in the eastern sector is an absolutely illegal line. But we are willing to recognise it on the basis of mutual adjustment. There is a dispute over Aksai Chin in the western sector. We can sit down and talk about that also. But you do not mention the eastern sector and speak only about the Western Sector. Isn't the conflict on our border a single issue? Why talk only about one sector and not be willing to talk about the other sectors? This is like 'What is mine is mine; we will negotiate what is yours.' Is that not a precondition? If we do not accept it, you turn around and attack us for putting preconditions. Mr Banerjee, please tell me frankly, is my parable correct?

Banerjee (having heard the translation in stunned silence): What parable?

Chen Yi (smiling): A thief crying "Stop thief".

Polite translation of this created some problem but it was done. Banerjee's face turned red and purple. He is obviously offended.

Chen Yi (continues quite bluntly): On the 1st of October, your Defence Minister shouted that he wanted to fight a limited war and expel the Chinese troops from your territory. On 4 October, Nehru had just returned from England and at the airport (itself) he spoke carelessly about waging a war with China. You have gone ahead to formulate some 'Operation

Ravena' and sent your Chief of Staff Kaul to the front. At the same time, you have urgently re-deployed your forces originally stationed on the India-Pakistan border to the Sino-Indian border. It seems to me that you are sharpening your knives. Do you want a fight?

Banerjee (weakly but contentiously): If China recognizes the McMahon line in the eastern sector and agrees to negotiate over the Western Sector, India will certainly not use military force.

Chen Yi (severely): You are mistaken. The McMahon line was thrust upon us by British Imperialism. It has never been legal. To think that we will recognize it and sign a treaty over it! If you are unwilling to give us even this bit of face, how can you speak of sincerity? Use of military force? It is a joke. I, Chen Yi, have fought more than 20 wars, (now that) I have rested for some ten odd years, my arms are itching again. Don't think with all those tens of thousands of troops and the great America and England behind you, you can do what you like. You simply cannot do it. I accept that though the Chinese troops are not as well equipped as yours the quality of our military technology is not as high as yours. But Chinese troops are difficult to gnaw at. Chiang Kai-shek had eight million troops, but they could not take a bite off us. It was the other way round; we made them flee. America put in half a million troops, all of them battle-hardened in World War II [into Korea]. And what was the result? They too could not take off their front teeth. Tell Nehru that they [Indians/Nehru] have cut off the last thread of hope about negotiations and banged the door shut. We will [now] meet on the battlefield. We will fight to the finish. In my opinion, you will still have to come to the negotiation table.

About the same time Mao called a military conference in the evening in his Shungquing villa in Peking. Present are besides Mao, Premier Chou En-lai, Foreign Minister Chen Yi, Defence Minister Lin Piao, Marshal Ye Jianying, Marshal Liu Bocheng, Chief of the General Staff Luo Ruiqing, Deputy Chief of General Staff Yang Chengiou, Director GPD Xiao Hua, Director GLD Qiu Huizuo, Commander of Tibet MD Gen Zhang Guohua, Commander of Sinkiang MD, Gen Jiachan.

Mao (lighting up a cigarette): I called everyone here today for a meeting on military affairs. Our border conflict with India has been bothering us for several years now. We do not want to fight a war. We had thought that it would be resolved through negotiations. But Nehru does not want to talk/ negotiate. He has mobilised a lot of troops. He is hell bent on fighting a war with us. It now seems that we cannot do without fighting ["it won't do, not to fight"]. If we have to fight, how should we fight ? Having fought, what will be the situation ? I invite all of you to contribute your thoughts and plans. Let me first ask Chen Yi to acquaint us about the situation in the foreign affairs struggle.

Chen Yi : You already know a great deal about the China-India border conflict through reports, newspapers etc. To put it simply, this is a bitter legacy left over by British imperialism. Nehru wants to swallow it up.

Although the border between China and India has not been formally demarcated, because of long-term harmonious processes and according to the administration exercised by both sides, it had become a traditional and customary boundary. After India became independent in 1947 it initially respected this boundary line. But in 1954 they changed their official maps and illegally made the McMahon line in the east as the already settled boundary. In the western sector they were plotting to separate Aksai Chin from China and incorporate it into India. In this way, they occupied some 125,000 sq kms of Chinese territory.

During the past several years, they have transgressed many times into our territory and air-space and have continuously created bloody incidents. In August 1959, they attacked our border guards in the Longju area in the eastern sector and caused bloodshed. In less than one month, they killed or wounded 47 of our officers and men.

We, at our Foreign Ministry, have worked hard in different ways but Nehru is unwilling to sit down to negotiate. He has swallowed the bait of " Forward Policy" and is determined to carry on with it. It seems that it will be better to see what happens on the battlefield.

Mao : A war between India and China will indeed be an extremely unfortunate thing. Recently, I have read a few books on India. India's ancient civilization is truly worthy of our admiration. Tang dynasty monks brought sutras from the western heaven [India], all 675 sutras were brought back from India. Chen Xuan Zang also blazed a trail for China. In those days there was a Brahmin monk who wrote down the 40 scrolls on Hindu religion and put them up on the door of the Lantu temple built by him. He declared that whoever broke one of those would........

I have beer looking up things. In history we have fought only one and a half wars with them [Indians]. That was in 648 A.D. i.e in Zhen Guan 22nd year. Tang Taizong had sent Wang Xuance as his chief emissary. The second occasion when missions were sent to the Jie-ri empire i.e today's India, we didn't imagine that the king of Jie-ri had already died a year earlier and there was a great rebellion in the country. A minister called A-lo-na-shun had usurped the throne, sent his army to attack the Chinese emissaries and killed 30 odd men from the mission's escorting troops. Wang Xuance fled in the night to Ni-po-Lo[Nepal] country, borrowed some troops and returned for a counter-attack. He defeated A-lo-no-shun. They maintained good order there, won over the people and withdrew the troops. A-lo-na-shun was exiled to Chang'an but was treated well by Tang Taizong. After that A-lo-na-shin did not return to his country. After his death, people carved his likeness on Tang Taizong's grave. He thus survived in name for ever.

The half war was when Taimur invaded India. In 1398, Taimur led a large army and went right upto Delhi. India had 40,000 troops, 1,000 cavalry and 120 elephants. For defence Taimur played a trick; he placed camels loaded with straw in the front line. When the battle began, he set fire to the straw. India's elephants were afraid of fire and seeing camels on fire they fled in all directions. In the process, they trampled upon troops on their own side. Taimur won a victory. The Mongol soldiers killed over 100,000 prisoners of war and completely sacked everybody's possessions. We call it a half-war because aren't there Inner and Outer Mongolias? This time when we go to war , in my opinion there will be two rules: one is to fight and win and drive

Nehru to the negotiation table. The second is that there should be a reason, benefit and moderation.

After Mao had finished, Dy CGS General Yang Chengwu outlined the enemy deployments.

"The eastern sector is an important one where India has made preparations to make a major attack against us. At present they have more than 100 posts inside our territory, some of them only a few meters from ours. Some are between our posts and some actually are behind our lines. According to intelligence reports, India adopted Operations 'Leg Horn' at the beginning of October to make a large-scale attack against us. Nehru has publicly ordered Kaul..... to expel Chinese troops."

Mao (interrupts him): "Jianying, haven't the newly appointed front-line commanders demonstrated for you their tactical plans ? Tell us about them so that our vision will be broadened."

Ye Jianying : Five years ago, I led a military delegation to India. Kaul was then Commander of the 4th Div. When he was young, he had graduated from the Royal British Military College at Sandhurst. He had probably participated in war in Burma during World War II but he probably has no experience of a real war. His colleagues ridicule him as a General who has never fought a war. During our visit the reason why he put on a demonstration of tactical offensive was, from one point of view, for building up his own image.

At that time, the demonstration was very well conceived, very tight, as if there was nothing left out. But precisely because of this, I felt that it very much resembled a staged play. Every little detail of whole plan was held in his head. On this point, I admired his intelligence and meticulousness. I did not have much contact with Kaul but generally felt that he was a determined and sensitive person. He was inclined to listen to the opinions of his officials and soldiers but not to those of the Generals. That was the fatal flaw in him. He liked music, plays, and trekking; he often went on inspection tours of posts in the snow-bound Ji-jie high mountains. He has experienced danger on quite a few occasions. Those who like him call him a 'brave spirit/devil', a mysterious character in Indian mythology. Last year, he received the Vishisht Seva reward 1st class from Nehru himself. That is high merit!

Mao : All right. Let him show his merit this time again.

Zhang Guohua and Jiachan then described war plans on the Chinese side and the difficulties in executing them. The most important problem : the enemy was relatively stronger and the Tibet Military District was finding it difficult to reinforce the troops and their war-making capacity.

Zhou : Can we transfer one army from another Military District ? The best would be one experienced in fighting on a high plateau and their bases should not be too far from the war zone. That way they can join the war rapidly.

Mao (lighting up another cigarette): Jianying, have you thought over this ? Which army can we transfer ?

Luo Ruiqing : In my opinion, we should send the 54th Army. For one thing, their base is the Jia-jiang, Ya-an area of Sichauan, relatively near the war zone. Secondly, they have fought on the Tibetan plateau while putting down the rebellion(1959) .

Liu Bocheng : Mr Chairman, do you remember Ding the courageous who encircled the 7th army ? That Ding Sheng should be the Commander.

Mao (scratching his head): Yes, yes the one who led the Heng-bao campaign. That was the battle with Bai Chongxi which created a pocket battle formation, using 7 Divisions to encircle Ding Sheng's single division . He wanted to fight a battle of extermination and could not imagine that it was too much to bite Ding Sheng's small combat units. This dashed (Bai's divisions) into pieces. Bai Chongxi was stuck with napalm ; he couldn't spit it out nor could he swallow it. In the end 7 Divisions were..... one by one..... yes. Let us use him. Between Ding-the-courageous and Kaul-the-brave. Let us see who finishes/topples the other.

Zhou (En-lai to Qiu Huizuo): I hope that comrades(here) will really think hard to resolve the logistical problems just mentioned by Guohua and Jiachan. At present, the Himalayan areas are just about to be cut off (due to winter). A lot of troops will be required to move about and fight in areas above the snow line. The Korean war taught us a lesson : Never allow extra casualities because of logistical difficulties. Besides, the 500 vehicles meant for defending the 54th Army and those already in the war zone must be quickly dispatched.

Mao : If China and India get into a war, not only the two major powers America and Soviet Union, but also many other countries who have no clear understanding will stand on their [Indian] side. Even Chiang Kai-shek may act. We will get a bit isolated. I think, not to worry. If we fight the battle at the front well, we will get into an advantageous position [allowing us to take the initiative]. I still believe in saying : rather than dying while kneeling down, it is better to die standing up. If they want us to die, it won't be so easy. This time, if we do not get into a war, it is OK but if we do, we will fight to project our might. We will have secured 30 years of peace.

[Mao's words have been proved right. It is already over 30 years since the war and no war has broken out between China and India .]

18 October, 11 p.m., there is an emergency meeting of military officers of the Eastern Front. Some 80 commanders participated. Deng Shaodong transmits the order of the Military Committee for launching the war.

Instruction to the Tibet MD front and Sinkiang MD reserves and for the information of Chengdu and Lanzhou MDs:

> In order to counter the arrogance of the Indian reactionaries and to protect the security of our borders and in order to create conditions for a negotiated settlement of the border problem, the Center has decided to undertake military action to counter-attack. Our forces already deployed in the Tibet MD should first destroy the invading enemy north of the 'McMahon line' in Nam Ka Chu area and also prepare to follow up with further action in order to destroy enemy reinforcements coming in from Tawang. In order to

> coordinate with the above actions, the Sinkiang MD forces already assembled along the western sector of the China-India border should first attack the enemy in the Galwan valley and the Red Mountain Top. Then they should prepare to sweep away the enemy from.........

Gen Zhang Guohua then gave instructions to the assembled commanders:

> In order to destroy the enemy in Nam Ka Chu area, I approve the plan contained in the telegram of 9 p.m., 16 October, sent by the Tibetan MD front.

Zhang Guohua then explained the military situation on the Indian side and added :

> Remember that the assignment for each of our units is to launch the main thrust against the right front. From 55 Div one regiment is to cross Nam ka Chu river and attack completely sealing the enemy. They are then to proceed to Tawang. Understood.
>
> The 87th Regiment, 61 Div is assigned the task of penetration. They are to cross Nam ka Chu river from the west. After that they will meet with difficulties but they are to destroy the enemy Headquarters, occupy the landing strip and the artillery base at Tsangdhar. At the same time, they are to hold the enemy's escape route to the rear. This is a difficult assignment. Those who find it so, should let others take it up.

The commander of 87 Regiment got up and said "Commander, how can you say such things. I, Shen, have carried out all kinds of assignments. Ask me to fight right up to New Delhi. If I, Shen, do not make it first, you can have my head."

Zhang : Big Shen, Don't boast before hand. 7 Brigade is India's elite formation. It fought in World War II. It is not enough to defeat them. Your assignment will be complete only when you capture Dalvi alive.

Shen: What if he commits suicide?

Zhang: He may but I make it clear that then your action will not have been dashing and sudden.

Shen: Commander, I understand. We shall capture Dalvi alive.

Zhang then authoritatively added:

> "I order that at dawn tomorrow at 5.20 am an artillery barrage will open fire. The main attack will start at 5.50 am. Adjust your watches. Right now it is 1900 hours 54 minutes and 27 seconds. Go back to the units and make battle preparations. The sign for the attack is three red flares."

On the following day i.e. 20 October, 1962, at Peking's Great People's Hall, Chou En-lai had a meeting with the British journalists.

Chou (looking at his watch): Today, we delayed the publication of our newspapers because they were to carry an important news item. Right now our radio stations are broadcasting the news. From dawn today, our government has decided to launch a counter-attack against the large force of Indian invading troops.

A British journalist: Premier Chou En-lai, how will the war end, with whose victory and whose defeat, please give us your evaluation.

Chou (smiling): This is a war. So there will be victory and defeat. The participating sides in a war decide to fight because they want to win. But the situations on the battlefield can change many times making the causes for victory and defeat extremely complex. It is too early to speak of victory or defeat. But we believe that the dispute over the border has gone on for several years and having shown our tolerance to the world, if China now launches a counter-attack in the face of a large-scale invasion, it was something which was bound to happen. It is just some friends from other countries who do not understand this point. I hope you can help us explain our side of the matter better. The invading Indian troops have surrounded many posts and their strength is relatively dispersed. This I believe has harmed the morale of the Indian troops. Add to that the impediments and the

> difficulties faced. The difficulty of transportation and low morale of troops. I believe that their defeat is certain.

Author's Comment

Since it is more or a less a sponsored book and that too from a totalitarian communist country, not everything can be taken at its face value. One has to make allowance for propaganda and rhetoric. Yet because it's a victor's account written after nearly thirty years after the war, barring some censorship, the credibility index is pretty high, unlike the Indian versions where there has been much to hide or twist facts for various reasons.

The following aspects about the Chinese side get easily highlighted and are worth taking note of:

- China was beset with its own problems. There was widespread famine in 1962. KMT had not been defanged.
- China was wary of the overwhelming diplomatic support enjoyed by India and there was the apprehension of the USA and UK jumping into the fray.
- Mao appreciated Nehru's role in championing China's cause and was aware of Nehru's compulsions at home and was keen to give him sufficient time to resolve the issue through negotiations.
- What stands out about the Chinese leaders is their vast military experience, poise, clarity of thought, clear national aims and objectives.
- At no stage did they underestimate the Indian Army. They did their homework well and made deliberate preparations to achieve their military objectives.

- At the same time the Chinese commanders, it seems from the above quoted piece, appeared to be unaware of the Indian force's near total lack of logistical support -- that they were going to fight a major enemy with 50 rounds in their pouches. It would show that the Chinese intelligence system wasn't all that good -- quite contrary to what we believed. Surely the Chinese could see that our troops had no entrenching tools, no saws or other cutting implements, no wire, no sand bags? On 9 October, our attack across Nam ka Chu was not supported by artillery or even MMGs. Did they not make any deductions ? If not, then they were not smart (or professional) after all. We may say that they were not prepared to take the Indian Army with its awesome reputation (Second World War days) lightly. In a way they were not wrong.

5

Topography of NEFA

The Himalayas along most of its length are over 300 kms wide but in Kameng sector the width is only about 200 kms. These ranges can be said to have been formed in a three-tier system. The highest tier, called the Greater Himalayas, runs as the northernmost border with Tibet. Here the mountain peaks are the highest and the passes are found at heights varying from 14,000 to 18,000 feet. The next tier, located approx 50 to 100 kms to its south, can be called the Middle Himalayas; and after a similar distance are the Lesser Himalayas. These three tiers are a series of near-continuous crestlines, or a conglomerate of peaks, ridges, spurs and passes, enclosing small and big valleys. Each tier forms its own watershed[1] drained by rivers that have over the millenia cut their way across these ridges as they rush downwards into the plains of India. There are big river valleys which are broad and fertile but there are also sections where the rivers pass through narrow precipitous gorges. Traditionally, therefore, trade routes follow valleys and periodically have to cross over passes before moving into the next valley.

NEFA (now the state of Arunachal Pradesh) constitutes the easternmost tract of the Himalayas. Lying between Bhutan and Tibet borders, it measures approx 50,000 sq kms.

Till the 1950s it was a wild and isolated region inhabited by several savage tribes of Indo-Mongoloid origin practising animistic cults. The great Brahmaputra, called Siang within the region and Tsangpo in Tibet, flows through it into Assam. The other major rivers east to west are Lohit, Subansiri, Kameng, Bharaili and Nyamjang Chu (Manas) and their numerous tributaries all having abundant water. The lower Himalayas are full of thick tropical rain forests. Higher up, the vegetation turns coniferous and alpine. Its northern borders with Tibet are marked by high mountain peaks, the range being highest in the central region marked by Gaurichen, Kangto, Nyegi Kangsang group of peaks, the highest being Namche Barwa around whose massif the Brahmputra takes a southward bend into India. Namche Barwa, in fact, forms the easternmost rampart of the mighty Himalayas. The McMahon line runs for most of its length along the Himalayan crestline, except at its westernmost extremity where it runs south of the now famous Thagla ridge, the highest crestline in that area and the bone of contention that finally led to the war.

North of the crestline is the Tibetan plateau, which southwards gives way to broken mountainous country. The monsoon is very heavy in this region, lasting from May to the beginning of October, and there is a fairly heavy snowfall later in winter and during the spring months. October to December is dry and clear, in fact beatific. Passes do not generally close till end-January. The precipitation on the Tibetan side is light.

From the operational point of view the region can be divided into three sectors, the eastern, central and western sectors. Of the three the western sector is the most accessible as the grain of the country is easy-going.

The central sector extends from Lho La to the Brahmaputra gorge at Gelling. Being extremely wild and mountainous and least developed of the three, this sector even now remains very difficult for movement on both sides of the border.

The eastern sector extends from Gelling to the trijunction of the boundaries of India, Tibet and Burma. The terrain here is also difficult. There used to be a track to Walong from Teju, with the Chinese casting their covetous eyes on the Mishmi tribe here; but a violent earthquake in 1950 had caused large-scale ecological damage and the route had become non-existent in most places. A journey from the roadhead at Teju to the border in 1962 took over two weeks. Walong nevertheless continued to enjoy strategic importance.

Road building on the Indian side was a frustrating process because of the shallow nature of the rock faces, and therefore, slow. The few roads that were built with great effort virtually became closed to vehicular traffic during the monsoons. On the other hand road building on the gentle sloping Tibetan plateau was easy. The Chinese had commenced construction of strategic roads and airfields after moving into Tibet in 1951. By 1960, they had built lateral all-weather roads in the Tsangpo valley capable of taking heavy vehicles. Their feeder roads at most places reached to within 5 to 10 kms of the McMahon Line.

Because it was in Kameng sector that both sides concentrated maximum forces and the operations there being the chief objective of this book, we need to have a more detailed look at its topography as it played a significant part in the trouncing of Indian forces.

KAMENG SECTOR

In the Kameng sector the McMahon line runs along the crest of Greater Himalaya from the eastern boundary till it reaches the Thagla ridge in the west. Presumably because the watershed principle no longer holds good in this region, the actual demarcation was not easy, leading to different interpretations by India and China, both claiming Thagla, the highest ridge in the area, though the line marked by McMahon was perhaps meant to be nearly 10 kms south of it as the crow flies.

The various routes that run through Kameng sector are shown in Map 4. As the reader will notice, there are three major passes on the McMahon line; Thagla (near Khinzemane), Bumla and Tulungla. The routes from the former two converge on Tawang, but it is also possible to bypass this township and proceed directly to Sela. The most traditional route from Tibet to the plains of India ran from Bumla to Tawang, Sela, Dirang, Mandala, Kalaktang, Bhairavkund and Udalgiri. However, by 1959 the civil administration had forced a new route from Misamari in the Assam plains (80 kms east of Udalgiri) to Bomdila (the headquarters of the Political Officer responsible for Kameng Division). This route (a jeepable track) went by way of foothills, Chaku, Eagle's Nest and Tenga Valley to Bomdila and beyond that a mule track led to Dirang, joining the bridle path of Udalgiri - Kalaktang - Mandala. (The middle tier of the Himalayan range (14000 - 17000 feet) in this area is made of the massifs around Sela, Poshingla and Changala. Finally there are the Lesser Himalayas (8000-10,000 feet) around Bomdila and Mandala.)

Sela, 13500 feet, at first appearance looks formidable and at a commanding position, a focal point for large-scale movement into Dirang valley, but the appearance is deceptive. It can be invested from nearly all directions and also bypassed from the north, east and the south. The bypasses not only allow the enemy to infiltrate to various points in the Dirang valley, there are some which go straight to Bomdila. The most significant of these tracks was from Tawang-Mago-Poshingla-Changla-Thembang-Bomdila also known as Bailey's Trail, which later played a key role in the winding up of the Indian defences. Having reached Dirang and Bomdila, the enemy has numerous options to head for the plains of Assam provided Bomdila and Mandala are not occupied by defending forces.

Western Kameng sector had great significance and not only because the traditional route from Tibet passed through it, it was also better developed and inhabited by a civilized, peace-loving people, the Mompas. There was a distinct Tibetan influence and control in the Tawang salient extending upto Dirang. Mompas practise Buddhism but had disliked their erstwhile Tibetan masters and were thankful to the Indians when the Indian government extended its administrative control over Tawang by driving out the Tibetan Dzongpens (1957). By 1962 most Mompas (Tawang) and Sherdukpens in Bomdila spoke Hindi.

Of the townships, Tawang was culturally and politically the most important place, with its 400-year old monastery that commemorates the birthplace of the Great Fifth Dalai Lama. Shakti on the Khanzamane-Tawang route was a sizeable village as it also linked Tawang with Bletting and Tashigong in Bhutan. Rearwards, Dirang was a bustling settlement. Besides, a string of villages (Nyukmadung being the most prominent) was sited on the slopes that overlooked this valley. Bomdila as the headquarters of the Political Officer was fast emerging into a reasonably modern settlement. Along the old traditional routes around Mandala lay the important villages of Phudung, Rupa, Shergaon, Morshing, Kalaktang and the lesser known monastery of Lagyala Gompa.

By 1962 the fair weather jeepable road to Bomdila had been extended up to Tawang and widened to one-ton capacity, but during the monsoon, the journey beyond Dirang Dzong had to be accomplished on foot as slush and landslides made movement of vehicles near impossible. The journey was nevertheless a great wilderness experience through lush green mountain country, cascading streams, charming tribal settlements and the numerous military stations that had sprung up along the line of communication, mostly manned by the Border Roads Organisation code-named 'Tusker' in this part of NEFA. Abundance of leeches and the dim-dam fly, whose sting left you with a week-long itch, were just two major irritants on the way. From the foothills one climbed 9000 feet to reach Eagle's Nest via Bompu and Chaku before descending nearly 4000 feet to Tenga valley. From Tenga valley one climbed 4000 feet to Bomdila township, the pass of the same name being a further five kilometers to the north. From Bomdila pass there was a gradual 50 km descent along a long loop followed by a straightforward run to Dirang Dzong situated at a height of 5500 feet by the bank of Dirang river. It had a salubrious climate and therefore was the most comfortable place between Foothills and Tawang, but militarily the place was a death-trap being dominated on both sides of the river by high mountains and a labyrinth of tracks that the enemy could use to bottle up troops located there. At the west end of Dirang valley one began the long and tortuous ascent to the top of Sela (13500 feet) windswept and forlorn, from where one descended first to the picturesque Nuranong valley and then to Jung located at 6500 feet just above the Tawang Chu (river). One crossed the bridge below Jung and headed west for the last leg of the journey to Tawang which is situated well spread out on a largish plateau at 10000 feet. The place is something of a Shangri La and the view memorable, but a defender's nightmare.

It was obvious that the terrain imposed extreme limitations on the administrative capacity of the Indian forces. The further one went from the plains, the more difficult became our maintenance capability, and beyond Bomdila it was desperate. As far as Tawang and all posts forward of it are concerned, they could only be maintained by air and the Indian Air Force's capacity was already overstretched, considering its commitments in Ladakh and elsewhere. This factor (beside the uncertain weather conditions) decided the manpower ceiling. In addition, there was the question of the animal transport companies engaged in multifarious administrative duties, cutting into the fighting strength that could actually be kept supplied up there. The situation as far as the Chinese were concerned was just the reverse. They had built all weather roads on the flat Tibetan plateau, capable of taking heavy traffic to within a few kilometers of the McMahon line. A terrain analysis should clearly have ruled out any forward posture by the Indians till land communications had been developed sufficiently. But no senior officer in the Government or in the Army had ever bothered to go up there or to have a terrain analysis carried out.

There was yet another hazard, quite unknown to the Indians then, of high altitude sickness, of acclimatisation and the need for snow clothing. It's not that these matters were something totally new for the Indians, because mountaineering had by then become fairly popular amongst a section of Indian Army officers; the Himalayan Mountaineering Institute at Darjeeling had been in existence since 1954 catering essentially to the increasing demand of Army enthusiasts. (In 1960 India had organized its first expedition to Mt Everest in which over fifty per cent members were from the Army.) But unfortunately mountaineering remained essentially an exclusive hobby. For the vast majority of Indian troops, high altitude was to remain a closed book and an unknown hazard - and in the event caused much hardship and demoralization. On the other hand, nearly two Chinese armies stationed in Tibet and Sinkiang had been operating at altitudes above 14,000 feet since 1959. It is a fact about acclimatisation that it is possible to get permanently acclimatised up to a height of 17,000 feet and it becomes very comfortable living at around 14,000 feet after one has been operating there for a few months. Permanent habitations are to be found in the Himalayan regions reaching up to 16,000 feet. The Chinese therefore enjoyed a tremendous advantage over the Indians when it came to operating at high altitudes. No wonder they were able to jog and even run, causing awe and demoralization amongst the Indian troops, who huffed, puffed, panted and shivered, not because they were unfit and the Chinese were superfit. It was the lack of acclimatisation manifesting itself. The solution would have been to minimise the debilitating handicap by avoiding the high altitude areas to the maximum extent until full acclimatisation achieved.

NOTES AND REFERENCES

1. In the strictest sense 'Himalayan Watershed' is a geographical fallacy. All rivers across Himalaya flow southwards from Tibet to India: the Tsangpo-Brahmaputra, the Nayam-Jangchu-(Manas), the Teesta, the Ganga, the Indus. The real watershed is one stage north of Himalaya: the Karakorams, Kuenlun-Changtang. Geographically, therefore, the Tsangpo valley in Tibet is an Indian subcontinental entity and is not indeed a part of China.

6

The Hunter Becomes the Hunted

The Debacle at Nam Ka Chu

As already mentioned, soon after the Longju incident in August 1959, the NEFA border was made the responsibility of the Army. 4 Infantry Division, which was stationed at Ambala Cantt., was ordered to move to NEFA. On arrival in Assam in November 1959, it established its headquarters at Tezpur. XXXIII Corps under Eastern Command came to be raised in mid-1960 with its headquarters at Shillong with its area of responsibility being the entire north-eastern region -- Sikkim, Indo-Bhutan Border, NEFA, India-East Pakistan border and Nagaland. Indian Army's main occupation before had been fighting the insurgents in Nagaland. General Officer Commanding of XXXIII Corps was the bland and bald accordion-playing Lieutenant General Umrao Singh, known for enjoying a good drink and naughty limericks. But when it came to professional work, he was basically a no-nonsense, straightforward man, clear headed and professionally competent. 4 Infantry Division now came directly under HQ XXXIII Corps.

Its 7 Infantry Brigade under Brigadier (later Major General) D.K Palit, VrC, moved to Misamari (about 15 kms from Tezpur near the foothills[1]) and was tasked to look after Kameng Division of NEFA. 5 Infantry Brigade was allotted the relatively less threatened area comprising Subansiri, Siang and Lohit frontier divisions. 11 Infantry Brigade moved first to Sikkim from where it later moved to Nagaland.

There was absolutely no infrastructure available in the area other than some reminders of the US Forces' presence during the Second World War -- mainly large numbers of cemented plinth areas and concrete forward airstrips. Having become fully experienced in house-building after Project Amar at Ambala where the Division had constructed 1450 houses with troop labour in record time, the formation now embarked on a similar project for building bashas (thatched huts with intermeshing bamboo walls). It was again a job well done but hardly the kind of thing a formation meant to assume operational readiness in an unfamiliar area ought to have been engaged in. In consequence, no conversion training from plains to mountain warfare could be carried out. Needless to say that valuable time was lost. The onset of winter and numerous logistical problems slowed down the move beyond Foothills.

In October 1959, Lieutenant General SPP Thorat, D.S.O., General Officer Commanding-in-Chief, Eastern Command, with his headquarters at Lucknow in central Uttar Pradesh (1800 kms from NEFA) and known for his professionalism and soldierly ways, had recommended a three-tier defence for NEFA. According to his plan, small outposts were to be established as near the McMahon line as possible to keep a watch and give early warning, but they were to fall back before a Chinese advance. The second tier was to consist of strong delaying positions, which would force the enemy to halt, deploy and fight, thereafter be made to regroup and bring his supply bases forward before resuming his advance.

The main battle was to be fought on the third line, which was to be organised on tactical ground of our own choosing around positions that could be built up and supplied easily from the plains, thus enabling our forces to crush the invader by turning the difficulties of terrain to advantage and leaving the Chinese the prospect of fighting with extended lines of communication. Accordingly, the defence line drawn by General Thorat was Tawang-Bombdila-Ziro-Daporijo-Along-Roing-Teju-Lohitpur-Hayuliang-Jairampur. It was an excellent concept somwhat flawed by the fact that it was drawn off the map and ignored the terrain as it actually existed. In Kameng Division, the line actually denoted a line of withdrawal rather than a defence line because Bomdila was 100 kms by road in depth of Tawang on the most likely axis of advance of the Chinese. The line actually ought to have run from Mandala (30 kms west of Bomdila) to Bomdila, and should have been separately defined for each anticipated ingress line in the various divisions as there was absolutely no lateral communication between these points.

Nevertheless its political implication must have been unpalatable as it amounted to surrender of territory even though temporarily. Also, would the Chinese bother to advance any further than India's second tier of defences, having taken whatever they could annex conveniently? Anyway, militarily this was India's best option under the circumstances, the other being a total rout right down from the crestline to the Foothills, as eventually happened.

Brigadier Palit, Commander 7 Infantry Brigade, was one of India's rare military thinkers, strong, confident and physically fit. He carried out a thorough reconnaissance of his sector right upto Khinzemane and Bumla, and he visited Dirang Dzong, Sela and Tawang. He made his staff traverse the Bailey trail through Mago valley over Poshingla to Thembang. He was convinced that the Bomdila-Mandala area had to be the Division's vital ground. In his book *War in*

High Himalaya, published in 1991, he has, however, confessed that at that stage he had not fully appreciated the great defensive potential of the Sela massif, as his reconnaissance of that massif had had to be cut short on account of a sudden illness just as he was crossing Sela, and the weather too was foggy, reducing visibility considerably. And thereafter he had been posted out to Army Headquarters. But that lurking feeling had remained, to be ignited later in October 1962, when he as the Director of Military Operations at Army HQ was to be relentless in according Sela the prime importance for the defence of NEFA. But we will come to that later in its appropriate stage in the book.

Brigadier Palit's recommendation that his brigade be permitted to hold defences based on Bomdila-Mandala was not accepted by the Division Commander, Major General Amrik Singh, M.C. Orders came instead to push upto Tawang. By February 1960, the first company of 1/9 GR, one of the battalions of the Brigade, made it to Tawang, braving blizzard-like conditions over Sela, and by August the complete battalion had concentrated there. By November 1960, 7 Mountain Battery of 22 Mountain Regiment (the author's unit) and some Engineers and other elements had also reached there. Brigade Headquarters (under Brig Ranbir Singh, M.C.) moved up in April 1961. The effective strength of the fighting troops was only forty per cent of the overall holdings, the rest being on leave, or on courses of instruction or deployed along the line of communication to service it (which normally is the responsibility of the next senior formation.) The formation could hardly have been termed battle-ready.

Brigadier Ranbir Singh, M.C., who had succeeded Brig. Palit, had to be evacuated just after a year in command of the Brigade. Brigadier J.P. Dalvi, a high profile officer with great credentials as far as courses and appointments go, assumed command of the Brigade in March 1962. It didn't take him long to get disillusioned with the state of affairs. In fact, he was simply swept away by events beyond his control as the "forward policy", code named Op Onkar, gathered momentum and culminated in the infamous Dhola Post incident in September 1962. There was as we have seen a mighty flap and political uproar with Nehru issuing carelessly rash threats. The tragedy is that the Indian top brass instead of keeping their cool and sticking to their original aim, docilely accepted political interference. They became disoriented and heedlessly plunged 7 Infantry Brigade into Nam Ka Chu valley.

Gone was the Thorat plan, or any thought about the defence of NEFA. 7 Infantry Brigade was being made to act almost as an expeditionary force out on a limb by itself. Lieutenant General L.P Sen, D.S.O., the Eastern Army Commander, who was riding roughshod over lower commanders had brusquely overruled the Corps, Division and the Brigade commanders, without ever having visited the mountains even once, was mentally re-living October 1947 (his moment of glory) when Indian troops under him were airlanded at Srinagar to throw out the Pakistan-sponsored invading tribals. His mental block obviously prevented him from appreciating the vast difference between the two tactical situations, especially the military might of China. For Lieutenant General B.M. Kaul, the all powerful CGS, Headquarters, IV Corps was specially created for him to execute a quixotic mission and ease out Gen Umrao Singh, who had placed his objection in writing, it must have appeared to be just the opportunity to prove his mettle as a field commander. He was hoping to be back in his original seat in Delhi in a couple of weeks. It appears totally amazing that there should have been such false over-confidence and military naiveté among our top generals. There is a well-known saying that "whom the gods want to destroy, they first make mad." Only in this case it was a shade worse, it was a combination of madness and the military sterility of our top brass.

Nam Ka Chu was no military battle. It was a gross miscarriage of a limited political aim set by Prime Minister Nehru and a mindless coterie of consultants. It must be appreciated that politicians will always have their compulsions and sometimes because of them, plunge nations into war. Once the war starts, however, it should be the generals' business to fight it as per their best plans. The political leaders once the war starts seldom interfere. There is therefore a major difference between peace time posturing and the actual conduct of war. There should always be freedom for commanders at every level in the field, if only they have the gumption and the flair to demand and exercise it.

Dalvi's Brigade was simply sacrificed. Underequipped, unprepared and in uncalled for haste, it was made to occupy a most unsound tactical position, strung out down on a river-line, seven to ten days beyond road-head. It provided the Chinese with an ideal opportunity to launch their premeditated attack (counter-attack in their words) for which they had so meticulously prepared for the last four years. The people to be blamed are General P.N Thapar, Lieutenant General L.P Sen, Lieutenant General B M Kaul, Major General Niranjan Prasad and Brigadier John Dalvi, in that order. As for Nehru, he would surely have given in if a forthright Chief of the Army Staff (COAS) had stated the military facts candidly and bailed him out. Crying off is not an unheard of expedient and is, in fact, quite the recommended thing for politicians in certain untenable situations.

It is not the intention here to dwell any longer on the fate of 7 Infantry Brigade. That is beyond the scope of this book. Our concern is about the military battles which were fought (or left unfought) after 7 Brigade had been overrun, when the onus rested entirely with the military leadership. So far one can grudgingly concede that political and diplomatic interference and pressures had our compliant generals in a bind; but this was not so after 20 October, 1962, when in a matter of three hours 7 Brigade had disintegrated, and the Chinese unleashed their grand offensive to reach the very foothills of India. After Nam Ka Chu, a shattered Nehru did allow the generals to take military decisions -- and any bungling from then onward was of their own making.

7

Personal Interlude

Marching With Mules to Tawang

I was commissioned in December 1961, and joined the Regiment of Artillery. After a five-month long Young Officers' course at Deolali, two of us Akshey Kapila and I were posted to 22 Mountain Regiment at Misamari in the foothills of Assam. It was the month of July, the monsoon was active and the area was lush green. There were miles and miles of tea gardens. The scenery was exotic inspite of the somewhat sticky weather. We were lucky to have got 22 Mountain Regiment, with its glorious history. It boasted of the only Victoria Cross in the Second World War in the entire Commonwealth artillery - Havaldar Umrao Singh of Kaladan Valley fame. The Regiment enjoyed the official designation of Corps d' Elite. We were the only ones who wore the lanyard in the Artillery then. It was a life straight out of Kipling's ballad 'And we all love the screw Guns.......'

The Regiment had four very famous mountain batteries, then located in far flung corners of the Himalayas. This was nothing unusual as there were in those days only two mountain regiments (two more were under raising) in the entire Indian Army. Of the Regiment's batteries, 2 Derajat

Mountain Battery (Frontier Force) was in Nagaland and 7 Bengal Mountain Battery was at Tawang. Only the headquarters of the Regiment was at Misamari with a large rear party of 7 Bengal because Tawang didn't have the capacity to sustain many troops and animals. Both Kapila and I were, for the time being, retained with the headquarters under the watchful eyes of our imposing looking Commanding Officer (CO) - Lieutenant Colonel Iqbal Singh, M.C. Our Second in Command (2IC) was Major Shiv Singh, with a handlebar moustache and a similar growth over both ears and, like most 2ICs in those days, he was superseded but a teetotaler, which was unusual. We had a young adjutant in Lieutenant Bharat Inder Goswami, a gentle vegetarian who had been recalled from Tawang because of a torrid love affair with a Mompa belle. (Appearances can be rather deceptive!) Our quartermaster was Captain Pritam Singh, a Sikh officer from the ranks, who had represented the services in hockey. We had a silent looking medical officer, Captain PP Nandi and a cheerful and slightly fat but handsome veterinary officer (VO), Captain RN Kakkar -- which was a good thing, because mules like their doctor to have a sense of humour.

It was a hectic but enjoyable life, a lot of riding, marches, grooming parades, pack gun drills, promotion cadres and a unit's many other chores. On Saturday evenings we all went to the Thakurbari Planters Club where we sampled the British Raj as most of the Planters were still British. It was a groovy life but we were looking forward to being sent to one of the batteries. It happened quite suddenly.

On 8 September,1962, there was a sudden flutter in Thakurbari Club where many Army officers including the GOC of 4 Division had gathered for the Saturday evening drinks and dinner when a staff officer arrived with the news of the Dhola post incident. As a subaltern I had only a vague idea about its implication but on 9 September, I became wiser when I was called up by the Commanding Officer and informed that I would be marching up with a mule column to Tawang. There were 50 mules and about 100 men of 7 Bengal Battery then at Misamari who had to be sent up immediately as a clash with the Chinese was considered imminent. We were to cover 300 kilometers in seven days and I was given just four hours to get organized. The route, the stages and the administrative arrangements had been worked out by the adjutant and the quartermaster. I was briefed in detail and handed over a proper move order including wireless instructions with day and night frequencies to report regularly on each day's progress. I was excited and looking forward to my baptism. The day's average worked out to a march of 40 kilometers and there were a couple of days when we would be covering 60 kilometers.

It was late in the evening when we reached the Foothill's camp of the Border Road Organisation. Doimara, our night's destination, lay another 10 Kms beyond among the low hills and a thickly canopied jungle. The night sounds of crying hyenas, flights of flying foxes, a herd of elephants crossing a nearby stream and the brisk rhythm of our marching steps and the silence of the mules was reminiscent of my favourite jungle movies. A little before midnight we reached Doimara. My duty for the moment was over. The colour party under Jemader Hardwari Lal had already laid out the camp. The mules were tethered after being watered. I walked across to the 40 pounder tent, my lodging for the night. Next day was going to be a 30 km walk along a steadily rising gradient to Bompu at a height of 5000 feet.

The journey to Bompu was an uneventful affair but for the dehydration and the exceptionally heavy afternoon downpour. I felt sapped and dog tired. On reaching camp I took out a packet of glaxo D and took many spoonfuls in a tumbler of nice cold spring water. The energizing and refreshing effect was instantaneous. This is what we used to do in the Academy after hard work-outs in swimming and cross-country runs and it always worked wonders.

Today was my first evening with the Ahir (Yadav) boys, the previous one having been spent on the march. I learnt a little about their homes in the countryside of Haryana, Uttar Pradesh and Rajasthan. They made no bones about their sedate lives and simple taste in food, dress and music. A jawan sang a *ragini* for my benefit. Jemader Hardwari Lal told me that the Ahirs looked after their officers much better than the others (implying no doubt the Sikhs of Derajat Battery to which I stood notionally interposted). It was an impromptu welcome and probably a sign that I had measured up to their standard during the day's gruelling march. Years later I came firmly to believe that the Ahirs have been one of Indian Army's finest fighters and asset but have remained unsung because of their unglamorous lifestyles. I am not surprised that they have now begun to flex their political muscle.

It was a country of oak and rhododendron beyond Bompu, but no conifers. The reason could be that the Piri range that we were now crossing lies in an extremely wet zone. We had a brief halt at Chaku which had a small camp of the Tuskers and a cluster of civilian huts. There was a tea shop adjoining the road which was nothing unusual but what straight away attracted my attention was that it was being run by a strikingly beautiful girl of Mongoloid features and what a figure! The Ahirs who are generally celibate people were not interested. It would be a pity I told myself if I didn't give this girl a closer look. I later heard much after the debacle that she was a Chinese agent and her so called father who ran the shop with her had a radio transmitter concealed in the hut behind the shop. He regularly passed information about the induction of troops into NEFA. His ravishing daughter no doubt had played her part by gleaning information from the lusty army men. I bought a packet of biscuits from her and strode back to the head of the column exchanging many a 'Ram Ram' on the way with the Ahir boys. It was obviously a lovely morning. There was an interesting jawan in our column, a swanky little fellow, who smoked a briar pipe. He was Piare Lal, a sweeper by trade, who now had a mule in his charge to whom he was deeply devoted. Everybody in the battery seemed to like him. He became quite attached to me and I sometimes shared my tobacco with him. How could I know that a few days later I would be the cause of his death? Sometimes nature brings about these encounters to add poignancy to tragic moments.

From Chaku there was a steep climb to Eagle's Nest (9000 feet), the highest pass on the Piri Range, and then a steep descent all the way to Tenga valley. We had covered 60 kilometers in about ten hours at a scorching pace of 6 kms per hour. That was the normal speed of the mountain gunners. It was said that the Infantry had to run to keep pace with the gunners. It had been a tiring day but then Kolhatkar, my coursemate whose battery was located next to our camp, took me to his officers' mess. A few bottles of chilled beer banished the day's fatigue. After a delicious dinner I returned to my small tent. When I look back I can't but feel amazed at the power of recovery of those youthful days.

On the third day we passed through Bomdila township in the early hours of the morning. It was a sleepy little town those days. The place had a school and a playground and on its northern end on the fringe of the pine forest were the elegantly built inspection bungalow and the residence of the Political Officer.

There was wood smoke coming out from the chimneys and a freshness in the air as we made our way through the pine forest above the town. Local labour made up mostly of Mompa women were on the road carrying out maintenance and chanting their Buddhist prayers. The women had rosy cheeks and were beautiful to look at.

After crossing the lower Bomdila pass we reached km 9 and overlooked a big bowl-like valley formed by the confluence of the Gang River with one of the lesser streams flowing east from Mandala Ridge. The road took a long detour of 13 Kms and emerged on the opposite slope at km 22, at the crow-flight distance of only 3 Kms. In the centre of the bowl was Rahung village. Across the valley in the north-eastern direction at roughly the same height as km 9 area was the village of Thembang on the route to Tungri and Poshingla. From where I was standing I got a grandstand view of the entire valley including the Thembang feature. There was a bridle path that ran down via Rahung to km 22. It saved us nearly two hours of marching.

Our camp at km 22 was sited in the premises of a Border Road's detachment. The Malyali overseer vacated his cabin for my night's lodging. His transistor radio was more prone to catch Chinese stations and particularly one where a female voice in very good Hindi was hurling admonishments at the Indians for acting as the running dogs of imperialists. If one listened to this kind of thing for too long, there was a likelihood of getting indoctrinated.

The following day I took a day off while the men marched. Well into the afternoon I travelled in a one ton vehicle and went past Munna camp and Dirang without stopping. The journey was all along the stream which interestingly had numerous names. Gang changed to Khouma near Dirang and it became Khou Khouma near Bridge 2, our day's destination. The valley was open and rich with maize crop and jumbo sized radish, which along with green chillies was the staple vegetable of the locals. It narrowed beyond Bridge I and opened up slightly on reaching Bridge 2, a stretch of 8 Kms, where 62 Infantry Brigade would subsequently get ambushed. Our destination for the day was Bridge 2 Area. From here began the grinding climb of over a hundred zigzag turns to Sela. The column had already settled down when I reached there just as it was getting dark. I wasn't happy with the camp area. Refreshed after a day's rest, I decided to subject my men to an eighteen Kms night march to Senge. I wasn't being fair but the men took it on sportingly. We were now entering the high altitude zone. We were in our summer clothing and it became cold. Luckily it didn't rain, in fact the moon was out and it became quite a pleasurable walk. It took us quite some time to find a reasonable area for tethering our animals. Men slept wherever they could find some shelter. As for me I got into an one ton vehicle and snuggled into a cosy corner which had bundles of tents and slept like a log.

The place because of the recent rains was all slush and crawling with horse leeches. When morning came we found that all mules and many of the men had collected those blood-sucking creatures. It took us a while to sanitize the mules and men. I moved into a basha of the transit camp mess and the men into their tented accommodation. No one complained. The fitness level was indeed very high. There had been no falling outs or any sickness so far. But our arrival at Senge also marked the revival of the rains with a vengeance. Some called it the parting kick of the south east monsoons. For four days it rained incessantly. There was no vehicular traffic being allowed beyond Senge as yet and as per orders given to me I was to shed the administrative vehicles here and move self-contained over the next two days' journey to Tawang. Meanwhile more troops (mainly Infantry) arrived at Senge and likewise got stranded. When it didn't stop raining even on the fifth day, disregarding advice of people who had experience of crossing Sela, I decided to move on with my men and now heavily laden mules, hoping to take the rain and the high winds of Sela in our stride. The men were game and eager to join up with their battery at Tawang. Mountains can be merciless with the inexperienced and the unprepared.

It was raining moderately as we made a delayed start at about 11 am. The road labour was out in full force as the Border Roads Organisation had a date-line to keep. In that bleak weather the loud chanting of prayers of the Tibetan labourers sounded more like a wail against the unrelenting rain gods. It was ominous. The rain became heavier as we began our march and the labourers soon abandoned work and went home. A thought that we should do like-wise occurred to me but I dismissed it as it would have meant a loss of face. We had our first break when we reached Shukla camp (now called Shangrila) to readjust mule loads and take stock. We were now climbing above 10,000 feet and for the first time the men began to feel difficulty in breathing. The forest was thick with dripping cedar trees. Most men wore jersey pullovers over angola shirts but there were a few who were in their summer clothes. The army raincapes that we were wearing are effective only to a point. We were soon all soaked to the skin. The wet woollens do help to retain body heat to a great extent but the plight of the couple of the boys in cotton shirts was really bad as they began to shiver in the chilly weather. Feeling concerned I gave my raincape to one and my jersey pullover to the other. When Jemadar Hardwari Lal, who was bringing up the rear learnt of what I had done, he hurriedly caught up with me, removed his smock denson jacket and insisted that I put it on and that the column wouldn't move till I had done that. It was a touching gesture and goes to show the loyalty and affection of Indian troops towards their officers specially when you are roughing it out with them.

We were now just a few kilometers short of Sela at nearly 13,000 feet and had climbed above the tree line. The landscape turned harsh with rocky escarped features dominating the sky-line. A fierce wind began to blow, dispersing the clouds. The sun's last rays cast their golden magic on the simmering water of the lake at Sela and the rock features shone out in their stark nakedness. It was a desolate place with not a soul in sight and the howling wind made the whole experience eerie and a trifle frightening. I now realised first hand what the wind-chill factor can do to the human body. It was a dangerous situation as many of my men were on the verge of hypothermia and Piare Lal was one of them. His face seemed to be drained of all blood, his lips had turned blue and he shivered uncontrollably. Even a minute's halt at Sela would have been suicidal and so I began driving my men and mules on a fast pace down hill to Nuranong, eight Kms away where a platoon of the animal transport company was located. It was a trial of an extreme kind. The column began to break up as the stragglers couldn't keep up with the rest. I somehow hoped that they would reach Nuranong where they would get some warmth, food and shelter. Two kilometers beyond Sela, we found a tribal camp with a blazing camp fire. I thought that our stragglers could spend the night here and warm themselves over the rhododendron fire. Battery Havaldar Major Ram Singh stayed back with them. All survived except Piare Lal. In his case hypothermia had set in to a degree where revival becomes impossible. How do I describe the look in his eyes, as I left him behind. Was it fear of death, a farewell, or an accusation? I would never know because thereafter I simply sped down to Nuranong. Ironically it was by then a clear starlit sky and I silently cursed myself for not having waited a day longer to begin marching from Senge.

I directed Jemadar Hardwari Lal to take charge of the Column and proceed to Tawang which was just a day's march from Nuranong and myself began hitch-hiking with the dead body to the L of C headquarters at Dirang. The Major in charge simply washed his hands off and asked me to move on. He told me that I was guilty of having caused a death by a rash or negligent act. But he would give me no transport nor any guidance. But then this world is full of many good people. Just as I was feeling in the dumps and helpless, Lieutenant Manvir Singh of the EME arrived on the scene in a 1 ton vehicle on his way to the foothills. A Fifteenth Ex NDA course officer (two years my senior), Manvir even then in those days of ragging and punishment in the Academy was known for his compassion and elan. He told me not to worry and made his men prepare a proper place in the vehicle befitting the dignity of the body of Pyare Lal. He generally took charge and we drove off to Bomdila the night's destination. Manvir knew Major Johri, the political officer, and his wife well. We were put up in the circuit house and we were invited for dinner by the Johris. It was a simple homely meal. I found Mrs. Johri to be a graceful hostess. Manvir had seen to all the formalities like inquest, no objection certificate, etc., and that I no longer felt morose or guilty. To this day, I can never forget this act of kindness on Manvir's part. The man was inherently good. But what makes people so good? A Sherwood College product, Manvir was a truly handsome person in every sense. I asked him if he had a girl friend and he showed me a picture of a very beautiful girl. But fate often plays cruel games and with wrong people.

Next morning we were off to Misamari. Enroute I encountered Lieutenant Colonel Bhupinder Singh, my new CO, who was on his way to Tawang. Bespectacled, strong jawed and lively, he gave me no peptalk nor admonishment after he had heard out my brief description of the fatal incident. He put his hand over my shoulder, and said that such things must be taken in the stride. He gave me a firm handshake and departed. I suddenly knew that I was going to like this man through thick and thin.

After a post-mortem Pyare Lal was given a befitting funeral with military honours. I told myself that I would one day visit Pyare Lal's family and pay my condolence. It's something I have failed to do and the guilt remains like a small wound that won't heal.

NOTES AND REFERENCES

1. Later a camp north of Tezpur was named "Foothills".

8

The Fall of Tawang

To recapitulate: by the middle of June 1962, Operation Onkar (establishing posts on the Himalayan crestline) was in full swing in the Kameng Division. A string of 24 new posts were in the offing and some of these were rather sensitive from the Chinese point of view. Apprehending Chinese reaction, battalion strength bases had begun to be developed to back these sensitive posts. There were, as we have seen, severe logistics constraints. One such case was the post at Khinzamane, backed up by a battalion (9 Punjab) located at Lumpu. Tawang had been declared a 'Vital Area' and was being developed into a brigade defended sector (7 Infantry Brigade under Brigadier J. P. Dalvi). Major General Niranjan Prasad had just a month before taken over as GOC 4 Infantry Division. A sensitive and intelligent person, he had come to 4 Division on promotion. As Napoleon has written, 'Some generals are lucky and some not'. In this war, he was to prove to be one of India's unlucky generals.

On 8 September, the incident on Dhola Post led to a total change in previous plans. Brigadier Dalvi, who was in Tezpur and about to proceed on annual leave, was rushed back to Tawang. One can imagine the state of his morale at this contretemps. The very next day Army Headquarters ordered

7 Infantry Brigade to Dhola post (Nam Ka Chu) area to prepare to capture Thagla Ridge! This uncovered the Tawang defences, which were left temporarily unmanned except for 1 Sikh with 7 Bengal Mountain Battery in support. On 13 September, Brigadier Kalyan Singh, Commander 4 Artillery Brigade, moved to Tawang and was appointed ad hoc commander of this sector, with hardly any additional resources, for the next three weeks. The Commanding Officer of 7 Mahar, the machine gun battalion, was made commander of all line of communication elements from Foothills to Tawang.

It was autumn, with blue skies. An uninterrupted period followed when Indian Air Force Dakotas and Fairchild Packets literally flooded the Tawang Dropping Zone (DZ) with clothing, rations and ammunition. On 1 October, Headquarters 22 Mountain Regiment and 2 Derajat Mountain Battery (Frontier Force) less their mules joined the Tawang garrison. 4 Garhwal Rifles of 62 Infantry Brigade also arrived on 8 October, while its parent formation headquarters and 13 Dogras were under orders also to move up. Artillery support got a distinct fillip with the arrival of 97 Field Battery(ex 5 Field Regiment) with their 25 pounder guns and a troop of 116 Heavy Mortar battery equipped with 4.2 inch mortars.

By 20 October, Tawang garrison had the following troops positioned there in various stages of operational preparedness:

a) 1 Sikh

b) 4 Garhwal

c) 7 Bengal Mountain Battery and 2 Derajat Mountain Battery (FF) (four 3.7 inch Howitzers each)

d) 97 Field battery (eight 25 pounder guns)

e) One Troop of 116 heavy Mortar Battery (four 4.2 inch mortars)

f) 18 Field Company - Ex 'Tusker' force (mainly to defend Jung bridge and prepare it for demolition).

There was something about Brigadier Kalyan Singh, his calm and confident disposition and, the easy ambling gait of a tall well-built Rajput, that seemed to give a lot of reassurance to the people around him. The mere presence of such a commander prevents panic from setting in and the atmosphere remains healthy. It was just as well he was the sector commander at Tawang because Tawang was a defender's nightmare and only a cool person could have handled the situation once the Chinese put in their attack.

Tawang with all its political and religious significance was spread over a wide, sloping plateau, and impossible to defend with a brigade level force. Brigadier Kalyan Singh had only two battalions under him. The Chinese could invest Tawang from any direction and also bypass it. Their roadhead was only a few kilometers across the McMahon line. The force level the Chinese could use against Tawang was entirely discretionary. It could be one division (three regiments) or two divisions. Logistics was not a problem for them in northern Kameng.

After 7 Brigade defences had been overrun on 20 October, a Chinese attack on Tawang became imminent. On 22 October, based upon the information available with Headquarters IV Corps, the enemy was expected to launch a multi-pronged attack on Tawang during the night on 23/24 October, with nearly two divisions as follows:

a) One regiment with one in reserve on axis Bumla-Tawang.

b) One regiment along Track Khinzamane-Samatso-Tawang.

c) One regiment along axis Shakti -Lumla -Tawang.

d) Strong columns to be detailed to cut off Tawang from the rear, at Jung, Sela and various suspensions bridges on Tawang Chu.

At this stage the defences organised by the ad hoc 4 Brigade of Tawang were as follows:

Bumla - Samatso - Tawang Axis

a) Two platoons of Assam Rifles	-	One on the pass at Bumla, one at Sulla.
b) 1 Sikh		
One platoon	-	IB ridge area (2 kms south of Bumla)
One company (less a platoon)	-	Tongpeng La, 3 kms south of the IB Ridge
Battalion headquarters with one company	-	Milakteng La, 5 kms south of Tongpeng La (Milakteng La is about 10 kms north of Tawang)
One company	-	On the Sulla-Samatso-Tawang track
One company	-	On a high feature west of battalion headquarters
c) 7(Bengal) Mountain Battery	-	Area Milakteng La
d) Troop 116 Heavy Mortar Battery	-	On the Sulla-Samatso Track

Tawang - Mukdangla (Landa) - Geyshe La Area

a) 4 Garhwal Battalion Headquarters with one company	-	at Tawang
One company	-	Mukdangla (Landa) on the track Penkingtang,-Jung, bypassing Tawang
One company	-	Penkingtang with a platoon at Geyshe La

(One company less a platoon was deployed away from Tawang at Chutangmu north of Ziminthang for the defence of Tactical Headquarters of 4 Infantry Division. After a brief encounter with the Chinese it made its way south of Tawang Chu in a cross-country move to the plains of Assam evading the Chinese). It took no further part in the operations.

b) 97 Field Battery	-	North edge of Tawang, where the road to Bumla then ended.
c) 2 Derajat Mountain Battery(FF)		
Battery less 2 guns (without mules)	-	In transit at Lao Basti (short of Tawang towards Jung)
Two guns with their Detachments but without ammunition	-	Mukdangla (Landa), with C Coy 4 Garhwal Rifles

The Chinese column advancing along the Khinzemane axis had managed to cut off the Indian troops at Lumpu, made up of stragglers, wounded men and non-combatants, who nevertheless had put up a brave resistance. With his tactical headquarters closely threatened, General Prasad ordered Ziminthang to be evacuated on 21 October (FN). While he was trekking to Tawang (his helicopter having been earlier shot down) he received the order, out of the blue, appointing him officiating Corps Commander whose HQ was more than 200 miles to the rear and about a week's journey away! He reached Tawang on the evening of 22 October and found General L.P Sen already there (his first visit to the mountains). It was a far from an amicable meeting and it is believed that Prasad blamed his army commander squarely for causing the fiasco. Gen L.P Sen was impatiently waiting for a helicopter to come and rescue him. He appeared helpless and considerably rattled and would do nothing to help or advise. But it's never difficult to jump down the throats of one's juniors.

After passing through Shakti, the Chinese column reached Lumla, 15 kms from Tawang, at 9 am on 23 October. At dawn of the same day the Chinese launched their main attack from the north on Bumla. The Chinese pincer was to close on Tawang, and it was a matter of time before Chinese elements would fully entrap Tawang garrison by cutting off the road behind them, thus preventing them from withdrawing to Jung, Jungle or Mago.

At 4.30 am on 23 October, Chinese opened up with a heavy barrage of guns and mortars and overwhelmed the Assam Rifles post at Bumla. Our artillery could not support our forces because it was said Bumla was out of range of the howitzers. This is quite wrong, because 7 Mountain Battery had its mules and their pack guns could have been deployed anywhere even right on Bumla itself and withdrawn literally in a jiffy after having accomplished their task. The Chinese had been making preparations for the attack for the past two or three days and even had had the audacity to occupy assembly areas in the open and carrying out morning PT (physical training) right under the noses of the Indians. Their intention by now ought to have been obvious, having overrun

7 Brigade on the 20th. If only our artillery had engaged them, they could have been killed in their hundreds. Orders for opening fire had to come down from the highest authority, in this case HQ Eastern Command whose intention was not to provoke the Chinese. There is a saying in Hindi about the futility of a he-goat's mother's prayers for her offspring when it is inevitable that the butcher's knife must eventually do its job. There is also the 'Dilli Door Ast'(Delhi is still far) syndrome that afflicts us from time to time. It's a kind of mental paralysis, quite in evidence in peace-time, when people are simply afraid of taking a decision without the senior's OK, who in turn looks to his senior and so on up the chain; and at the end of it is a no and in any case it is already too late by then. Everybody has played safe and saved his skin, so what if the organisation, the Army or the country, suffers in the bargain. This point is stressed here but this was only one of the many instances in the '62 war, two glaring ones having been the failure to re-site first the Dhola post and later 7 Brigade itself .

At about 5 am the Chinese launched their attack on the Sikh platoon on IB Ridge, commanded by Subedar Joginder Singh. Captain Gosal, the Forward Observation Officer with the battalion, now insisted that artillery fire be brought down immediately. The permission was at last given by the Army Commander, who happenned to be present at Tawang at that time. This tiny force under this gallant subedar beat back at least three attacks and mowed down a good many of the enemy. Only four men of this platoon managed to get back to the company position at Tongpeng La. Subedar Joginder Singh was badly injured, taken prisoner and died of his wounds while in captivity. He was later awarded India's highest gallantry award, the Param Vir Chakra.

At 7.30 am the Chinese made contact with the Sikh company defences at Tongpengla, now reinforced with a platoon from Milakteng La. For four hours the company held on doggedly, inflicting heavy casualties, under the inspiring leadership of its company commander, Major Hari Pal Kaushik (an ace forward of the Indian Olympic hockey team). Artillery support from our artillery was deadly accurate, as the company had one of the finest gunner officers (Captain G.S Gosal of 22 Mountain Regiment) as an OP officer, who was not only a tremendous shot but had had the presence of mind to have recorded the various possible targets as accurately as it was possible on his quarter inch map. The battery had also previously fired in the area after creating an ad hoc firing range, and this had helped to determine meteorological corrections for ensuring greater accuracy. This was a breach of orders but it paid dividends quite out of proportion.

Hari Pal Kaushik's company had given a bloody nose to the Chinese and blunted their attack, inflicting casualties and making them temporarily halt their operations. At 11 am the company was asked to fall back on Milakteng La. Consequently 1 Sikh managed to make a clean break with the Chinese, a prerequisite for the execution of withdrawal operation, always a very difficult thing to achieve in war. A few pertinent points need to be made with regard to the excellent showing of 1 Sikh. It was in sharp contrast to what happened, three weeks later at Sela, where their withdrawal became a disorganised rout; but we shall record that episode later.

1 Sikh had been in Tawang sector for nearly six months and their reconnaissance of the Bum La area, including likely enemy approaches, had been detailed and thorough. They had had sufficient time to prepare their defences, while the rest of the 7 Brigade was out on the tramp in Nam Ka Chu area. Furthermore what undoubtedly gave them heart and the ability to stand and fight was the timely and accurate artillery support. This battle-winning (and often battle-redeeming) factor seems to get glossed over time and again in

histories of wars and battle scenarios. It is a fact that whenever artillery has been given its due importance, the result has been a happy one. It is not often realised that many more enemy are killed by guns than by rifles, machine-guns or bayonets. In this case 7 Battery fired over 2000 rounds during the day out of 6000 available at the gun position. The heavy mortars did a fine job too. 97 Field Battery engaged a Chinese concentration at Gyamyang firing off 300 shells from each of the eight guns.

Another Point: It's the initial reaction that makes all the difference. Fear is the key factor, which causes one to fight, flee or freeze. The reaction can be modulated by leaders by their personal example, and can be contagious. 1 Sikh's marvellous show took place because there was a Subedar Joginder Singh and a Major Hari Pal Kaushik among their forward elements on that day.

According to General N Prasad's account in *The Fall of Tawang*, Sen was panicky because his helicopter had not returned for him. Yet in a fit of misplaced bravado he had said that he wanted Tawang to be held at all costs. He was talking big. He was going to send two brigades to reinforce the garrison. He was merely building castles in the air, because considering the logistics, it would have taken a minimum of two weeks for this to have materialized, but then he had never been acquainted with logistics. The Chinese might have liked to thank him for his abetting their operations at Nam Ka Chu, but were definitely not going to oblige him by allowing him a month or so to bring in his two brigades. In the event, within just 12 hours Sen (who was on his first visit to NEFA) changed his mind once he learnt that three enemy regiments with as many in reserve were converging upon Tawang. As it happens in such situations, rumour had it that the Chinese coup de force to capture Jung bridge had already advanced upto Mukdang La and brought the Garhwalis under heavy artillery and mortar fire. But actually nothing like that had happened. 1 Sikh's stout defence had caused an appreciable delay on the enemy. Their cut-off force made it to Mukdang La only in the early hours of 24 October.

The orders to withdraw from Tawang were given to 4 Brigade between 7 and 9 am on 23 October. After that Generals Sen and Prasad left Tawang, the former by helicopter to Tezpur and the latter by road all the way to Sela and then Dirang.

Withdrawal from a position or a theatre is never an easy thing. There is always much confusion and chaos. In this case, besides the fighting troops there were hundreds of pioneers, Assam Rifles personnel and civilians including lamas, as also a few Chinese agents streaming down the road. There were hardly any vehicles, and the narrow road to Jung had become a quagmire. 97 Field battery had to abandon their guns as the towing vehicles got badly bogged down. 2 Derajat Battery's two guns at Mukdang La had to be left behind as there were no mules to bring them back. But the guns at Lao Basti were manhandled all the way to Jung by the sturdy Sikh troops.

4 Garhwal was given the task of covering the withdrawal of I Sikh from Milakteng La as late as 4 pm on 23 October. They too had to leave behind a good deal of their equipment, but 7 Bengal Battery was better off as they had their mules. The troop from 116 Heavy Mortar battery carried their mortars on their backs up to Pankentang. It would have taken them a few days at their going rate to reach Jung. The only answer was to roll them down the hill at staggered points.

All in all, large numbers of guns, mortars, medium and light machine guns, wireless sets, ammunition of all kinds were lost to the enemy. What was ironical was that very sizeable stocks of supplies and ammunition that had been air dropped by the Air Force with such a diligent effort were gifted to the Chinese inspite of a hasty effort to destroy them by burning before leaving. The items included rations for 2800 mén for 21 days, over 2000 sleeping bags, about 1500 each of blankets and mattresses, one and a half second lines of small arms ammunition and over two thousand shells and cartridges of 25 pounder guns. A large quantity of ammunition dropped on October 22 in a bid to hold Tawang 'at all cost' lay scattered on the DZ.

1 Sikh and 7 Bengal Mountain Battery reached Tawang as late as 11 pm on the night of 23 October. Many bashas and stores were on fire though the Chinese were yet to follow up. By about 8 am on 24 October, all troops from Tawang sector had crossed over Jung bridge. They made a transit halt at the convoy ground at Jung from where, in various modes, they began moving up towards Nuranong and Sela. 4 Garhwal was left behind to guard Jung bridge. Towards the evening the Chinese established contact, deployed four of their mortars on the slopes opposite Jung. Just before last light the Chinese made a rush for the bridge. The Garhwals panicked and ran but 18 Engineer Company personnel under Second Lieutenant Kailash Dhingra managed to blow up the bridge just in time. Simultaneously the Chinese mortars opened up, a salvo of star (flare) shells followed by a number of high explosive ones, sending a few hundred Indian troops still lingering on in the convoy ground scurrying for cover, followed by a run towards Nuranong and safety. The casualities on the Indian side just were four killed and a few more wounded.

In the final analysis, Brigadier Kalyan Singh handled the withdrawal from Tawang in a fairly cool and collected manner. There were losses in materiel but the formation and it's units came back intact and in fairly good morale. 4 Garhwal Rifles after its temporary lapse at Jung, recovered admirably and three weeks later gave a masterly performance as covering troops at Nuranong.

9

Personal Interlude

A Gunner's Shame

By first week of October, I was posted back to 2 Derajat Battery, which has been withdrawn from Nagaland and was now at Tawang but without its mules. Derajat had a fantastic war record, having won more battle honours than most Infantry battalions in the Indian Army. Its troops were Jat Sikhs, serving with whom is not every officer's cup of tea. You need to be tough, mean and large-hearted yourself. It can be disastrous if weak or meddlesome officers are put in command of Sikh troops. I was hoping that our chemistry would work.

On 15 October, I was ordered to proceed with a section of the Battery (2 guns and 24 men) to Mukdang La, a mountain feature at 12,500 feet, north-east of Twang over which passed the track from Bumla to Jung, bypassing Tawang. Company of 4 Garhwal Rifles was located there and we were to move up to give them artillery support. From Tawang we had to travel back towards Jung to a village by the name of Lao Basti, from where a mule track went up to Mukdang La. We were loaned 20 mules from 7 Bengal Battery for the carriage of guns and about a similar number of local ponies for the carriage of essential administrative loads. Because of the paucity of animal transport, no artillery ammunition could be carried. It was expected that this would be done in subsequent ferries, but in the event that never really could take place. All that we were carrying was pouch small arms ammunition amounting to 50 rounds of .303 rifle on each man and my loaded pistol.

Lao Basti, located at 8000 feet, had a colourful arch at its entrance, an impressive stupa and a row of walls. The houses were big with massive doors but little ventilation. There were spacious courtyards where matronly women were spinning wool and old men with peaceful faces sat on the pavement rotating their prayer wheels. Small children with running noses and Tibetan apso dogs were the only ones to feel excited about our intrusion. There is something very fascinating about Buddhism, and I sometimes feel sad that it got wiped out from mainland India a millennium and a half ago. We would have been a disciplined nation in place of the existing anarchy, a state of affairs synonymous with Hinduism.

Once out of the village, the mule track climbed gradually over a series of spurs till we came to a major nallah coming down from the Geyshila feature. The scenery opened up. A clear sky and a refreshing breeze added to the gusto of the climb. There is a saying that a mule can go where a man can. I, therefore, decided to take a short cut to try this out. I was taking Kiplinges verse "The monkey knows where the road was, the wild goat knows where we pass......", rather literally. Allowance has the to be made for sufficient clearance on narrow ledges. On one of these a chase mule (called so because it carried the chase or the front half of the gun barrel) fell down a thousand feet precipice. It gave a frightening cry as it went cartwheeling down on the rocks and then lay motionless at the bottom of the cliff. Naik Ajit Singh, a burly six footer, scrambled down the precarious slope because the half-barrel had to be retrieved at all cost. In a remarkable feat in this high altitude, single-handedly, he retrieved the half-barrel weighing 200 pounds. Fortunately there was no other casualty and after sometime we rejoined the bridle path on the crest of the main spur of Mukdang La and confronted a breath-taking alpine landscape of meadows and pinewoods, of grazing yaks and yak huts. The track was now so broad that you could drive a jeep over it. Mukdang La feature was covered by a pine forest. To its east, about 500 yards away, was a big meadow, our gun-position-to-be. The company defences were neatly dug and well camouflaged by smart and sprightly Garhwali troops. I went to meet Major Rai, the company commander, to report our arrival. I found the Major sitting outside his bunker on his camp chair, reading a letter from his wife with an army balacalava on his head, looking smug and handsome. He was quite pleased to see me but became a little disconcerted when he learnt that we had brought no artillery ammunition. I told him "not to worry sir, my battery commander has assured me that it will be sent up in a day or two" I enjoyed some tea with *shakarparas* and left to site my gun position.

The men quickly dug up the gun pits and rigged up a log hut from the piles of pine sleepers from an adjacent logging area. For myself I selected a yak hut at the far end of the meadow. I had a very innocent young jawan named Bhajan Singh as my batman, who true to his name added to the serenity of the place by singing his gurbani in the early hours of the morning. Indeed there was nothing war-like in those surroundings.

A dull life it was for the next five days; and the intended ammunition didn't arrive. I got to know Major Rai a little more intimately. He and my BC Maj Devinder Goswami were batchmates from the IMA, and good friends. He was an Academy blue in football, but that was twelve years ago. What I saw in front of me was someone who had gone slightly soft. He didn't like this life away from his wife and children and the prospect of spending a most bleak winter in this isolated position. Nature's beauty, which was so evident, apparently interested him not. He was missing his peace-station life.

Meanwhile, unknown to us, 7 Infantry Brigade had been overrun and ceased to exist as an entity. But we were far away from Nam Ka Chu and even the distant echo of gun and mortar fire that had briefly erupted there didn't reach us. We learnt about the rout only on 23rd October, on the company wireless set. It was obvious that the Chinese would now advance for capture of Tawang. Maj Rai asked me, "Where is your ammunition?" I did my bit and informed my BC on the set.

I woke up in the early hours of 23 October, to the distant sound of artillery fire and realized that battle had broken out at Bumla. A little later MMG bursts could also be heard. I was vaguely excited. I was certain that the Chinese were being given a bloody nose. I was sure that the Indian Army would, in keeping with its great exploits in the Second World War and the Kashmir operations, stand up resolutely in the face of a Chinese offensive. The thought that we would be asked to withdraw was unthinkable. I was obviously lost in blissful ignorance.

At about 9 am I went across to meet Major Rai. The company was at stand to. We could still hear the distant boom of the guns and mortars and the sound of automatic fire. I thought that the Chinese had been beaten back but just then a disheveled junior commissioned officer and an equally shaken jawan of Assam Rifles from the Bumla post came running into the company position. One would have thought the Chinese were hot on their heels. They narrated a harrowing tale of how wave after wave of the Chinese had overwhelmed their position. They could well have been deserters but their arrival was hardly a good thing for our troops and the morale, even though there was no doubt that they were exaggerating. The lesson is that such people must never be allowed to mix with troops in defences.

At about 1300 hours C company received orders from its commanding officer to abandon its position at 5 pm and withdraw to Jung. My BC then came on the set and instructed me likewise. He said that efforts were being made to send up some mules of 7 Bengal and that I was to wait till 5 pm and in case they failed to turn up by then, I was to spike the guns and withdraw with the Garhwalis.

After tying up with Major Rai that the company headquarters would be the rendezvous for the withdrawal, I walked across to the gun position to break the news to my men. The fate of our guns depended upon whether 7 Bengal mules would turn up. I discussed the feasibility of man-carrying the guns, but found that the eight mules loads that a single gun could be broken into would itself require over twenty men to carry it. It was all very well to do so over a few hundred yards but a 20 km carry with the Chinese most surely catching up with us made the exercise unthinkable. A string of local ponies arrived at the gun position bringing our weekly rations. They definitely could have carried back some of the less cumbersome parts of the guns and we cajoled a most reluctant head of the ponymen, who finally agreed to give it a try. But he was a clever fellow because on the pretext of grazing his ponies an hour later we found no trace of the ponies or the poneywallas nor of their leader. They had given us the slip. The leader should have been kept as hostage but we had allowed ourselves to be duped by their hill cunning. Of course at the back of my mind was the belief that 7 Bengal mules would turn up.

By 4 pm, we had burnt everything that we weren't going to carry back with us. These were mainly rations and some personal effects (in my case a suitcase containing winter clothing including an elegant combination suit made by 'Selections' the regimental tailor at Deolali, for which I was even then paying monthly instalments through post-dated cheques. A couple of jawans advised me not to burn these brand new clothes and offered to carry them for me. But that was not the point. I told them that it would be a disgrace if I were to take these and leave the guns behind. (It was quite stupid of me to have carried all these to the operational area but then I had been told that there was little chance of war and one could always wear them at Tawang on Sundays.

When the mules didn't arrive and it was nearing the time for the rendezvous with the Garhwalis, I decided to walk across to the company location to ask the major if we could wait a little longer. It was all quiet and peaceful and I couldn't see a single Chinese anywhere near us. When I reached the company locality a few minutes before 5 o'clock, our appointed time, I found not a living soul there. There was a queer silence in that pinewood forest, with dying embers among a few heaps of burnt down stores emitting smoke and the occasional crackle. Obviously the place had been vacated some time back. I felt let down by the company commander. Surely, the least he could have done was to have sent a word through a runner before leaving. I walked back to the gun position and was in a for a worse shock. All but two of my jawans had also decamped. The two who had remained were Havaldar Mukhtiar Singh, the senior gun number one, and Lance Naik Jagir Singh, my wireless operator. Mukhtiar Singh, who was the senior most person after me, shed silent tears as I lambasted him for letting the men walk away without orders. He blamed it all on Naik Swaran Singh, the other number one. After I had left, Swaran Singh had talked the others into walking down the mountain. He had seen the Infantry departing from the defences and must have told the others that their Lieutenant Sahib had followed suit. Naik Swaran Singh was a very handsome, tall and well-built jawan and the ace sportsman of the battery. He obviously enjoyed a tremendous sway over the others, much more than the soft spoken but stolid Mukhtiar. Courage and cowardice have indeed very little to do with physical appearances. Had I committed a tactical blunder of leaving the gun position at a crucial juncture? A more shrewd leader would have taken Swaran Singh along.

Unlike the Infantry, the gunners do not have any regimental banner or colours (because we pride ourselves that we are everywhere, at every battle, *Ubique* or *Sarvatra*). The guns are our colours and men have fought to their end to protect them. I was aware that it would be a disgrace to abandon the guns even though I had my battery commander's authority to do so. That I wouldn't be the only one doing so was of very little consolation. What I was not aware of at that time was that the battery had never before lost a gun in battle. I was new to the battery. Maybe if I had known that, I would have shown a lot more initiative and ingenuity in getting the guns out from there and escaped this inglorious distinction of having been the first gun position officer of the Battery who abandoned his guns. We Indians have very little sense of history. My shame is nowhere recorded and would probably never have been known, but I feel I must own up for all its perversity.

We must have waited till 5.30 pm. The two 3.7 inch guns were in the gun pits just as we had deployed them. Guns are generally destroyed with explosives or by ramming an artillery shell and having another pushed down from the top thereby causing a premature explosion in the barrel leading to the gun's destruction. When this cannot be done, the guns are "spiked" which means that the sights and range cone/drum of the guns are damaged by striking at them with pick-axes and by generally removing the crucial parts. We had no means to carry out the first option and so proceeded to spike the guns. We removed the dial sights, the breech and firing mechanisms and spiked the range drum. Ashamed and angry, we retreated from there. Mukhtiar had tears rolling down his face. Jagir, the only heavily laden person amongst us, asked for my permission to discard the heavy 22 AH battery he was carrying in addition to the generally useless wireless set No 62 of Second World War vintage. He threw the battery down the khud and in the creeping darkness, when everything around us was quiet and peaceful, we resumed our most undistinguished withdrawal.

The three of us had hardly gone a kilometer when Naik Swaran Singh with the others suddenly appeared from their concealed position around a bend in the track. Towering over me with his great height, I must admit that I found it a trifle undignified in giving vent to my anger while looking up at that mighty figure, specially when he told me that they had not run away but had in fact taken the initiative to occupy an ambush position in order to surprise the Chinese. The truth, however, was that on catching up with the Infantry and learning that I wasn't with them, he had thought it prudent to wait for the three of us. I let it be for the time being and was relieved that I had now my complete party under me and we could move down in an organised manner. I would apprise my BC about Swaran Singh's conduct on reaching Jung.

After another hour we reached the shortcut junction and caught up with C company, which had halted there for a break. The company commander said that he was glad that we had come as they had been waiting for us. He said it with such a straight face that I began to doubt whether I indeed had got the rendezvous wrong. The company began moving laboriously, occupying tactical bounds every kilometer or so copy-book style. I found that quite ridiculous and painfully slow. The Chinese were most probably still at Bumla and I told him so. Because he had ditched me earlier, I decided now to part company and told him what I thought of him in no uncertain terms and headed down the short cut with my men at a brisk pace.

While we were on the short cut, the 7 Bengal mule column was moving up from Jung along the bridle path and thus we failed to meet each other. C company too was on the short cut at this time. It transpired that the mule column had been delayed in setting out for our position, but because there was no communication between us, this information never reached us. The column under an exceptionally brave Naik by the name of Joga Singh carried on steadily on the track to Mukdang La. The fact that they didn't meet any one on the way, convinced Joga that the position was still intact and held by our troops. As per Joga Singh's account when they reached Mukdang La at about 10 pm they found no one there. Obviously even the Chinese had not yet followed up. Lacking the expertise to dismantle the guns and more pertinently the implements viz wrenches and other tools, he retreated from the scene and led his unloaded mules back to Jung.

In the event the Chinese left the guns alone. Reports are that these were discovered just as we had left them by troops of 5 Mountain Division when the formation moved up to Tawang and Bumla in the seventies. A road had been built all the way to Landa (which is the name the erstwhile Mukdang La is now known by). In 1995 I thought I would go and take a look myself but when I reached there I was told that the guns had been removed by some unit who must now be using them as souvenirs in some peace station. I have yet to locate that unit.

A DOSE OF BATTLE INOCULATION

There was predawn darkness when after a cross-country descent we reached a rock escarpment above the road near Jung bridge. We decided to skid down the near vertical slope and in the process surprised a column of 1 Sikh being led by Second Lieutenant Surinder Dagur, my coursmate from the NDA. He greeted me with an impish smile made more so by his nicotin stained teeth. An unusually handsome officer, Dagur was known for his guts and his mischief-mongering at the Academy. His battalion had done exceedingly well at Bumla but Dagur having been in a depth locality had not been directly involved. He was itching for more action. When we reached the convoy ground at Jung, we parted company after I had smoked one of his Gold Flake cigarettes. His battalion moved on towards Sela and I went looking for my battery commander in the milling crowd that had gathered there. The scene was akin to a cattle fair in India. Hundreds of men with a sprinkling of officers sat around in aimless groups. Some were making up for the lost sleep but the enterprising types were brewing tea. The privileged ones, which included Brigadier Kalyan Singh, the Commander of the Brigade, Colonel Bhupinder Singh, our Commanding Officer, and a few staff officers had occupied the elegant premises of the Border Road's Officers' mess. I searched out my BC there and was rewarded with a welcome cup of tea. The Battery, with the two guns that it had been able to bring back, had now been ordered to deploy at Bridge 3 near Nuranong to cover the withdrawal from Jung. We were given a couple of one ton vehicles for ferrying our loads. I moved with the first ferry on a journey involving numerous zigzag turns of the road above Jung, till we entered the beautiful Nuranong valley through which flowed a stream with crystal clear water teeming with rainbow trout. Half way up, in perfect sylvan surroundings, was located the exotic rest house of the forest department. After unloading the vehicles I started on my return journey to Jung.

While moving back down the numerous zigzags, the mountain slopes across the Jung valley, the one my party had come down the previous night, was constantly in view. Something odd was happening out there. Surely, I said to myself, there couldn't be any of our troops on the other side still. So, who were those characters moving around in a determined and purposeful manner? Sometimes the obvious doesn't strike one straightaway. A careful scrutiny revealed that they were Chinese deploying their heavy mortars in full view of our troops, some of whom were still languishing on the convoy ground in their wishful wait for transportation to the rear areas. The Chinese activity had aroused considerable spectator curiosity. Brigadier Kalyan Singh, my CO, and the staff officers were enjoying their evening tea in the verandah of the mess (and there were salted almonds to go with it). A gunner of repute, Kalyan sent for his binoculars and in his phlegmatic manner gave out a running commentary of the enemy's action, as the Chinese took their compass bearings, aligned and then loaded their mortars. Our CO, who had been an instructor in gunnery, thought the performance was praiseworthy. The intention of the Chinese should have been quite obvious but the tea session, if anything, grew more animated. The scene around the convoy ground was equally curious. Most of the men had had no food the whole day and they were bored.. The appearance of the Chinese on the other side had helped to break the monotony. A decade plus of peacetime unrealistic training against dummy enemy in exercises and camps had dimmed the warlike instincts of our army. I wonder what the Chinese must have thought of us as they waited for the dusk, or last light in the army parlance, to start the fireworks. They must have thought we were the stupidest of donkeys.

It was about this time that I reached the convoy ground. It had just begun to get dark when a few illuminating shells lit up the sky above us. Soon thereafter salvoes of high explosive bombs burst all around us. The Chinese intentions instantly became clear, causing a fair amount of panic though few casualties. The Brigade Commander, who had fought against Romel in the Second World War, jumped off the verandah and took cover in a nearby ditch. Within seconds at least twenty others also jumped in, mostly on top of him. A strong well built man, he silently rose shaking off that terrified lot and walked over to his Willis jeep. My CO who was otherwise quite a fidgety person had kept his cool. He had with him his black labrador named, Quonde, on the leash. He too got into his jeep with his dog, orderly, and Ajit Singh his driver, and drove off behind the Commander's jeep. Nearly everyone else ran uphill towards Nuranong, away from the shells. Before I could realize it my driver too had bolted leaving the one-ton behind and I have never seen him since then to this day. My driving skill in those days was limited to a couple of lessons taken at the Indian Military Academy. I was what could be termed a dangerous driver. There was no way that I could have negotiated those hundred odd uphill bends. After going a few hundred yards I gave up and took to my feet and in no time had caught up with the fleeing lot. Once out of mortar range, I looked back and found that the Chinese had lit up their camp fires. They must have been very pleased with themselves.

It was a dark night but climbing uphill in the dark isn't all that problematic, it's the descent that is dangerous. When I reached the inspection bungalow, it was full. In one of the rooms that I managed to make an entry into, our adjutant Captain Pillai and our senior Subaltern Charanjit Dhillon slept soundly. Quonde was sprawled comfortably between them on the double bed in equally blissful sleep. A dozen odd empty beer bottles were littered on the floor. I didn't have the heart to displace Quonde. I looked around and located a small storeroom that was stacked with gunny bags which made a very comfortable mattress and also substituted for a sleeping bag and very soon I was in deep slumber. I had not slept for nearly two nights.

It was late in the morning when I woke up after a most refreshing sleep. The main room was without its previous night's occupants, only the empty beer bottles remained. For a moment I thought I had missed the bus and didn't particularly relish the idea of having to walk all the way to Sela, specially as I had had no solid food for fortyeight hours.

As I moved out into the open I was relieved to find my BC and Lieutenant Dhillon who informed me that the Battery had, deployed there in support of 4 Garhwal. All others had moved on to Sela and beyond.

After a day's stay in the rest house, we moved a kilometer further down the valley and occupied a proper position near Bridge 3, in the midst of the battalion defences. This was necessary because our guns had a planning range of only 4800 yards. We had other problems too, as we were without a "director" (a super compass mounted on a tripod) nor artillery boards and maps (which had been left behind at Jung). While a prismatic compass can perform the function of a director with reduced accuracy for laying the guns in the required arc of fire, without an artillery board and a map, engaging targets by indirect fire (which is the norm for artillery engagements) can be quite tricky. We resorted to a variation of what the gunners call the Oscar Tango Bravo Tango procedure. The observation post officer directly gave out the gun position officer's fire orders. It worked quite well and very soon the enemy mortars started getting the treatment. We were soon sufficiently emboldened to occupy a roving position ahead of the battalion's defences during the day and carried out harassing fire whenever we detected any Chinese on the slopes opposite.

Logistically we had still not stabilized, having left most of our stores behind at Lao Basti and the remainder at Jung. We were for a time without even cooking utensils. That the Border Roads' camp at Jung was well stocked and that they had an excellently furnished officer's mess has already been made known to the reader. My BC was an enterprising type and he began using me for foraging trips to Jung for retrieving our equipment and replenishing stocks of rations and other items.

My first trip was made with just two Sikh jawans accompanying me. For official consumption it was a reconnaissance patrol, but the actual mission was to retrieve artillery equipment (artillery board and director) and my BC's leather briefcase which contained twenty thousand rupees, the unexpended amount of the imprest money which the Battery head-clerk had left behind when the Chinese had begun mortaring the convoy ground on 24 October. Twenty thousand rupees were quite a big sum those days, equivalent to nearly Rs. 20 lakhs these days. The mission was accomplished successfully and I was particularly happy because my party was the first one to re-visit Jung. I found it quiet and peaceful. The Chinese were still across on the other side of the Tawang Chu. There had apparently not been many casualties because of the Chinese mortar fire. I came across only two dead bodies bloated and surprisingly left untouched by scavenging animals and birds though stray dogs were very much around. Possibly because enough food was still lying about, the dogs had not felt compelled to turn to eating human flesh. For all I know because of the dog's inherent loyalty to man, they may well have been guarding the dead bodies against other wild animals.

We were in full view of the Chinese but somehow no mortars opened up. They were only about a thousand yards away, across the gorge. It was quite uneventful. I had a good look around and was convinced that our Battery would gain immensely if we could bring a vehicle to load up the abandoned goods, viz bottles of Scotch whisky, crockery and special items of rations like sugar, dried fruits, tinned fruit and meat. I went and reported my findings to my maverick BC who was delighted to send me down again after a couple of days, in a one-ton vehicle. The first priority was to be our essential artillery equipment.

4 Garhwal troops had regained confidence and had fire in their eyes. The battalion had been reinforced by a company of 4 Sikh LI and a platoon of 13 Dogra. Major Rosario, the Sikh LI company commander, a Goan, sported a

turban and a thatha (a piece of cloth worn over the beard). He spoke fluent Punjabi. It was difficult to distinguish him from his Sikh troops. He was a soldierly fellow and, like most Goan officers, very witty and was indeed great fun to be with when out patrolling in no-man's-land.

Charanjit Dhillon (Cherry to his friends) was my immediate senior in the Battery. He was easy going, slack and the couldn't-care-less type, but with the fitness of a wild animal. He seldom changed his clothes and often went to sleep with his boots and jungle hat and, when required, would be awake and active in an instant. It was said that while serving in Nagaland, when his party had once come under ambush, he had leapt with the speed of lightning on a well armed Naga and overpowered him. The Sikh troops simply loved him. A shaven off Sikh himself, with a wisp of a moustache, he chain smoked. The troops didn't seem to mind, indeed his batman made sure that the "Laftain" Sahib's stock of Gold Flake cigarettes that came as part of army rations never got exhausted. Cherry liked to get tipsy with whisky or rum in the evenings but his behaviour was never offensive or obnoxious. He was a happy man, at peace with the world. Consciously or subconsciously he seemed to have modelled himself after the archetypical hero one saw in the Holywood westerns. I had begun to adore him.

Dhillon and I took turns to accompany Infantry patrols. None of us were any longer in any awe of the Chinese. That our 3.7 inch guns dominated the forward slopes of Geyshila and Mukdang La features was a decisive factor that allowed aggressive patrolling on our part. Weatherwise, October and November are the best months in the Eastern Himalayas. The sort of campaign we were engaged in was proving to be a fulfilling experience.

10

The Build Up

Operations South of Tawang Chu

After the withdrawal from Tawang, the logical step should have been to pull out the 'Thorat plan' from the office drawers and act on it after incorporating certain changes as the situation demanded. But it is natural that there was ample confusion among the top brass. Ad hoc decisions continued to be taken. General Sen's first reaction was to fall back upon Bomdila and orders to the effect had to be countermanded in less than 24 hours when the decision was taken by General Prasad to hold Sela. An hour before midnight on 24 October, a telephonic message arrived at 4 Division headquarters stating that 62 Brigade with 1 Sikh (from Tawang) and 4 Sikh LI, would hold Sela. 4 Garhwal Rifles and 2 Derajat Mountain Battery (now reduced to just two guns) and 18 Field Engineer Company were halted at Nuranong, 8 kms ahead of Sela. There has been great controversy ever since as to whether holding Sela was a right decision.

Meanwhile General Sen had managed to convince the Army Chief to sack Major General Niranjan Prasad, whom the former had accused of running away from Tawang on 23 October. It is quite normal to look for a scape-goat, when things go wrong, but in fact there was no justification for replacing Niranjan Prasad.

Major General Anant Singh Pathania, MVC, MC, Director of the National Cadet Corps in the Ministry of Defence at New Delhi, was hand-picked because of his gallant record in the Second World War as a junior officer and later as a commanding officer in Jammu and Kashmir operations in 1947-48. He arrived on 25 October, and took over from General Prasad. It must have been quite a shock for an aging general to have been pulled out from a very cushy noncombatant job to the rigours of a high-altitude warfare. It would have been bad enough during peace-time but in the midst of operations, ordering this change simply because Pathania had been awarded gallantry medals twenty years previously, was simply criminal. No wonder then that soon after assuming command of the formation, Anant Pathania looked for the most comfortable site in the entire sector to spend the winter, hoping that the Chinese would be good enough to oblige by not attacking him, or, to scoot to the plains in case the Chinese made things too hot for his comfortable stay.

The appointment of Lieutenant General Harbaksh Singh,VrC, as the new GOC IV Corps, was on the other hand a totally welcome development. This tall and handsome general had a natural gift of vibing with the soldiers. During his visit to Sela on 25 October, he met numerous men of his old battalion, 1 Sikh, and others, and pepped them up after their harrowing withdrawal from Tawang. For Indian jawans such chats with a senior commander can compensate for any amount of physical hardship. And word of his presence soon passed around in that inexplicable way. But the moral assurance and the joy of the rank and file was short-lived when news came on 29 October of the return of General B.M Kaul, who resumed command of IV Corps and General Harbaksh was posted to Siliguri as GOC XXXIII Corps.

The Army Chief had met the Prime Minister on 25 October to brief him about the war situation and his future plans. Nehru made it clear that he left it entirely to the military to execute the war and evacuate areas if necessary; and that hopefully the Army would win back what they lose or surrender temporarily. No Chief could have asked for more, even if this latitude was given a couple of years too late. At the time the Army needed a Chief who could assert himself: General Thapar was not that man; he was too overwhelmed by events to start thinking and acting in a clear and positive manner. He acquiesced to the return of a not-yet-so-fully-recovered Kaul to IV Corps because Nehru felt that it would harm Kaul's reputation, which would suffer if he was not allowed to return! This treason- like decision, where the personal interest of one general was made to over-ride that of the country, virtually sealed the fate of the troops in NEFA. The omen was all too clear from the gloomy faces of the officers of 4 Division when it was learnt that Kaul had returned. The common refrain was "God save us now that Kaul is back".

To go back a bit, from October onwards, a large number of troops from various parts of India had been ordered to move to NEFA. Various formations and units were converging on Tezpur and Misamari though without their first line transport, defense stores including digging implements (to save on railway rolling stock or space in the civil and Airforce aircrafts). There were frequent changes in grouping and regrouping. No formation retained its original orbat. In order to get an idea about the induction of units and formations into Kameng Division or 4 Division Sector, it's best tackled from the time they left their parent stations in India.

62 Infantry Brigade

62 Infantry Brigade was a newly raised formation in 1959. In 1962 it formed part of 20 Infantry Division and was located

at Ramgarh near Ranchi, equipped and trained for mobile operations in the plains against East Pakistan. The formation left Ramgarh for Tezpur on 15 and 16 September with the following units:

a) 4 Sikh

b) 4 Garhwal Rifles

c) 2/8 GR

The special trains carrying 4 Sikh and 2/8 GR were diverted en route to Johrat (2/8 GR was placed under command of 5 Infantry Brigade and 4 Sikh under 11 Infantry Brigade). Thus 62 Infantry Brigade less two battalions reached Charduar (near Tezpur) on 19 September. On 8 October, 4 Garhwal was also taken away from the Brigade, leaving brigade headquarters with absolutely no troops to command!

Subsequently HQ 62 Infantry Brigade moved to Tawang on 21 October, only to fall back on to Sela on 25 October, with 1 Sikh placed under its command. Additional troops had soon begun to arrive. 4 Sikh LI ex 48 Infantry Brigade and 2 Sikh LI from Southern Command joined the brigade on Sela.

The initial reconnaissance for the deployment of the brigade in Sela was carried out by Brigadier N.K Lal, the commander of the brigade. On 29 October, Brigadier Hoshiar Singh, IOM, till then Colonel Administration, NDA Kharakavasla, arrived on promotion and relieved Brigadier Lal. It was yet another dramatised posting. An ex-Second World War hero (Hoshiar had won his awards twenty years previously as a Viceroy's Commissioned Officer) he had been specially picked up to conduct what was expected to be the most fierce battle of Kameng Sector. All cadets with the Commandant and all officers had lined up at the Pashan gate at the NDA to give Hoshiar a would-be saviour's send off. On reaching Sela, he had pronounced it as impregnable. In Hindi he had said *Arre Bhai yeh Sela nahin Shila hai* (Brothers, this place is not Sela; it is a Rock). A few days later he visited covering troops defences at Nuranong and gazed at Tawang from a vantage point. He found it most fascinating. In examining its easy southern slopes he had done some loud thinking about how he would go about recapturing Tawang in the spring of 1963. As a side thought, he felt that one could make a good polo ground out there, a reminder no doubt of NDA life, where polo is such a popular and prestigious sport. But life is full of ironies and Brigadier Hoshiar was destined for a fate which is the lot of those who fail at the crucial time in war. Or, put more bluntly, the old warhorse had been pushed up beyond his level of competence.

65 Infantry Brigade

65 Infantry Brigade had been located in Hyderabad (Deccan). It left for Siliguri on 14/15 October. On reaching Barauni, its destination was changed from Siliguri to Misamari where it arrived on 23 October with its original complement of units; 19 Maratha LI and 4 Rajput.

After a briefing at Corps HQ, the reconnaissance groups left for Bomdila and the formation completed concentration in Bomdila by 27 October, but troops were not committed to ground as there were plans to move it further up, possibly for beefing up the Sela defences. Eventually by 30 October, 65 Infantry Brigade was moved to Dirang. The brigade was commanded by the aging Brigadier G.M Sayeed. On arrival at Misamari, Sayeed was replaced by Brigadier A.S Cheema. It is believed that the divisional commander didn't like Sayeed. It was also felt at the IV Corps Headquarters that like NK Lal at Sela, Sayeed was too old and unfit besides being 'under-moralled if not demoralised'[1].

48 Infantry Brigade

48 Infantry Brigade had been part of 17 Infantry Division in Ambala (a Punjab plains oriented formation) with the following units on its orbat:

a) 5 Guards

b) 1 Sikh LI

c) 4 Sikh LI

d) 6 Field Regiment

On 21 October, the brigade received its warning orders for move to NEFA. 5 Guards was at this time undergoing training with the Jungle Warfare School at Clement Town near Dehradun. General P.N Thapar, the COAS, had visited the battalion there. The impression he left in the minds of the officers was that of bushy eye-brows, an old retiring general who spoke well.

The brigade was commanded by Brig Gurbux Singh, a gunner, son of a rich building contractor knighted by the British for his contribution in building Lutyen's Delhi, and brother of the now famous author and journalist Khushwant Singh. Brigadier Gurbux was a polished, dignified man, somewhat reserved and retiring with a warm disposition. The commanding officers were: Lieutenant Colonel Munshi Singh Brar of 1 Sikh LI, Lieutenant Colonel Nanda of 4 Sikh LI and Lieutenant Colonel Jai Singh of 5 Guards.

The first of the brigade's military trains left Ambala on 23 October. By 28 October, the brigade had concentrated at Misamari. On 4 November, one platoon of B Company 5 Guards under Captain Amarjit Singh was dispatched to occupy a patrol base at Poshingla. On 6 November, the brigade left in a jeep convoy for Bomdila. On reaching there 4 Sikh LI was detached from the brigade and sent to Sela to be part of 62 Infantry Brigade. In its place 1 Madras on arrival from Nagaland was given to 48 Infantry Brigade.

Artillery

By the beginning of November, the division had the following artillery units in the Kameng sector.

a) Headquarters 22 Mountain Regiment with 2 Derajat Mountain Battery and 7 Bengal Mountain Battery.

b) 5 Field Regiment less guns of 97 Field Battery (abandoned at Tawang).

c) 6 Field Regiment.

d) Elements of 34, 116 and 135 Heavy Mortar Batteries.

The guns were deployed piece-meal by batteries and even troops and sections in order to cover the entire sector. Their actual layout will be given out when we come to the detailed deployment of troops.

Armour

Armour being the seniormost arm in the army is normally listed as number one when giving out the orbat of a formation. But in Kameng, the terrain didn't at all suit the employment of armour. It was somebody's hare-brained idea to use it as a tactical surprise, specially in the defence of Sela! 7 Cavalry (less a squadron) was ordered to move from Varanasi in the last week of October. It had World War II Stuart Tanks. On arrival at Misamari one squadron was inducted into Kameng sector, one of its troops to be deployed at Bomdila, another (with squadron headquarters) at Dirang and the third at Sela. The narrow, bad road, steep climbs and descents took their toll of the obsolescent Stuart tanks. Two tanks and some men were lost on the way. The squadron commander, Major S.S Jamwal, discovered that the climb to Sela was beyond the capacity of his tanks. The strain on the engines was too much. The tanks at Bomdila and Dirang Dzong, when they got there eventually were practically useless. But our armored lads have generally a tremendous gift of the gab and can be great 'Sheikh Chillis'. For the reader who has a sense of humour, it is recommended that he read the official history of this squadron.

NOTES AND REFERENCES

1. However, many old officers of the brigade interviewed by the author, hold the view that Sayeed was a good and a committed commander and that the formation would have done well under him.

11

The Imperatives of Deployment

There was, as we have seen, a difference of opinion about the relative importance of Sela and Bomdila leading to the initial confusion when orders for falling back to Bomdila had to be countermanded. The BGS Corps Headquarters was convinced about the prime importance of Bomdila, but surely he did not imply that Sela was to have been left unguarded! It was a question of relative importance and about that there can be no doubt that Bomdila as well as Mandala ought to have had priority over Sela. Eventually one of the main causes of 4 Division defences foundering in the face of the Chinese pincer attacks was that the Bomdila defences had been neglected and Mandala area had been left unoccupied. Yet, Sela was no death trap either as has been made out by certain analysts, but neither was it so formidable as to call for the major part of the division defences to be based upon it. Firstly, it was too near Tawang, which was to act as the launching pad for the second phase of the Chinese offensive. The Chinese would have simply battered away without having to regroup or redeploy their forces for a month or two if necessary even if we had built up Sela defences to two brigades. They had sufficient forces to accomplish their mission. Massing three or even four divisions was no problem for them. They had ensured that by extending the road from

Bumla to Tawang. Secondly, there was mis-information being bandied about that 'Old Father Winter' would put an early end to the operations. In fact Sela and Bumla do not close till end-January and that too not for long. The precipitation in Kameng is much less than in the Western Himalayas, an aspect which was generally not fully understood by our military planners. The Chinese therefore had ample time at their disposal. Thirdly, Sela could be bypassed and cut off, and worse, invested from nearly every direction. Finally, there was the risk of infiltration into the big bowl like interior of Sela defences during bad visibility or, once one of the forward localities was driven in.

There were other disadvantages too, the foremost being almost total dependence on air maintenance, which itself was subject to disruption by weather as well as likely anti-aircraft action by the Chinese. It has also been said that the biggest weakness of the Indians at Sela was the failure to cater for the effect of extreme cold (the wind-chill factor) and high altitude would have on troops suddenly rushed up from the distant plains. But this is not true. Indian troops are a hardy lot. The troops that had been suddenly rushed in were 2 Sikh LI and 4 Sikh LI and they acquitted themselves well. The de-motivators were the officers, and unfortunately most of them were the ones on the staff.

On the other hand, the imperative of holding Sela should not have been in any doubt. The question is of the force level and whether it should have been designated as vital ground, or a delaying position strong enough to make the Chinese redeploy and regroup for launching their offensive against the main defences around Bomdila. Indeed, any worthwhile delay by the Indian forces would have placed the Chinese in a fix in the overwhelmingly pro-Indian world opinion which would have been inevitable.

What it really boiled down to was 'After Sela What?". But this question was never posed or answered.

Irrespective of the above, once the decision had been taken to give top priority to building up Sela as the major defensive locality, and so much effort put in nearly every manner, it could never be imagined that a commander would simply abandon the defences and walk out with his troops because his senior had panicked; and then gone on to blunder and undertake a most inept kind of withdrawal.

Courage is, as we all know, of two kinds, physical and moral. Of the two, physical courage can be of questionable merit. It has a lot to do with the circumstances. Even a rat will fight back if cornered. And then we also know that a fair percentage of citations in war are motivated and even cooked up. There is the saying that generally the second best get the awards, the real brave die unsung. The intention, however, is not to decry physical courage but to emphasize that a physically brave man need not necessarily be morally courageous. Moral courage is a rare commodity and is the hallmark of a true leader, and therefore cannot and must not be confused with the other. This is where we went wrong in 1962 in Kameng division in NEFA.

Locating the division headquarters in Dirang Dzong was the real bloomer; because it was a death trap. Moreover, a valuable part of the force (a whole brigade) got sucked into the valley for the defence of the divisional headquarters, yet a sense of security always eluded the GOC. General Palit has written in his book that as the DMO he was under the impression, after his detailed discussions on 25 October at Sela, Dirang and later Tezpur, that the second brigade was also to build up on Sela by occupying defences around Senge and that the divisional headquarters would be sited there. It had come as a rude shock to him on 17 November to learn that HQ 4 Division had all the time remained at Dirang Dzong, as also 65 Brigade because Anant Pathania's penchant for headaches did not permit him to remain at Senge! High altitude headache is a fairly common occurrence but it disappears after a few days once a person gets acclimatized. General Kaul, it is believed, had given permission to General Pathania to move his HQ to Dirang when the latter pleaded headaches. Kaul consulted no doctor; just a personal *meharbani* (kindness) on his part, as was his wont (and to hell with national security). Kaul, one is told, could be very considerate and kind towards his juniors, and in any case hadn't he himself commanded IV Corps for nearly ten days in October from his sick bed in Delhi! It must have been a unique instance in modern warfare that the health of a GOC outweighed all tactical considerations. But there is a counter-point; perhaps Kaul was hoping that the Chinese would not be putting in any attack that winter. The scenario is both sad and farcical.

Someone in Corps Headquarters ought to have woken up to this serious lapse and done something about it. It is believed that Pathania's GSO 2 SD of HQ 4 Division had been sent by him to Tenga valley to reconnaitre a site for even a further pull-back of his HQ! But by then it was too late and Major Ummat (the staff officer in question) who knew what the game was all about (i.e., the plan to upstick and run), instead of wasting time on a futile effort had ensured his own safety by making straight for the foothills.

Brig. K.K Singh, the BGS IV Corps, had correctly appreciated the strategic importance of Bomdila. After Sela it was inevitable that the final battle would have to be fought at Bomdila, where the Indians enjoyed all the advantages. Bomdila was only a three-day march from Foothills in the sub-Himalayan belt, whereas for the Chinese maintaining even one division engaged in an offensive operation of war 250 to 400 kilometers away from their bases in Tibet would have been highly problematic. It sometimes happens that one leaves the easiest problems to be tackled last, thinking that when the time comes the needful will be done. This can be not only dangerous but robs one of the fruits of sure success.

Officer-cadets at the Military Academy are taught the principles of war; the first and most important of them being the selection and maintenance of the aim. Where things go wrong is when one fails to visualize the likely course of events in a realistic manner. If that is not possible, the simple advice of hoping for the best and preparing for the worst is highly recommended, and can compensate for a whole lot of gray areas in the information about enemy strength and intentions.

It is said that the Intelligence capability of the Indians about the Chinese was literally zero. This is not true. What is true is that commanders were loath to stir out of their comfortable billets and therefore tailored the Chinese threat entirely to suit their wishful plans, the bottomline being that the Chinese were unlikely to launch their second phase of the offensive so soon. However, even if we grant that there was indeed very little known about the enemy's intentions then, there was another way of solving the problem as long as the aim was to defeat the enemy.

If we consider the ground factor alone, it would be seen that Bomdila and Mandala areas needed to be occupied by about two brigades. At those lower heights, these formations would have needed no special equipment or snow clothing. A combination of mule and mechanical transport columns supplemented by air transport support would have ensured adequate and continuous supplies of arms, ammunition, rations and defence stores.

The Chinese would have required a minimum of two divisions to capture the Indian defences at Bomdila and Mandala. They would have been further required to bring up their artillery, with all the attendant prerequisites of forward dumping of ammunition and moving up of their logistics bases, a problematic expedient if you consider that a brigade group would have been operating in Sela and Poshingla, fighting all the way back to the main defences from prepared delaying positions. Add to this the inherent capability of the Indians to reinforce Bomdila with more Infantry and artillery. The Chinese trapped in the Rahung bowl and the Dirang valley would have suffered incalculable losses from Indian artillery fire.

It was a question of putting the 'Thorat Plan' into practice. But one can understand why it was not done. Headquarters IV Corps had been raised overnight on 3 October, 1962, and was immediately overwhelmed by events in Nam Ka Chu; and now all the emphasis was on Sela. The staff had had no benefit of previous knowledge and were given no time to do its homework once the Chinese increased the pressure; furthermore, our offensive in the Walong sector gained prominence. It is worth considering whether things would not have been different had HQ XXXIII Corps, even with a change in the GOC, continued to look after NEFA, because it would have ensured a much needed continuity in planning and execution.

With the above as background knowledge we can now take a look at the deployment as it actually was in the first week of November 1962.

12

The Deployment of 4 Division

By 10 November, all troops earmarked for 4 Infantry Division had been deployed in the areas allocated to them. General Pathania had estimated that within a fortnight, as soon as the Chinese built up their lines of communication from Bumla to Tawang, they would bring against him a force of approximately two divisions. In his appreciation, which he is believed to have given to General Thapar, the Army Commander and the Corps Commander on 6/7 November, he had asked for six brigades (17 battalions to be precise) for a successful defence of the Kameng sector. What he had under him instead were 10 battalions with another brigade (67 Infantry Brigade) awaiting induction near Tezpur. General Pathania was asking for the moon, considering the time and space factor. And when he didn't get what he wanted, his major concern became ensuring the security of his headquarters, in other words his own personal safety.

General Pathania had appreciated that to effectively stop any Chinese offensive along the main approach Tawang-Sela-Bomdila-Foothills, two pieces of vital ground had to be held; the Sela-Senge complex and the Bomdila feature. He totally failed to take into account the Mandala feature guarding the old traditional route to the Assam plains, the one he himself with his staff followed after deserting his headquarters on Dirang, and which the Chinese later used with impunity to ambush the retreating columns of 62 Infantry Brigade.

The real problem was the zigzagging 98 km distance between Sela and Bomdila and the certainty that the Chinese would cut this line of communication at numerous points. There was no dearth of mountain tracks for the enemy to use. This was the real trap the Chinese were to lay; yet, all that the road-bound Indian Army (which was so vulnerable psychologically, or rather paranoid of being cut off) needed to do was simply to absorb this Chinese inroad. Trying to counter it by sending troops occupying vital defences, proved fatal, definitely not with the available force level. The negative (defeatist) outlook would be to think about where the Chinese could cut one's own lines of communication (L of C). The positive (aggressive) attitude (which Harbaksh had displayed on 25 October) would be to determine the places at which we could cut the Chinese L of C, or ambush their infiltrating parties bypassing Sela. Perhaps force level, time and space made this option difficult. A cooler answer would have been to starve out the infiltrating force and to react chiefly with accurate artillery fire and our own jitter parties. In any case Sela was being maintained mainly by air, only partially by road. It was, therefore, essentially psychological warfare at work and Indians were just not mentally prepared for it.

DEPLOYMENT AS ON 10 NOVEMBER 1962

Sela

62 Infantry Brigade Sector

a) HQ 62 Infantry Brigade	South of Sela at km 90
b) 4 Garhwal Rifles (Covering Troops)	Area Bridge 3(Nuranong)

c) 4 Sikh LI	
i) Two companies	Two Lakes area (occupying a screen position on Track Jung - Chabrala - Senge)
ii) One company	Km 108(Near Nuranong)
iii) Battalion less three companies	Left shoulder of Sela
d) 2 Sikh LI	
i) Two companies	Kye La
ii) Battalion less two companies	East and forward of Sela on the feature between km 102 and 104
e) 1 Sikh	Right shoulder of Sela
f) 13 Dogra	Senge (on the high ground overlooking the DZ)

Artillery

g) 2 Derajat Mountain Battery (FF) (less one section)	Bridge 3 (Nuranong)
h) 86 Field Battery of 6 Field Regiment	Km 107 (Near Nuranong)
i) 95 Field Battery of 5 Field Regiment	Km 96
j) 96 Field Battery of 5 Field Regiment	Km 90
k) 116 and 34 Heavy Mortar batteries	Sela

Engineers

l) 19 Field Company — Km 76(Shukla Camp)

Services

m) Mobile Dressing Station(MDS) — Km 76

n) Advance Dressing Station and Strecher Bearer Company — Km 90

o) Composite Platoon — At the DZ at Senge

p) Advance Workshop Detachment(AWD) — Senge

Dirang Dzong

HQ 4 Infantry Division

HQ 4 Infantry Division occupied accommodation consisting of a stone building and a cluster of neatly built bashas on the south bank of the Khouma river, constructed by the Tusker Force (Border Roads). For some in-explicable reason it was not considered necessary either to prepare or to occupy proper defences. HQ 4 Artillery Brigade was co-located with it. Brigadier Gurbax Singh Gill was the new commander of artillery brigade, Brigadier Kalyan Singh having moved over as Commander of IV Corps Artillery Brigade in Tezpur.

65 Infantry Brigade

a) HQ 65 Infantry Brigade with normal ancillary units — Ewang

b) i) 19 Maratha less two companies — Ewang

	ii) One company	Point 2900 (south of Khouma river)
	iii) One company	Point 2090 (north of Khouma river)
c)	4 Rajput	
i)	Battalion HQ with one company(for defence of the bridge. The company was deployed on the feature astride the bridge)	Bridge 1
ii)	One company	Dangsikpu on Bhutan border
iii)	One platoon with a section section of mountain guns from 7 Bengal Mountain Battery	2 kms east of Ding Pksu
iv)	One company (To guard route Dzalungala-Nyakma-dung)	Point 3582 on the Sela road
v)	One company	Point 2898 and Lubrang

Artillery

d)	i) HQ 6 Field Regiment	With 65 Brigade Head-quarters at Ewang
	ii) One Field Battery	Near Sagor village along the road.

Armour

e)	A Troop from 7 Cavalry Squadron	Ewang

Bomdila

48 Infantry Brigade

a) HQ 48 Infantry Brigade	In and around the Circuit House at Bomdila (It too never occupied any defences)
b) 5 Guards	
i) One company with the Battalion HQ	On the slope between Brigade HQ and Political Officer's bungalow
ii) Two companies	In bashas short of the power house. Their task was to occupy a defended area on the Wango ridge to the south east.
iii) one company less one platoon	In bashas near the cinema (It was dispatched on 12 November to build up on the patrol base at Poshingla)
c) 1 Sikh LI	
i) Battalion less one company	Bomdila feature(slope between Point 2902 and the Political Officer's Bungalow)
ii) One company	Phudung (on the western flank to guard against the Mandala approach)
d) 1 Madras	In linear defence east of the road to Dirang - (east of Bomdila pass).On 16 November, one of its

	companies was later sent to Dirang to further shore up the defence of Division HQ!

Artillery

e) A Battery from 6 Field Regiment	Area helipad, south of circuit house
f) 7 Bengal Mountain Battery less one section but with a section from 2 Derajat Mountain Battery.	South of Brigade HQ
g) Troop from 135 Heavy Mortar Battery	North of the Political Officer's Bungalow

Armour

h) One troop (only two tanks were serviceable)	Near Brigade HQ.

N.B. Indian artillery units in NEFA were deployed by sub-units (batteries), troops and even sections. For the benefit of civilian readers it is considered pertinent to give out in brief the organisation of these elements.

(a) Mountain Regiment	Mule-based, with batteries operating independently. Each battery had four 3.7" guns with a maximum range of 6800 yards. Could be split into two sections each of two guns.
(b) Field Regiment	Twenty-four 25 pounder guns with a maximum range of 13000 yards (three

	batteries of 8 guns each. A battery had two troops, each consisting of four guns).
(c) Heavy Mortar Regiment	Twenty four 4.2″ Mortars (Organisation, same as a field regiment).

13

Assessment of Chinese Strength and Offensive Pattern

During the Second World War, two Kuomintang Chinese divisions had operated as part of the allied forces in Burma and their performance was not at par with others. They had made a poor impression on the Indian Army. Many ignorant people in India including those with fossilised minds in the Army, may have still thought of them as opium eaters, though our leaders should have known better after the Korean campaign. General K. S. Thimayya and General SPP Thorat had both been to the NNRC in Korea and had acquired a fair picture of the military tactics and capabilities of the PLA. Even General Kaul had been there. Ignorance about the Chinese tactics is therefore baffling. Perhaps the Government of India's policy of keeping the Army out of the picture in its border dispute with China for a decade from 1950 to 1959 helped to perpetuate an information blackout on the Chinese army.

But there was a way out in case military leaders had meant business. They could have used Japanese tactics in Burma as a template for planning counter-measures and operations, and they wouldn't have been far off the mark.

On 7 October, 1962, IV Corps war diary records the assessment of Chinese deployment in Tibet, opposite NEFA as follows:

a) One regiment on the following two axes:

   i) Tsona Dzong-Le

   ii) Tsona Dzong-Shao

b) One regiment less one battalion concentrated in Lhontse Dzong - Chayul Dzong with one battalion in area Longju.

c) An Infantry division in area Tsela Dzong deployed along the south bank of the Tsangpo river opposite Lhola-Nayu-Milling.

d) An estimated Infantry division in area Shugden-Drowa, Gompa-Tithang and Rima.

That amounts to a total of two divisions and two regiments opposite NEFA. If we take into account the Chinese version as given in *The Snows of the High Himalayas*, they had another division (61) also available, as also 134 Division of their 54th Army held in reserve. There is also a mention of "Chengdu Force", which may well be the famous 419 unit.

It was estimated that the enemy had deployed one division against 7 Brigade in Nam Ka Chu area. On 22 October, when the battle for Tawang was being joined, HQ IV Corps had sent a message informing HQ 4 Infantry Division that the threat to Tawang was assessed at one division plus one regiment.[1] On 9 November, IV Corps war diary records that the enemy was soon expected to build up his strength in Tawang area up to two divisions and launch an offensive. The road Bumla-Tawang was completed on 10 November, with a vehicle convoy arriving in Tawang on 12/13 November.

There have been other exaggerated claims. It can however be taken for certain that the Chinese had one more division (134 Infantry Division) in immediate reserve and, in all likelihood, the capability to induct an extra division into NEFA, if required. This is to suggest that they had plans to apply their famous human wave tactics and that they would have been prepared to go all out in case the Indians put up a stiff resistance at Sela. That in the event they ended up not even using one full division, because Indians failed to put up a fight, was a bonus they had not expected.

PATTERN OF OPERATIONS

The general assessment of a Chinese offensive at HQ IV Corps, was as follows (War diary of HQ IV Corps):

a) They would first drive in the covering troops at Nuranong and gain contact with 62 Brigade's main defences at Sela.

b) Then capture Senge by sending forces from the western flank on Chabrala axis and attack Sela from rear.

c) Capture Dirang Dzong, and simultaneously attack Bomdila via Poshingla Tungri-Thembang.

It would be prudent to take the actual plan of the Chinese forces as follows:

a) 419 unit less one battalion to advance along track Rho-Melling-Tsela-Poshingla-Changla-Tungri-Lagam and after Lagam split into two columns as follows:

   i) A battalion group to Sangti and Munna, to threaten Dirang Dzong by establishing a road-block at Km 31 and thereafter exploit up to Mandala.

   ii) A Regiment less one battalion to proceed to Thembang, cut off the road at Km 9 and attack

Bomdila if the situation permits and thereafter be prepared to exploit up to Rupa and beyond as follows:

Rupa-Tenga Valley

Rupa-Pirila-Chaku

Rupa-Morshing-Lagyala Gompa

b) 11 Infantry Division to operate as follows:

   i) One regiment to maintain pressure on the covering troops at Nuranong and Sela defences around Kyela and the east flank of Sela. One regiment to be in reserve at Jung to exploit any unexpected success.

   ii) A regiment less one battalion to operate along Track Yangyapla-Nykmadung-Bridge 2 and the Bridge 1 area.

   iii) One battalion to move along track Jung-Chabrala-Jungle and join up with the Yangyapla column at Bridge 2 Area.

c) 55 Infantry Division to launch the main attack on Sela once 11 Infantry Division has accomplished its task.

The Chinese troops carrying out the outflanking moves had to be self-contained with very little dependence on animal transport (as it takes away a lot of useful loads). The Chinese soldier fought and slept in the one pair of padded uniform he was wearing. He carried no bedding or pack. Most of the troops were armed with either a self-loading rifle or a carbine. Their light machine guns (with a drum magazine) were belt fed. They had trolley-mounted heavy medium machine-guns as well as 57 millimeter recoilless guns and medium mortars. The soldier carried his rations in a cloth tube which he tied round his waste. These seemed to consist mainly of rice, thupka, groundnuts, tinned pork and dehydrated vegetables.

The Chinese soldier was remarkably fit. A hip-swaying walk-jog seemed to be his normal pace or rather method of movement. He could carry on thus for hours together.

The Chinese had done their homework well. Evidence gathered from locals suggests that their key personnel, including guides, had acquainted themselves during earlier clandestine reconnaissances of all routes of ingress upto Bomdila and beyond, without the Indians having been any the wiser about their presence in Indian territory.

They always had interpreters in English, Hindi and India's major regional languages like Tamil close at hand for ready interrogation, permitting prompt action on information gathered.

What is most unflattering as far as Indians are concerned is that the Chinese planners had soon begun to read the psyche of the Indian rank and file, specially that of senior leaders, rather well. Did they really believe that just a brigade worth of their forces (419 unit) would put 28,000 Indian troops to flight ? It couldn't have been otherwise. Even for taking a big gamble, the probability factor has to be taken into account and a certain margin of safety catered for. And of course we all know that audacity pays in war.

NOTES AND REFERENCES

1. It is generally believed that Indian intelligence on Chinese strength and intentions was scanty, yet by comparing the actual Chinese action, the IV Corps assessment was fairly accurate and based upon some definite information. It is worth mentioning that Lieutenant Colonel (later Major General) Shabeg Singh was the GSO 1 (Intelligence) at HQ IV Corps. He was an extremely resourceful, unorthodox and intelligent officer but a somewhat shady character, who was later court-martialled as a major

general. Knowing Shabeg, it is possible he had developed sources on his own (there were enough Tibetan and even Chinese agents in Kameng and Foothills area). Shabeg may not have even kept his superiors informed of his clandestine activities.

Lieutenant Colonel (later Major General) B.M Bhattacharjea, who commanded 4 Garhwal Rifles, and was taken prisoner-of-war, had managed to warm up to his captors citing his CPM connections back home in West Bengal, so that in the course of conversations with them he gathered that the Chinese had employed their 11 and 55 Divisions and 419 unit. 419 unit was a specially trained regimental group.

14

Chinese Interlude II

Snows of the Himalayas

(Mao's study in Zhongnauhai. Mao is sitting on a sofa, his legs comfortably spread out. He is smoking. He has been reading a report about the enemy situation on the China-India border. Zhou En-lai, standing behind, him watches him attentively).

"Really, one can say the black clouds are pressing hard to push things over. It looks as if the whole of the Himalayas mountain is being turned upside down". Mao says smilingly.

Zhou: Mr Chairman, India's forces have increased by two additional divisions, altogether 9 brigades and bloody incidents have gone up rapidly.

Mao: It seems that (Nehru) does not care two hoots about an old friend's face or feelings. It seems that sweet-talking and persuasion do not work; they do not get registered on him.

Zhou: We have already worked very hard on the diplomatic front. But now America is putting its fingers in this. Imperialism hopes that the larger the war, the better.

Mao: When two marine creatures fight, doesn't the old fisherman benefit ? (Mao put out the cigarette and got up.) The American capitalists are highly principled. When it comes to opposing communism, they come up with money and weapons. Nehru has just to stretch his hand and Kennedy wholeheartedly agrees. He will give everything he (Nehru) wants, a lot of weapons and new ones too. Has our elder brother also given him anything?

"It is because he has these behind him that Nehru's backbone has been straightened."

Mao (looking out of the window at the trees, with a strong gesture of his hand): "We don't have what they have (A. bombs). We don't have them now but may have in future. But they can never have what we have."

Mao's sentiment immediately affected Zhou.

Zhou: "Mr Chairman, you are right. They have planes, high guns, atom bombs. We have the revolutionary spirit."

Mao: One must always have the spirit. Weapons can never be the deciding factor.

Zhou (nodding his head): Now some are using the UN to step up public opinion to send UN troops to India as was done during the Korean War. They are looking for an excuse to send the troops.

Mao (laughing): The honourables are really forgetful ! If it comes to the worst, they will once again prove that imperialism and all the reactionaries are paper tigers. It is difficult to rattle the Chinese people.

He sat down on the sofa and remained silent for some time deeply lost in thought. Zhou also did not speak; he knew that this was not the time to interrupt Mao's chain of thinking. Mao Zedong, as if talking to himself: "Paper tigers, even when they raise the wind (fart) loudly, they can arouse a lot of fear!"

Zhou: Mr Chairman, we will win this war. The question is whether we should, at a small price, achieve a big victory. If we want national prestige, military prestige, then we should not fight a war we are not confident about (winning).

Mao: I have been thinking. War and peace are a pair of opposites. They are also a unity. If we fight this war well, we will have achieved at least 20 to 30 years of peace. That would be like older generations planting trees and later ones enjoying the share. We should take a slightly longer view, shouldn't we? Tell Zhang Guohua and Ding Sheng to prepare for a tough war, a fiercely mean war. Don't underestimate the enemy. The weather in Tibet is severe. Our preparations must be well executed. We must see to it that the troops do not suffer from cold and hunger. The logistic task will be extremely difficult.

Zhou: I have already sent people to speed up things. I have also asked for the dispatch of some newly made 'Liberation' brand vehicles to the Tibetan area.

General HQ's Instructions: 28 October, 1962

"In view of the latest situation, we must prepare for a tough and ugly war because the enemy is relatively concentrated. His numbers are comparatively large, his fortifications comparatively strong and the terrain favours the enemy in terms of defence. You must understand this point clearly and must make comprehensive preparations. Never allow yourselves to become overconfident. In order to achieve a quick and decisive defeat of the enemy, the following points are raised. Please study them carefully for implementation:

(a) Immediately organize a capability for closely investigating the topography of this area and also concretely study ways of attacking the enemy, outflanking him, encircling him, penetration and where all one can cut off the enemy on the road. Select a point for breakthrough. If the topography does not permit large-scale outflanking or encirclement, think about the ways to penetrate the enemy using specially selected men to divide the enemy and destroy him bit by bit. If flanking and splitting up is made impossible by topographical limitations, then frontally pin the enemy down in a relatively small area and then attack him under the cover of artillery.

(b) We must concentrate decisive and superior artillery fire. Besides massing 92 and 60 mm guns and 57 and 75 mm recoilless guns, 40 mm rocket-launching tubes and flame-throwers, we must find some way of pushing forward one or two liens battalions of 120 mm forward artillery. All kinds of artillery must have sufficient quantities of ammunition and we must have enough quantities of explosives. In short, we must explore every means to overpower enemy fortifications with artillery fire as well as to cause heavy deaths among enemy troops.

(c) Establish good communications network. Besides securing communication with higher echelons, all battle formations must establish a way to lay field lines as well as make wireless contacts. Ensure ways for making timely and reliable contact for proper command and control.

It is the first week of November 1962. Zhang Guohua, commander of the Tibet Military District, takes off from the Lhasa airstrip lost in deep thought. He has been summoned to Peking.

Zhang's plane lands at a military field in a Peking western suburb. People from the GS HQ are waiting for him. He is taken straight to a meeting where Zhou En-lai greets him. Zhang has a heart problem. So Zhou asks him about his health but is assured that everything is O.K. This is an important meeting. Foreign Minister Chen Yi, Chief of Gen Staff Luo Ralinquing and Director of GPD Xiao Hua are present as well.

Zhou asks Zhang to make a presentation. The curtain on the wall is pulled aside revealing a map of China-India border.

Zhang: On 23 October, after our forces went in and occupied Tawang, they built an emergency road from Bumla to Tawang. At present our divisions 11 and 55, the 21st Army and 61 Div have made all preparations for a counter-attack. We also have the 54th Army and 134 Div in reserve. The Indians have greatly reinforced their strength and deployment. Their 62 Brigade and five Infantry battalions holding the area between Xi-Shan-[Nuranog] and Shen-ge-zong, the 48 Brigade is at Bomdila. The 4th Arty Brigade, 65 Brigade and HQ 4 Division are at Xin-de-rang, the 67 Brigade is at Fute-shan [Foothills] and the 4th Army Hqs is at Tezpur. The enemy has opened a 100 Km line from north to south with Sela and Bomdila as the two strong points. Behind it are Fute-shan and Tezpur. The Indians have already received American and British weapons and equipment, tanks and heavy artillery pieces are there. Xi-Shan-Kou [Nuranong] lies to the west of Sela. The topography is narrow; it is easy to defend but difficult to attack; there are snow-covered mountains on both sides of the road or there is primeval forest, making it difficult for the forces to move."

Zhang Guohua explains on the map the deployments on both sides and the possibilities of action.

There is silence in the room. All the high military commanders are in deep thought. Marshal Liu Bocheng has not spoken thus far. But he gets up and goes to the map and takes a careful look at it. He raises his glasses a bit and says deliberately and decisively:

Liu: The enemy has a copper-head, an iron tail, a narrow waist and a thick chest. He looks awesome, like a poisonous snake, he can do you harm but he also has only seven inches. You cut off those seven inches and he cannot manage his head and tail.

Marshal Liu's clear vision enlivens the whole atmosphere. Foreign Minister Chen Yi enthusiastically responds:

> "Oh yes! For our strategists such as our old Marshal to go against Kaul is very unfair. He [Kaul] has never fought a war for a single day. Now you suddenly want to cut off his seven inches. Don't you have any sympathy for him?"

Marshal Liu laughs: "It is for great poets to express compassion in a big way, isn't it?"

Liu: We can penetrate along three different routes, one to pierce the Bang-di-shan [Bomdila], one to cut the link between Sela and Cou-shan-kou in the east and cut the road to De-rang-zong and the third to go south through Chi-ku [Chaku] cutting Bang-di-shan from the plains of Assam. The enemy all along the eastern front then becomes a fish in the net, ready to be finished.

[The high-strategy for the war is thus decided]

Zhou: Our military strength and equipment is no match, whatsoever, for the Indian Army. But if we choose the right strategy and tactics, we can achieve a decisive victory in this war.

Zhang Guohua: We must now rapidly draw up a concrete plan and make preparations to counter-attack to prevent the Indian attack.

Zhou: We must organize our troops well. They must fight when asked to do so and stop when asked to do so; they must also withdraw when so ordered. Not only must they fight well, they must become a model for respecting rules.

[Zhang Guohua feels relieved. After a few days, he and his staff take the plane and are back at the China-India frontline].

15

Personal Interlude

Honour Lost and Regained

On one of my trips to Jung, I had the vehicle parked in a defiladed re-entrant because the Chinese always found it quite a tempting target for their mortars. Having done so I made my working party, consisting of two of our jawans, follow me to the convoy ground. Just then my attention was drawn to the frantic barking of a local dog. He would bark and then run around a basha, peep in and start barking again. This made me inquisitive. As we reached the hut an emaciated jawan with splinter wounds in his legs came crawling out on his arms. He was a medical assistant from the Army Medical Corps and had survived, for six days now after being wounded, on crumbs of food his friend and savior the dog had brought him. The same dog now had organised his rescue mission. There have been many legends woven around this faithful animal's service to man and what I recount is only a small example.

It was a long uphill to the road where the vehicle was parked and I had yet to begin with my mission's various errands. I, therefore, told the wounded jawan not to worry and that in an hour so we would be back to pick him up.

About this time I spotted a patrol moving around about a kilometer from us. I signalled to them to come over to our position which they did. It turned out to be a 15-man patrol from 13 Dogras (one of their platoons was deployed with 4 Garhwal). A sleek looking JCO was in charge. I instructed him to have his jawans improvise a stretcher and carry the wounded man to the road above. To this he readily agreed and I proceeded to ferret around in the area. I was able to get nearly everything on my list less sugar and for this I decided to try the abandoned ration stores of the DGBR located a kilometer further down the road. I told the Dogra JCO about where I was going and that I would pick up the casualty once I returned from the adjacent camp.

The Chinese mortars had been quiet till then. They must have seen our vehicle coming down to Jung and disappearing inside the re-entrant. But our journey now to the lower camp was well within their range on a straight section of the road, where the vehicle made a perfect moving target. No sooner had we started our journey that the enemy began firing their mortars. We nevertheless reached the lower camp safely. We concealed the vehicle behind a hillock and quickly loaded a 100 kg sack of sugar. Mortar shells were coming down with quite an intensity and the first kilometre of our return journey was the most crucial one. In order to minimise the number of casualties should our vehicle get hit, I asked the two jawans to climb cross-country on foot and wait for me about a 1000 feet above on the road where the mortars couldn't reach us. Having marched them off, I asked the driver to drive hell for leather and in the process forgot about the wounded man. The Dogra patrol was waiting on the roadside. Fifteen jawans with a casualty on a stretcher would under normal circumstances be quite prominent but I simply don't remember having seen them. My mind was preoccupied with enemy mortars and the narrow misses every fifteen seconds or so. I have no doubt that if it had been a howitzer engaging us instead, it would surely have got us. It was only after we had negotiated a couple of zigzag bends and well out of enemy range that I became aware of the lapse. I asked the driver to stop the vehicle and found that the patrol was coming up the foot track carrying the casualty. The Chinese had now begun to target them. Determinedly but unscathed they crossed into the safe zone. On meeting me the Subedar Sahib said "*Wah Sahib Wah, dar ke bhag Aye*" (Bravo Sahib, bravo; you got scared and ran away). I thought the admonishment was not warranted and certainly not coming from a JCO. I got very angry and insulted him in unmentionable words and in a manner that I ought not to have uttered. This simply infuriated the entire patrol and I suddenly sensed danger. I had heard instances of mutinies where angry troops had shot their officers and also about unpopular and disliked officers being conveniently bumped off by their own troops in war, the term used is fragging. Instinctively I turned to the meanest looking man in the group and asked him why was he looking at me like that. He said that when they had done a marvelous job in carrying up the casualty while I had run away in the vehicle how could I have the temerity to insult their Subedar Sahib and that they won't take it. I said sorry to the JCO and to mollify him further I wrote out a well deserved citation for him in his diary. I had the casualty placed into my vehicle and drove off. Well this incident definitely left a scar on my ego even though within myself I was certain that it was a genuine case of forgetfulness.

Within a few days of this incident, the battalion was ordered to send a company patrol to destroy the suspension bridge over the Tawang Chu below Lao Basti. C company with Major Rai in charge was detailed for the task. Maybe my foraging escapades to Jung had given me a little reputation of sorts. HQ Artillery Brigade nominated me by name to accompany this patrol as the FOO. We were to be away for two to three nights and I was looking forward to an exciting adventure even though I suspected that with Major

Rai in charge, nothing daring or spectacular could be expected. But I had not taken Devinder Goswami, my bachelor BC, into reckoning. He was raring for some action and made it abundantly clear to the staff that he himself intended to go for this mission.

The road to our roving position passed through the battalion defences. Once one crossed the Bridge 3, one came across a stretch of a scattered minefield laid by the Engineers along the stream to act as an obstacle against a sneaking attack through the deep valley. There was just a strand of barbed wire laid along the road to indicate the inner boundary of the minefield. There were no other mandatory warning signals about the gaps and the extent of the minefield.

Invariably our day used to begin with either Dhillon or myself leading our small group of vehicles to occupy the roving position. On this particular day it happened to be Dhillon's turn. I was to follow a little later. As I reached the forward limits of the defences, I found a group of men gathered on the road side. One of the ASC drivers, who was new to the place, had unknowingly walked into the minefield to answer a call of nature a hundred yards below the road. He had stepped on a mine and blown up his leg. There he was lying in terrible agony, bleeding away to certain death unless he could be rescued. A kind of futile debate was on and there was a general air of helplessness. It was a non-pattern minefield and only the Engineers, who were located beyond Sela, had the map of its actual layout. A wireless message had been sent but the earliest the map would have reached us was not before three hours or so, and the jawan would surely bleed to death by then. Major Rozario of 4 Sikh LI was there. The medical officer had also arrived on the scene and there were some bright types shouting encouragement to the fellow. I have never liked to be a part of crowds when little is being achieved. I felt sorry for the injured man and wished I could help him but quickly realized the hopelessness unless someone was prepared to take the risk and walk into the minefield and lift him out of there. I was debating the pros and cons of this when I suddenly noticed my friend the Dogra JCO with some of his men in the crowd and my mind was instantly made up. I asked if anyone would volunteer to come down with me to carry back the casualty. There was a sudden hush and then a Sikh jawan from 1 Sikh, Ram Singh, said, "Sahib, I'll come with you". There wasn't much time to think. I simply looked for a firm piece of ground, which had not been dug recently to place my feet on, but basically I trusted my luck. We got away with it, Ram Singh and I lifted the wounded man by his arms and legs, one of which was just a stump below the knee. I retraced my steps avoiding trip wire and within minutes we were back on the road. The doctor took charge and after having been administered first aid, the casualty was rushed in the ambulance to the Dressing Station at Senge. I never came to know whether the man survived. There was much praise and many words of appreciation. Subedar Sahib from 13 Dogra came over to me, shook my hand and his men lifted me in the air. I was happy that I had been vindicated. Life suddenly became different. I was no longer just an officer but had became a bit of a hero admired and respected by the men.

Acts of bravery and cowardice are matters of chance and accident. I should know, because I have had more than my due share of honours and awards in mountaineering because luck was on my side.

On 8 November, I got a shock when Lieutenant Bharat Inder Goswami, the erstwhile adjutant since relegated to the post of orderly officer at the Regimental Headquarters, suddenly arrived, without any prior notice, to replace me. I was ordered to move to R.H.Q. at Bomdila to take his place. Goswami had been a favourite of our previous CO, but with the arrival of Colonel Bhupinder Singh, there had been a change in the dispensation. Captain KTM Pillai had been appointed adjutant. An orderly officer is a kind of aide-de-camp (ADC) to the Commanding Officer and acts as understudy to the adjutant. The job has its prestige but to my mind it was too far removed from the action and excitement of battery life, specially during active operations. On 9 November, the Commanding Officer arrived on a day's visit to the battery and overruled the protest on my part.

Guru Nanak's birthday fell on 10 November that year and for our Sikh troops it was a very special and a solemn occasion. It was marked by an *akhand path* which had begun two days earlier with the *bhog* or the conclusion ceremony being performed in the morning of the Guru's birthday. This was followed by the *ardas* and *kirtan* and the *karha parsad*. It was all very sombre, rousing and dignified. Those handsome Sikhs could be bawdy and boisterous in other times but now they all looked pious and grim. The Battery had a boy by the name of Kirpal Singh. He sang splendidly. My heart was heavy at the thought of leaving this very fine outfit. I would miss the action, the gallant Sikh troops and in particular Cherry Dhillon, one of the bravest officers of the Indian Army. How would I have known that some strange force was at work and that both Bharat Goswamy and Dhillon would get killed in an ambush at Bridge 2 and I would never meet them again?

16

Conduct of Operations

The Chinese decision not to cross the Tawang Chu and make for Sela immediately after the fall of Tawang was misinterpreted by the Indians. General Kaul, after resuming command of IV Corps, addressed all battalion commanders and above, at Sela. He said: "Only the Chinese and the Devil know whether they would cross the Tawang Chu or not" or words to that effect. It was hardly a positive statement coming from the level of a Corps Commander. A few days later the thinking took a more comfortable and self-serving turn. The Chinese, it was felt, might not attack after all. This diluted the sense of urgency and naturally operational preparations suffered. It is true that the Chinese could well have sent a regimental group (or even less) bypassing Jung and Nuranong as early as on 24 or 25 October itself. If they had done that, Sela till then held by only one mixed company (made up of personnel from 51 Mountain Regiment under Commander Corps Artillery Brigade) would have easily fallen. But that would have been a self-defeating exercise, pushing the Indians back to strengthen the defence of Bomdila and Mandala areas, from where it would have been difficult to dislodge them. One more reason was no doubt also to give the Indians no reason for transferring Indian forces from its western borders to NEFA. The arrival of 5

Infantry Division by the first week of November could have caused a lot of problems to the Chinese. Happily for them, the Indians interpreted the delay in the enemy follow-up wrongly. Mao, in one of his maxims, has said, "Make wiping out the enemy's strength our main objective ; do not make holding or seizing a city or place our main objective................." That is what they were after.

FALSE OPTIMISM AND SLUGGISH PREPARATIONS

As the Indians began building up for the defence of Kameng, an air of optimism gradually began to waft over India. Shock, outrage and astonishment at China's "treacherous" attack, turned to a vigorous display of Indian unity specially among politicians and the urban masses. Characteristically Nehru, carried away by this emotional upswing in the country, began issuing confused and conflicting statements justifying the war and thanking China for "unveiling the true face of India; strong and yet calm and determined, an ancient face which is ever young vibrant on the other occasions." He kept harping on the peaceableness of the Indians and the depth of the national commitment to non-violence.

There was frequent mention of Chinese "treachery". But what is "treachery" in war? Are armies meant to go into war with benign intentions? Aren't cunning, deception, surprise and ruthlessness all essential ingredients for success in war? Don't they together add up to what we deprecatingly refer to as "treachery"? We Indians have always been allegedly a war-mongering people but with mixed-up values and vague ideas on warfare.

From 24 October for a period of two weeks there was a lull in the campaign. The Chinese forces needed to regroup and as already mentioned it also suited their design to try and confuse the Indians. Meanwhile 4 Garhwal Rifles, up forward of Nuranong, unaffected by wishful thinking, had begun carrying out aggressive patrolling in no-man's-land around Jung (on our side of the Tawang Chu) helped by the fire of our mountain battery from roving positions ahead of the Battalion's defences. Some 2000 feet higher up and eight kms away, a myth-like belief in the invincibility of Sela slowly gained ground and this got a distinct fillip with the arrival of Hoshiar Singh, with his chestful of gallantry awards. Morale was gradually building up but it was of the fragile kind, built in a vacuum of enemy inactivity and not backed by solid preparations on the ground. Even an invincible place needs defensive preparations. This will become amply clear later in the narrative. A party of press reporters visited Sela in the second week of November and carried back a good impression of the troops. But there were contradictions. On 12 November the Corps Commander addressed all Commanding Officers at Sela exhorting the troops to be administratively prepared for the coming winter at Sela. As an extension of this thinking, Brigadier Hoshiar Singh, during one of his visits to our roving gun position ahead of 4 Garhwal defences, got excited on sighting Tawang and shared with us his thoughts on the spring offensive that would most surely be launched after the coming winter. He once chided the Commanding Officer of 4 Garhwal for spending more time in preparing defences than in taking adequate measures for ensuring that the men have a comfortable winter. (Winter was in fact not that worrisome a problem, Nuranong appreciably being lower than Sela with its wooded slopes acting as a buffer against high winds.)

All this was happening while hectic 24-hour road-building activity including blasting was going on at Tawang since 25 October, day after day, and powerful bangs could be heard round the clock at Nuranong. During the night one could see the beams of powerful searchlights of road-building equipment near the Pankengtang heights. The Indian Border Roads had earlier estimated that it would take them six months to complete the section of road from Tawang to Bumla. It was therefore, quite logical to think that the Chinese would take roughly about the same time. The reality on the ground was disregarded. Was it because this would have called for some uncomfortable thinking? What after all is tactical surprise in war? The Chinese were out to achieve just that under the very noses of Indians.

The Chinese increased their pressure on Sela defences even as their road to Tawang neared completion. Their advance elements were out prowling, feeling the Indian defences and scouting the infiltration routes.

It's not that the Corps or the Divisional Commander had not visualized that the Chinese would infiltrate along the flanking tracks. What they had failed to appreciate was the strength of the force that could outflank Sela. The Indian commanders felt that the Chinese would attack only along the road axis from Jung to Nuranong and onwards to Sela, and they were preparing for it. This would also explain the peacetime profile of the Divisional HQ at Dirang Dzong. They didn't know that the Chinese would use the side-door via Poshingla with such amazing results. So the Poshingla detour simply became a side-issue and was treated accordingly. It had been assessed by Divisional HQ that the Chinese would be unable to bring more than a company along this approach. This was authenticated by the Army Headquarters and the Intelligence Bureau, based upon Captain FM Bailey's report submitted after his journey along this route in 1913. All travelogues, even official military reconnaissances, have an element of drama and exaggeration about them. Military history can produce so many instances when determined armies have achieved the impossible, from Hannibal's crossing of the Alps with elephants to the Japanese invasion of Kohima. The lesson of the Kohima-Imphal campaign, where the Japs had brought up two Infantry divisions into Manipur across the Chindwin, along difficult mule tracks and footpaths, when it was estimated that the maximum they could bring was a brigade, should not have been forgotten.

AN ILL-FATED EXPEDITION TO POSHINGLA

As mentioned earlier, 5 Guards while still at Misamari, had been directed to send a platoon under an officer to Poshingla. The platoon under Captain Amarjit Singh reached Dirang Dzong on 4 November, and because of shortage of porters and ponies could leave for Poshingla only on 6 November. Amarjit had under him one junior commissioned officer and 35 other ranks. The party was carrying just pouch ammunition and 10 days rations. On 8 November, the patrol leader reported on the wireless set that the porters and ponies had deserted the party and requested for replacement and further reinforcements.

He spent the next two days reconnoitering Poshingla, where he found four sections of Assam Rifles, whom he redeployed 1,500 metres to the rear. On 11 November, he began preparations for a company defended locality astride the pass. Meanwhile the Battalion, which was now at Bomdila, dispatched a reinforcement of 15 OR under a JCO with a few porters and ponies, more rations and ammunition. A few days later, the rest of the company followed.

On 14 November, Amarjit left on a reconnaissance of Topgey towards Tsela, on the look out for the Chinese, but it was they who spotted his party first and set an ambush. Amarjit's party walked into it at 9 am on 15 November. There were only four survivors and Amarjit's batman was one of them. Amarjit himself was killed in the ambush.

The Chinese approached Poshingla in the afternoon and mortared the place. The resupply column had just reached there a little earlier but after an hour's resistance the Indians fell back on Changla. The Chinese followed on their heels and at 7.30 pm the same evening evicted the Assam Rifles personnel manning the position, who did manage to pass on the situation report to their headquarters at Bomdila before leaving.

The withdrawing elements reached Lagam at 3.30 am on 16 November, and were met by the company headquarters and two platoons that had set out from Bomdila on 12 and 13 November. Their attempt to reach Tungri was preempted by the Chinese who had reached there earlier and now greeted them with mortar and machine gun fire. The men fell back and withdrew in small parties to an uncertain fate as the battalion they belonged to was itself soon to disintegrate. We shall come to all that later in the narrative and must now return to Sela and witness the happenings there.

A FORMIDABLE COVERING TROOPS POSITION

4 Garhwal had built up a commanding position in Bridge 3 area of Nuranong, deployed two companies up, A and D companies being forward. The Battalion not only dominated the road coming up from Jung but it was also not easy to bypass it, as on either side were sheer craggy vertical cliffs. From the many vantage points one could clearly observe the valley of the Tawang Chu, including the forward slopes of Geyshela, Rho, Sheo and Lao villages and also Tawang and its impressive monastery, all of which it could dominate by observation and partially by artillery fire. It could in patches also overlook the track going from Rho to Melling and Mago and the foot bridge over the Tawang Chu. The fairly large village of Jung and the sprawling 'Tusker' camp now lying abandoned were located 4000 feet below and formed a stretch of no-man's-land. Both Indians and the Chinese could bombard it with artillery and mortars.

After their temporary setback on 24 October, when the Battalion had briefly panicked because there was a weak company commander with the forward elements, a sense of shame amongst the officers and men had given way to determination and the will to vindicate their honour. The Commanding Officer, Lieutenant Colonel B.M. Bhattarcharjea, who talked like most Bengalis do with a rasagola in mouth and vociferously, with a disposition to buffoon around, was actually quite sharp and astute. As an act of penance he had shaved his head completely and his adjutant, Captain Dharam Pal, followed suit. Quite wisely he placed his suspect company commander in a depth position; the two forward companies were commanded by high-spirited young subalterns. The names of the subalterns in the forward companies were Vinod Goswami, Tandon and Deb. Vinod was short, smart and peppy, abounding in energy. Tandon, lean and wiry, with a slow and deliberate manner of speech and movement, was calm in a positive sense -- in that his approach to life was an antidote to panic. Deb was quiet, cheerful and stout-hearted. With these lively youngsters around, it was inevitable that the men would also become enthused and give of their best. What definitely pepped up the morale of the troops was the accurate and more than prompt support of 2 Derajat Mountain Battery (FF) guns, sited inside the Battalion defences. The gunners invariably occupied a roving position ahead of the defences, on the look out for enemy targets. The Chinese prudently laid low, their medium mortars silenced by the Derajat guns.

Soon thereafter a battery of 6 Field Regiment was deployed at km 107, 2 kms in depth of this Battalion and with this boosted artillery support the morale of 4 Garhwal rose even higher.A company of 4 Sikh LI and a platoon of 13 Dogra for a while also formed part of the defences. They were good troops on their own; their present association with the Garhwalis only made things better.

MIXED FEELINGS AND PREPARATIONS AT SELA

By 1 November, Sela had four battalions occupying defences. Sela proper was held by only two and a half battalions (1 Sikh, 2 Sikh LI and 4 Sikh LI less three companies) Two companies of 4 Sikh LI were in area of "Two Lakes" overlooking the Jung-Chabrala approach and one company was in depth behind 4 Garhwal at the junction of the main road and the track to Two Lakes area. 13 Dogra was at Senge, guarding the rear or the southern approach to Sela and affording a modicum of protection to the administrative elements located there.

To say that life was uncomfortable at windswept and frost-ridden Sela would be an understatement. Digging was difficult because the ground was hard rock. The troops had to resort to building sangars (walls made of stones) which can never shut out the wind and cold. They also provide inadequate protection against enemy fire. On the other hand there was a fresh water lake in the midst of the defences and hence an adequate supply of water. Rock features occupied by our troops dominated a huge area from all sides. Any Chinese approaching from Nuranong and Kyela would have walked into deadly killing grounds. For this it was essential to rehearse counter-attack plans and the occupation of contingency positions. Artillery defensive fire tasks should have been registered by firing. Also, it was essential that troops from each battalion should get to know the others (men and officers and the drills for passing through when required). None of this was done. Instead, Hoshiar had turned the concept of patrolling on its head. He sent out large unwieldy patrols which invariably walked into ambushes by stealthy shadow patrols of the Chinese. It was a mindless thing to do -- send troops occupying formidable positions on high features into unknown areas down below, where menacing Chinese parties waited to give them a hot reception.

India's caste system was also taking its toll at Sela. The Sikhs' tenets forbid casteism but right up till the recent upsurge in the Eighties, Sikh society was as caste-ridden as the Hindus. It had its subtle and not so subtle manifestations in the Army and it was up to good leaders to minimise its effect. At Sela there were two Sikh LI battalions, formed of the scheduled (Mazhbi) or low caste Sikhs, who literally lived in a state of apartheid back in the villages in the Punjab; and there was one Sikh battalion i.e 1 Sikh, formed of Jat middle-caste Sikhs, the most dominant class in the Punjab. They were all good troops but this caste prejudice, not too far under the surface, prevented a rapport from developing between 1 Sikh and 2 Sikh LI, neighboring battalions. 4 Sikh LI wasn't affected, being away and somewhat isolated from the brigade defences. On more than one occasion there were problems in cooperation when 2 Sikh LI felt that they were callously let down by their middle-caste colleagues.

In those days one could classify officers into three categories. Young and unmarried were fit, soldierly and by and large eager for battle. Fifty per cent of the married type were fit and competent, but the other fifty per cent had become mentally and physically soft. Their motivation level was low and they were a demoralizing element. They bemoaned the life on Sela without their wives and children and the prospects of spending a bleak winter at this isolated position. It may seem surprising but in the Academy quite a few amongst them had been outstanding sportsmen, but prolonged peace tenures had made them too used to a comfortable existence. Most of the staff officers fell in this category. The system was such that they had managed their careers in such a manner that they all had minimum regimental service. Two of the three Brigade Majors, the most key appointment in a Brigade Headquarters in NEFA, were graduates of the Staff College at Camberley in the UK and therefore the best as far as career profiles go. General Prem Bhagat, who was a member of the Henderson Brooks

Committee, had later as Corps Commander issued his standing instructions and there can be little doubt that the HB Report was very much in his mind when he wrote them. General Bhagat cautions the Commanders against being manipulated by the staff. It was therefore a deadly combination in NEFA — professionally rusty or incompetent commanders being manipulated by a staff; and fifty per cent of the commanding officers had no desire to stick on and fight.

Reverting to Sela, in those hostile weather conditions, specially at night when the wind-chill factor numbed the body, imagine the plight of the sentries — there had to be nearly two hundred of them at any one time in each battalion, inadequately equipped, weathering the winds that stung like a whiplash. Compare this with the atmosphere in officers' bunkers with bukharis burning where in the course of gossip, belly-aching and appraisal of events, rumour and bogeys were generated. Would the junior commissioned officers and men have remained impervious to this syndrome when patrol after patrol came back empty handed or worsted by the Chinese. An idle mind is the devil's workshop it is said. Hoshiar ought to have realized the seriousness of the situation aggravated by extreme cold, the harsh living conditions of the men and the continuing reverses in patrolling. It required action of a positive kind. He should have had his troops out with officers leading them first by day and later by night practising counter-attacks and various battle-drills. Instead, he wasn't even aware that he was being infected by the spirit of despondency.

The foregoing description is based upon depositions of people who were then present at Sela. I have intentionally refrained from naming any personalities because that would serve no aim which is to look for causes and effects and their possible remedies.

17

Activities Upto 16 November 1962

The Chinese were working at a feverish pace, day and night, with a large Tibetan labour force, to build a class 9 road (capable of taking 3-ton vehicles) from Bumla to Tawang. The road construction commenced immediately after the fall of Tawang and was completed by 12 November. The Chinese then began to improve the Tawang-Jung section of the road and by November 14, they had rebuilt the demolished Bridge 4 at Jung.

The Chinese did not, however, wait for the road to be completed before making their move. They unleashed their 419 unit on 11 November, tasked to threaten Bomdila and Dirang Dzong defences by 16 November. This special force was self-contained and remarkably fit. Animal transport (yaks and ponies) saw them off up to Mago; and thereafter this commando type force moved at blistering speed for six days carrying trolley mounted mortars and recoilless guns, limited ammunition (made adequate by exemplary fire discipline and neatly rehearsed and executed battle-drills). With Mao's Red Book in their breast pockets and his maxims on tactics in their hearts, the Chinese troops had to reach their immediate destination kms 9 and 31 on the Bomdila-Dirang Road by the 17th, and reach it they would. The commander of the force traveled on a sturdy gray pony with a couple of extra animals as back up. There was tremendous practical sense in this because this gentleman, well into his fifties, had to make a show of authority as also keep up with the pace of his young men. This was a tradition carried over from the days of the warlords.

Simultaneously two battalions also began infiltrating beyond the Tawang Chu, heading for Bridge 1 and 2 areas torwards Dirang to cut lines of communication and lay ambushes. The routes they followed were from the north via Yangyapla and Nyukmadung and from the south via Chabrala and Jangle. These two battalions most probably belonged to Big Shen's regiment, the same that had been used to infiltrate 7 Brigade's defences at Nam Ka Chu. Having reached Shakti on 23 October, they had been halted in their tracks till the start of phase 2 of their offensive; and they were now raring to go.

A regiment had meanwhile begun investing Sela from the direction of Dzalungala. It sent out patrols, jitter and shadow parties to probe the Sela defences from the north and east to determine the layout, specially the location of automatic weapons, and also to unnerve the Indians and entice their unsuspecting and cumbersome patrols into well planned ambushes.

Another regiment prepared itself for a frontal attack on 4 Garhwal defences, which they probably appreciated would be a hard nut to crack. The main Chinese atttack was to come later, to be launched by 55 Infantry Division, D Day being 20 November. But the Chinese must have hoped that 419 unit and Shen's units would do the job and the main attack wouldn't be necessary. In case Sela held out, there was going to be some very hard fighting ahead of them. They had made full preparations and it was for this reason that so much effort had been put in to build the road from Bumla to Tawang (so that they could bring up their artillery for the attack on Sela).

A sectorwise narrative of activities as recorded by the Indian side will show how the Indians reacted to these emerging Chinese moves.

62 INFANTRY BRIGADE SECTOR (SELA)

On 1 November, a company from 4 Garhwal under Major Rai was sent to destroy Lao footbridge on the Tawang Chu (which the Chinese could use to infiltrate into Dirang Valley via Jangle). They took a local guide, but he deserted them near the bridge, which was found to be strongly held by the Chinese. The Company Commander developed cold feet and called off the attack. Instead the FOO (Battery Commander of 2 Derajat Battery) who was accompanying the patrol, engaged the bridge and the Chinese on both sides of it. No damage to the bridge could be caused but some casualties took place amongst the Chinese. The patrol remained out for four days.

2 Sikh LI sent a patrol of one officer and four other ranks to observe enemy movement along Mago Chu. The patrol was intercepted by a strong Chinese patrol near Hanging Bridge on 5 November. Two of our jawans were killed; the battalion retrieved their bodies, not their arms, on 9 November.

On 7 November, a platoon patrol of 1 Sikh left for Lunguthang and reported a heavy concentration of 500-700 of Chinese troops. The Chinese moved swiftly and about 200 of them intercepted the Sikhs near Dzalungla. The patrol was extricated with the help of 3 inch mortars of 2 Sikh LI firing from Kye La.

On 10 November, the covering troops (4 Garhwal) reported about 70 yaks and mules moving from Rho to Melling.

Later in the evening, a company or more of the enemy was reported to have concentrated near the Depth Company of 1 Sikh at Sela. A jitter party of theirs climbed up the adjoining hill feature and opened fire. They achieved their aim, because our troops opened up with small arms, mortars and field guns as though the Chinese had launched a full fledged attack. But the firing was all into thin air and lasted for about two hours with much useless waste of ammunition, with no enemy casualty reported. Such panicky, blind fire is typical of demoralised troops.

While "the fireworks" were going on at Sela, beams of vehicle headlights were seen on the Bumla gap near Penkingtang heights, which indicated that the road to Tawang was more or less complete.

On 11 November, 4 Garhwal reported about 1000 Chinese moving in small groups of 20 to 30 men from Rho to Melling. It was assessed that more would have moved during the night as on the next day too this intense movement carried on. They were engaged by our artillery but without success because the valley was deep and defiladed which the field guns could not reach in spite of firing in high angle. The Chinese had taken necessary precautions by moving in small groups with adequate distances between them. Divisional Headquarters scoffed at the report sent in by 4 Garhwal, dubbing it as exaggerated. After all the Bailey trail was considered incapable of taking more than a company. This was illogical assessment because where a company can go, a brigade or even a division can go; it depends on logistics, not terrain.

At Bomdila, as a precautionary measure (grudgingly granting the Chinese a slightly higher capability), 48 Brigade was directed to build up the post at Poshingla to company strength by November 13, a case of putting in too little, too late. This was the time when orders should have been given to build up a battalion at Thembang.

On 13 November, a vehicle column was seen parked in the erstwhile Assistant Political Officer's office at Tawang. Our field guns fired two dozen rounds from a roving position but with only partial success.

Brigadier Hoshiar Singh, as part of his motivational drive for infusing an aggressive spirit, had wanted his battalions to capture a few Chinese soldiers. He announced a cash award of Rs 1000 for each Chinese prisoner of war. Only 4 Garhwal made a serious attempt to avail of this incentive though 4 Sikh LI did also manage to capture two Chinese during the thick of the battle. During the night of 13/14 November, the Indians launched perhaps the only daring raid in 4 Division sector. It was an indication of the final transformation of 4 Garhwal into a highly motivated outfit, with a few daredevils amongst its ranks. Second Lieutenant Vinod Goswami led a small patrol across Mago Chu to Rho village crossing the river with the help of an improvised log bridge. They captured a Chinese sentry guarding a hut and then lobbed hand grenades inside the hut, causing not only casualties but also alarm, alerting the remaining posts of the Chinese. In the ensuing scuffle unable to carry the prisoner across the precarious log bridge, it was regretfully reported that they bayoneted him to death and fled across the bridge, carrying his rifle with them which was later sent to Divisional Headquarters. A few days later Vinod Goswami was killed in action and was posthumously awarded the Vir Chakra.

So far the patrols sent out from Sela had fared poorly in engagements with the Chinese and most came back worsted. The only exception was 4 Garhwal and in a smaller way 4 Sikh LI. This fact was affecting morale, and to boost it

Brigadier Hoshiar decided to send a strong raiding party to give a hard knocks to the enemy, as he put it. What it implied was a reconnaissance in force. It was a wasteful effort, which instead of doing any good caused considerable harm in every way. Hoshiar should have realized that there was no fixed enemy disposition opposing him. Instead, the Chinese were perhaps lying in wait, in places, hoping to draw the Indians out of their prepared defences, so that they would walk into murderous killing grounds. The Chinese knew the ground and the routes and the habits of Indian patrols, which were more like nomadic force with little idea of where and how the Chinese would surprise them.

A composite force of two companies of 2 Sikh LI and one company of 1 Sikh under Major Jaspal Singh, second in command of 2 Sikh LI, was sent out on 15 November towards Luguthang to engage any enemy that they might find there. Artillery support was catered for and a forward observation officer and his party accompanied the force. While the company of 1 Sikh established a firm base at Dzalungula, the two Sikh LI companies proceeded towards Luguthang, near which they established their night harbour. At night the Chinese surprised them and, simultaneously, they also attacked the firm base at Dzalungula. 2 Sikh LI troops fell back on Dzalungula hoping to find the company of 1 Sikh there but the latter had been thrown back. Instead of getting the protection they had hoped for, 2 Sikh LI got a hot reception from the Chinese who had now occupied the firm base. 2 Sikh LI casualties were 1 officer and 60 other ranks killed or missing; and 1 Sikh had 2 other ranks wounded. Artillery support failed to materialize because the artillery forward observer could not establish communication with his gun position. This event caused bad blood between the two battalions because, rightly or wrongly, 2 Sikh LI felt let down by 1 Sikh.

At about 2 pm on 16 November, 4 Sikh LI companies reported more than 1000 Chinese moving between the Bhutan border along the Track Chabrala-Jangle. All three field batteries deployed in Sela opened up. Taking advantage of bad visibility, and the wooded mountainous terrain, the column quickly disappeared from sight.

It should have been obvious that the Chinese pincers were about to surround Sela, and that were moving to occupy preselected positions to cut lines of communication and lay ambushes. Their instructions must have been to avoid any major confrontation, bypass positions such as 4 Rajput company at point 3582 covering the track coming from Yangyapla to Bridge 2 area, and only undertake minimum actions to confound the Indians and draw them out of their entrenched positions.

DIRANG DZONG (HEADQUARTERS 4 INFANTRY DIVISION AND 65 INFANTRY BRIGADE)

The first fortnight passed off quite peacefully at Dirang Dzong. Camp life there was of the drugged kind and the deportment of the garrison was as though they were in a peacetime cantonment.. It was only a matter of time before these people would be jolted out of their lackadaisical reverie.

4 Rajput had arranged a party on the evening of 15 November in their officer's mess at the Sapper Camp overlooking Bridge 1 to celebrate their annual day (Zojila Day). GOC 4 Infantry Division with some of his staff besides other guests including the Commanders of the Artillery brigade and 65 Infantry Brigade attended this party. The celebration had barely begun when suddenly two Assam Rifles jawans who had escaped from Changla in the wake of the Chinese attack, claiming to be the two lone survivors, appeared on the scene. This brought the party to a sudden

end. Everybody dispersed and rushed to his respective headquarters. Thus was their reverie broken.

15 November was not a lucky day for the formation and the unit. A patrol of 4 Rajput with an artillery observer had been sent from Point 3582 to Yangyapla. The patrol returned the same day but the artillery observer (Lieutenant Chaudhary of 6 Field Regiment) with his party had insisted on a break enroute to brew up tea, giving away his position to a Chinese party lurking near by. He had broken the basic rule of camouflage and concealment, which says that smoke by day and light by night, can be seen at long distances. The patrol leader being a junior commissioned officer was quite helpless to overrule an officer. Out of *izzat* and concern he left five of his own men for added protection. All except one jawan of 4 Rajput were killed. This man came back and gave the information about the fate of the party. Worse was to follow.

News arrived at Divisional Headquarters late on 16 November that a battalion strong Chinese force had surrounded and annihilated the platoon of 5 Guards under Amarjit at Poshingla on 15 November. The harrowing tale narrated by the four survivors got General Anant Pathania, GOC, and his staff really worried. They now realized how serious this outflanking threat was. With his own headquarters located in peacetime bashas and tents, the reverie was now turning to panic.

The first task was to keep the Chinese at bay for as long as possible and then move out of Dirang at the earliest. Accordingly 19 Marathas were ordered to send out two columns as under:

a) One company under Major Parab left Dirang at 9 pm on the 15th along the track Dirang-Sangti and on the following day reached as far as Rengza. This company made no contact with the enemy and rejoined the battalion in the early hours on 18 November.

b) The other company under the second in command, Major Shaikh, with an artillery observer (Lieutenant, later Lieutenant General, Vinay Shankar) left on the afternoon of 16 November along the route Dirang-Munna Camp-Namshu- Changdor. They observed considerable Chinese activity in the area of village Changdor, which was engaged by our artillery. The shoot over, the company commander, instead of occupying a defensive position (with the aim of blocking the Chinese infiltration, the task he had been given) decided to return to Munna camp, a move that no doubt prompted the audacious Chinese to follow them hot on their heels. On 18, early morning, while this company was still recovering from the toil, resting and brewing tea, the Chinese put in their attack killing 18 of our jawans and capturing 22. With this surgical operation over in a matter of minutes, the Chinese detached a column to establish a road-block in km 31 area.

Major Shaikh's operation was an exercise in futility because nothing was gained and a lot was lost as the morale of 19 Maratha suffered greatly. Meanwhile at Divisional Headquarters, action had been initiated to vacate Dirang and make a bunk for Tenga valley. General Pathania sounded the Corps headquarters about his intention of running away, but was advised against it by the BGS Corps. Undeterred Pathania dispatched a layout party under Major Ummat, his GSO2 (SD) to Tenga valley to prepare a site for his new Divisional HQ. As we already know, Ummat didn't stop till he had reached the absolute safety of the Foothills! He was caught there by his AQMG, who had come down to expedite the move of 67 Brigade, and put under arrest (though not for long!).

Meanwhile the Chinese had also begun infiltrating towards Nyukamadung from the north, after bypassing Sela.

One platoon from 4 Rajput moved north from Point 3582 and gained contact with a company of the Chinese. In the ensuring exchange of fire, 11 of the Rajput force were killed. Only after the platoon was reinforced was the Chinese fire neutralized. After dusk, on orders of the Battalion headquarters, the company broke contact and reoccupied Point 3582.

Because of the development of the above threat, the Commanding Officer of 4 Rajput lifted his B Company, which was protecting Bridge 1 area, to reinforce Point 3582 with one platoon and, with the remainder, to occupy Gompachar to its rear. This was exactly what the Chinese wanted. Having drawn out B company, Bridge 1 was now ready for the taking. They thereafter left 4 Rajput alone for the time being, lying doggo near their ambush positions, ready to strike should the troops at Sela upsticks and try to withdraw towards Dirang.

BOMDILA (48 INFANTRY BRIGADE)

Bomdila had become the forgotten sector of 4 Infantry Division. This is surprising because only a fortnight earlier it had been considered to be the Divisional vital ground. The least its status deserved was that it should have been kept occupied by a brigade preferably from the very outset i.e mid-September onwards. The troops could have been staged up from here with the Brigade Headquarters staying put. Ideally it should have been 11 or 5 Infantry Brigade (originally part of 4 Division). Imagine what could have happened with commander like Rawley at Bomdila, whose 11 Infantry Brigade was at this very time putting up a heroic fight at Walong. Unfortunately, it was quite late in the operations when 48 Brigade arrived at Bomdila. By then the focus of attention was firmly on Sela, and later on the Poshingla axis, so that Bomdila never really got functioning. Brigadier Gurbax Singh was a mild non-pushy personality. What the situation demanded was a human dynamo.

The atmosphere prevailing in Divisional HQ at Dirang Dzong seems to have permeated down to Bomdila. The Brigade Commander chose to live in the luxurious Circuit House next to the Political Officer's bungalow. Brigade HQ was in barracks across the road. 5 Guards, which was to occupy a position in depth at Wango Ridge, was similarly billeted in barracks. Maybe subconscious minds were at work. Perhaps they all suspected that their's was a temporary stay and that they would eventually have to move out to Thembang; or even to Dirang, for further beefing up the security of Divisional HQ! Headquarters 22 Mountain Regiment had occupied the government school building, though its guns were in properly prepared gun pits. The two battalions occupying the forward defences, 1 Sikh LI on the main Bomdila feature (Point 2902) and 1 Madras strung out on the ridge running due east from the pass and across the Dirang road, had also dug in. The ground was soft and there were ample pine trees that could be felled for overhead protection. However, there was a shortage of defence stores like mines, barbed wire, pickets and corrugated iron sheets. These were by no stretch of imagination artificial deficiencies but the fact is that very few took the threat to Bomdila seriously. If they had, there were so many ways of overcoming the shortages. A positive commander would have refused to move into comfortable quarters and would have roughed it out, if necessary in a bunker. One can only imagine the galvanising effect that would have had on the troops, specially the officers. It was a matter of the state of mind. The climate in Bomdila in autumn time is alluringly delightful. The place had a hill station ambience and there was little physical hardship. Unfortunately comfort and ease do not a fighting machinery make.

Till 16 November, 48 Brigade's main occupation was to deal with developments on the Poshingla axis. In effect this meant executing instructions received from Divisional Headquarters for dispatching piecemeal detachments of the company of 5 Guards commanded by Captain Amarjit. A commander genuinely concerned about the fate of Bomdila would have done enough forward reconnaissance and appreciated that the importance of Thembang lay in being not only a screen or a covering troops position but a perfect cul de sac for Number 419 unit of the Chinese, who would either have had to turn back or perish hopelessly against the formidable defences at Bomdila. One has just to stand near km 9 ahead of Bomdila to appreciate how dominating the view from there is of Thembang, the river valley below it and the Rahung bowl. Artillery, mortars and machine gun fire would simply play havoc on the enemy trapped in this area. Zhang Gohua while exhorting his commanders before the battle had used the analogy of closing the door and beating the dogs and not let one get away. This is what the Indians could have done to the Chinese troops once they had contacted Thembang. The Chinese were self-contained for just one week, with no artillery support, very little reserve ammunition and a difficult line of communication behind them. It was essential that Sela had to hold on for at least a week and Dirang Dzong left to dummy positions. The Chinese *coup de main* would not only have petered out, the chances are that they would have been hunted down like fugitives. Commander 48 Brigade should have been clamouring for more troops instead of eking out a passive existence. The first priority should have been to occupy Thembang with a battalion and make available all artillery and brigaded mortars at Bomdila in the indirect as well as direct role. Km 9 area should have had a screen position. With carefully cited artillery observation posts in the screen and covering troops positions it would have been difficult for even a single Chinese to get away. Some readers may find it difficult to believe all this. Sceptics are advised to pay a visit to Bomdila, km 9 and Thembang and there should be little doubt left thereafter. In the event, the Chinese lost nearly 300 to 400 troops in a matter of half an hour because of direct firing of four 25 ponder guns that were deployed at short notice at km 9 on 17 November.

With one more battalion at Bomdila, there would have been a different story to tell. Two battalions were indeed on the way. One arrived a day too late and the other got inordinately delayed and never turned up. They should have arrived atleast a week earlier although the timidity of the GOC might have resulted in their getting sucked into Dirang Dzong. Pathania's appetite to throw troops around him was quite insatiable.

18

The Denouement

Sela Abandoned

By 17 November, Sela was undoubtedly a formidable redoubt, a strongly defended sector with five Infantry battalions, adequate artillery support, stocked for a minimum of a twelve-day battle. If one were to grade the state of combat worthiness of units, one would have noticed that it was a direct reflection of the quality of their officers, specially the commanding officers, and (I suspect) in reverse proportion to their distance from the brigade headquarters. Even in peace-time a good commanding officer likes to have his unit located sufficiently away from his brigade headquarters. For the ingratiating kind it is the other way round, because in the latter case the battalion's interests are secondary to his. Furthermore, troops who are nearer the enemy or in more regular contact with him have a higher state of readiness and there is less of that fear of the unknown. If one could be permitted to hazard a grading of the Infantry battalions of 62 Infantry brigade as on 17 November out of a total of 10 marks, I would put it as something like this: 4 Garhwal Rifles - 8, 4 Sikh LI - 7, 2 Sikh LI - 6 and 1 Sikh - 6. Why then should things have gone wrong? (The intention here is not to single out any unit for praise or criticism but to offer a plausible analysis why events developed as they did.) Battles normally lead to fluid situations. A unit that does well at one situation might fail in another or vice versa, because of the change in circumstances.

At 0500 hours on 17 November, a battalion of the Chinese attacked the forward company of 4 Garhwal Rifles under Second Lieutenant Tandon. The Chinese initially had tried a day earlier to deceive their way in by sending their leading group disguised as local Mompas. (This was in violation of the Geneva Convention, but then Communist China had till then not put its signature to that document.) When Jemader Udai Singh, the sharp and agile platoon commander, went forward to investigate, he found rifle muzzles sticking out of the loose Mompa kaftaan-like cloaks. He managed to rush back after lobbing a grenade at the enemy.

Now Udai Singh had the reputation of being quite a smart alec in peacetime. It sometimes happens that such people get totally transformed in crisis situations and give of their best. The man had both guile and guts and held his forward platoon firmly and resolutely. Their deception having failed, the Chinese regular attack now commenced in bloody earnest. Mines around the forward company began exploding as the Chinese launched their attack in frontal waves; on the sides were unnegotiable cliffs. A commando OP of theirs seemed to have worked his way into the valley, because accurate counter-bombardment came on to the Derajat Battery gun position. A few of our gunners fled for cover but the stout hearted Gun Position Officer (Lieutenant Charanjit Dhillon) restored the situation by coming out of his sheltered command post to help in the loading of the guns even as he kept passing his fire orders. The mountain guns remained fully active. There were no casualties. The first Chinese attack was beaten back.

At 10.30 am the Chinese put in a three-pronged attack, trying to sweep in from the exposed left flank of the company. This time they were able to bring two of their medium machine guns within 30 metres and began targeting a light machine gun of the Garhwalis that had been causing Chinese casualities. Three of the Garhwalis under Naik Jaswant Singh Rawat stole up to the Chinese gun position and lobbed a few grenades. Then Jaswant leaped in and grabbed the machine gun but was killed while he was running back with it, the second man with him (Tarlok Singh) was also felled by enemy fire, the third man (Gopal Singh) though wounded, brought back the weapon to Battalion HQ. Jaswant Singh was posthumously awarded the Mahavir Chakra, the second highest gallantry award in India. Tarlok and Gopal were awarded Vir Chakra, the former posthumously. A few years later, after the war, this erstwhile-defended locality of the Garhwalis was named Jaswant Garh, and a temple has been constructed. A kind of legend has been woven around this heroic jawan. There are no defences there any longer but you would always find passing vehicles halting there briefly, for the occupants to pay homage. The spirit of Jaswant seems to inhabit the place and serves as a reminder of one of the great deeds of valour of the 1962 war.

The battle continued till 4 pm, the Chinese using mountain guns and mortars. A further attack by the enemy had been repulsed by then. Tandon's company had faced the brunt of that attack. His coolness had given heart to his men. Captain PPS Bains, the Battalion Quartermaster, had swung into action and personally supervised ammunition replenishment, which proved vital. However, the Chinese had managed to obtain a foothold on the flanks. A few hundred Chinese lay dead in front of D and A companies of the Garhwalis. The Garhwalis own casualities were light, two killed and eight wounded[1].

About this time 4 Garhwal's line and wireless communication with Brigade headquarters had snapped. At about 5 pm two liaison officers sent by Brigadier Hoshiar Singh arrived and delivered orders to the commanding officer, to withdraw to Sela defences at night. They were told that 1 Sikh would be serving them a hot meal on arrival at Sela.

The Indian Army pamphlet on tactics does recommend that the covering troops having accomplished their task (i.e causing delay, attrition and if possible forcing the enemy to redeploy) should fall back to the main defences. But this is only a recommendation and not a mandatory procedure. Since the Garhwalis had done such an excellent job, it was all the more reason that they should have continued to remain there. It is said that in attack you never reinforce failure - that applied to the Chinese in this case. As a corollary to this, there is every reason to add that in defence success should not be frittered away. The Garhwalis should have stayed on as long as it was possible. Its withdrawal later, with one company of 4 Sikh LI holding a screen position at km 107, would have been not that problematic.

The question that nags at one unanswered is 'where?' after their withdrawal from Nuranong were the 4 Garhwal defences to be on Sela? (The truth is that a rear position for them in the main defences had never been sited or prepared.)

Hoshiar's plan now was to withdraw all troops into an inner perimeter of the main Sela position and hold it as a fortress. Earlier in the day he called back the two companies of 4 Sikh LI from the Two Lakes area. Till that morning this area was in the process of being incorporated into the battalion defended area. Then orders were reversed. Suddenly it was found that the two companies were no longer serving any useful purpose there and were ordered to move back into their previous positions. At 10.30 am Brigadier Hoshiar Singh accompanied by Colonel Budhwar,

Officer Commanding 5 Field regiment, arrived at the screen position near Nuranong and he personally briefed Major Kapoor, D Company Commander, to cover the withdrawal of 4 Garhwal, and A and C companies of his battalion, coming from Two Lakes and thereafter withdraw to Sela.

At about 5 pm General Pathania came on the phone and spoke to Hoshiar Singh to inform him that the Chinese had appeared in strength on the eastern flank of the Divisional sector and he was apprehensive that 62 Infantry Brigade may not be able to hold on to Sela for long, specially now that the enemy had attacked the 4 Garhwal position earlier in the day and the battalion had been ordered to withdraw to Senge Dzong. It is said that Brig Hoshiar declined to leave the Sela defences and told the GOC that he had already foreseen the possibility of being cut off, and he was quite prepared to fight it out, provided he continued to be supplied by air. At this GOC cut short the conversation and said that he would call up later.

Many people present at Sela have vouched for Brigadier Hoshiar's determination to fight it out at Sela, because he felt that the defences were very strong and could be held even if cut off. He used to motivate his troops continuously by telling them that they must be ruthless with the enemy and evict him from our sacred soil and that this was possible by having an aggressive spirit and having a will to win.

In actual fact, it may be that Brigadier Hoshiar's determination wasn't as strong as has been made out to be. It was to crumble in the next half an hour once the return call of the GOC materialized, when the latter informed him that air support could not be guaranteed and that he must withdraw during the night 17/18 November. Brigadier Hoshiar Singh told the GOC that it was just not feasible to withdraw that night as it was already late evening. However, if he was forced to abandon the defences, the earliest he could do so was on the following night. The GOC, as always concerned mainly with the need for his own safety, ordered two Infantry companies from Sela to be sent to Dirang by the fastest means for the defence of Divisional HQ. Two companies from 13 Dogra at Senge were sent during the same night.

This bit about guaranteed air support is intriguing. Didn't Hoshiar know that no one could guarantee air support? Why then this rider ? It suggests the obvious. He was inviting the GOC to commit him to withdraw from Sela. Yet, Hoshiar was a brave man and therefore there must have been other pressures weighing on him. Could it be that his staff and advisers had been working on him and softening up his resolve?

General Kaul was in Walong sector on the afternoon of 17 November trying to rescue stragglers of 11 Infantry Brigade. Meanwhile the COAS and the DMO (Brigadier Palit) had arrived at Tezpur and were met by Gen Sen at Tezpur airfield. They moved to IV Corps Headquarters. The COAS had a wireless message sent recalling Kaul to Corps headquarters immediately. They were briefed by General Sen about 4 Garhwal's heroic battle, who had since been "ordered to withdraw". The DMO strongly objected to the withdrawal of the battalion when it had just won four engagements -- and he asked General Sen to cancel the order to withdraw 4 Garhwal. General Sen refused telling Brigadier Palit that 4 Division's battles were none of his business -- or words to that effect.

The COAS and the Army Commander simply refused to give any decision in spite of the DMO's earnest pleas that they must intervene to save the situation at Sela -- that is, countermand the withdrawal order. This has been rightly assessed as the lowest point reached by the Indian Army. How indeed could there be such professional impotence? One of the plausible reasons could be that General Thapar and General Sen were afraid of Bijji Kaul. After all, his chief patron, Nehru, was very much in the saddle in Delhi. Low self-esteem can be a very debilitating thing indeed and General Thapar in spite of being an impeccable gentleman was now suffering from a bad attack of low self-esteem. As for General Sen, the outcome in Nam Ka Chu had shaken his confidence and he was steering clear of any decision that called for stiff resistance by the forward troops.

Gen Pathania rang up several times during the day, firstly to ask permission to pull back his HQ to Tenga valley, and later as he grew more paranoid, he painted such a dim picture that he wanted permission to withdraw 62 Infantry Brigade and all elements in Dirang valley to Bomdila. Surreptitiously, and without permission, he had dispatched an advance party (with Major Ummat) to Tenga valley to site his HQ (as already recorded). Furthermore, without consulting Corps HQ, he had already ordered Hoshiar to withdraw his brigade. Yet he had so maneuvered events that he was able to pass on all the blame to his brigade commanders; a dangerous man to serve under indeed. He had obviously tremendous guile in him. Unfortunately he used it for a wrong purpose.

With all these talks going on, over an open line with no security, would it not be correct to assume that the Chinese were capable and of more than just casual tapping or eavesdropping? Surely they couldn't have been gifted with such super intelligence as to know exactly how the Indians were going to withdraw. General Pathania's first talk with Hoshiar and later the numerous ones to Corps HQ must have given the Chinese just the information they wanted. No wonder they could lay their ambushes with such precision and to such deadly effect.

At 7.30 pm General Kaul returned to his headquarters in a state of exuberance after his hectic day in the Walong sector. After fifteen minutes, GOC 4 Division was again on the line seeking permission to withdraw from Sela. Kaul was eventually enthused by Brig Palit to urge Pathania to stick it out, but within half an hour he gave in to Pathania's alarmist request and a signal was sent ordering 4 Division to pull back from Sela and Dirang to Bomdila. It so happened that just then direct communication with 4 Division had been disrupted and the message had to be passed to Bomdila for being relayed to Dirang. This transpired during a short absence of Brig Palit from the operation room and when he learnt about it he created quite a shindy and, within minutes had the signal, which had yet not been yet relayed from Bomdila, cancelled. However, its contents wouldn't have done much to restore the morale at Bomdila, which was itself in the throes of a dire crisis of its own.

Subsequently (unknown to the DMO) Kaul drafted another signal and this was dispatched. All that it amounted to was military verbosity — beating round the bush. The central message was very clear: Pathania had been given the permission to withdraw. The following message was sent:

1. You will hold on to present positions to the best of your ability. When any position becomes untenable *I delegate the authority to you to withdraw to any alternative position you can hold* (Italics mine).

2. Approximately 400 enemy have already cut the road Bomdila-Dirang Dzong. I have ordered Commander 48 Brigade to attack this enemy force tonight speedily and resolutely and keep the road clear at all costs. You may be cut off by the enemy at Senge Dzong, Dirang and Bomdila. Your only course is to fight it out as best as you can.

3. 67 Infantry Brigade less one battalion will reach Bomdila by morning 18 November. Use your tanks and

other arms to the fullest extent to clear lines of communication.

Neville Maxwell has called it a masterpiece of military buck passing. A psychoanalysis of the message on the other hand, would reveal certain telling traits of the then higher command and its chief protagonist, General Kaul. The contents are reminiscent of a peacetime one-sided exercise, where the impact of words matter a lot more than the action and the reality on the ground.

At 6.30 pm at Sela, the Brigade Commander called a conference in his bunker which was attended by the commanders of 5 Field Regiment and 19 Field Company Engineers, his Brigade Major and the DAA and QMG. An outline plan was formulated for the withdrawal from Sela:

1. Covering Troops (4 Garhwal), on withdrawal, to move to Senge during 17/18 night.
2. 2 Sikh LI to withdraw during 18/19 night and occupy area Nyukmadung.
3. The remaining troops to withdraw in stages, till 1 Sikh finally abandons Sela after midnight 18/19 November.
4. All troops to be clear of Bridge 2 by morning of 19 November.

It is believed that later that night Pathania had yet another telephone conversation with Hoshiar Singh. It was thereafter decided to withdraw 2 Sikh LI immediately to within the inner parameter of Sela. Later the same night the battalion was ordered to establish a firm base at Nyukmadung. This was a most extraordinary order, pulling out a battalion in the middle of the night and then ordering it to proceed to a place never seen by anyone in the unit, even in day time. It was an invitation to chaos and confusion.

An indescribable muddle was in the offing at Sela. 4 Garhwal with 2 Derajat Battery bringing up the rear, reached Sela at about 3 am on 18 November. Here they learnt that instead of deploying at Sela they were to carry on to Senge where they would come under 13 Dogra. After having fought a hard day's battles, to be subjected to a nightlong uncalled-for withdrawal would have taxed the best of troops. Fatigue had set in; there were now many stragglers. The majority marched on to Senge even as a subedar sahib of 1 Sikh came out to request them for their meal — an offer they politely declined because somehow they had a feeling that all wasn't well at Sela. But the stragglers (about fifty of them) on reaching the lake slumped for a rest and began brewing tea, disregarding BC 2 Derajat's warning that the Chinese were not far behind. Soon thereafter these stragglers were overwhelmed by the Chinese. They were all killed or captured. Compare this with just two killed and eight wounded when on 17 November they had fought and beaten back four attacks!

Concurrently with the arrival of 4 Garhwal at Sela, 2 Sikh LI began upsticking from their defences. The Chinese, as though quite aware of this move, promptly shadowed them and came and occupied the vacated defences of A and C companies of 4 Sikh LI, who were themselves on the move from Tsogya Lakes. Probably orders had not been passed down to the troops of 1 Sikh. As a result when 2 Sikh LI was passing through 1 Sikh defences, their unexpected appearance caused panic and confusion and 1 Sikh also abandoned its position. Thereafter 1 Sikh and 2 Sikh LI all became fugitives, mixed up in the ensuing stampede.

This is about the time that Brigadier Hoshiar arrived on the scene and realized that the game was up. It became obvious that a rout had been precipitated. Under the circumstances, he followed the logical course. He legitimised the proceedings by giving a covering sanction, an order for all troops to withdraw immediately and concentrate at Senge. Somewhat fazed by these unexpected orders and developments, the gunners and the sappers had to hurriedly pack up and follow the retreating Infantry. Unfortunately this left 4 Sikh LI to its own fate because, the enemy had interjected itself between this battalion and rest of 62 Infantry brigade.

At about 0500 hours the GSO 1 of 4 Division spoke to the Brigade Major of 62 Brigade and was apprised of this premature withdrawal, which must have surprised even General Pathania.

PERSONAL OBSERVATION

In retrospect it is unthinkable that such a thing could happen. Surely it was not an empty boast that Sela defences were impregnable. The very fact that the Chinese had earmarked their 11 and 55 Divisions with 134 Division in reserve for the attack on Sela and also rushed 540 Artillery Brigade of 130 Division to Jung to support the attack, shows that the Chinese were leaving nothing to chance in order to capture this formidable redoubt. After all Marshal Liu Bocheng had referred to Nuranong and Sela defences as the copper head and a thick chest of the awesome snake to which he had likened the Indian defences in Kameng sector. It is a different matter that he had advocated that their forces should also target the narrow waist meaning Dirang (the seven inches of the snake). It could be argued that there wasn't just sufficient space for such a large-scale attack and nor could the Chinese be expected to sustain the mind-boggling rates of maintenance (war wastage rates) to support three divisions. It is all debatable, but knowing what the Vietnamese achieved in Dien Bein Phu in 1954 against the French or in the Tet offensive against the Americans in 1967 and the Chinese in North Korea in 1952, we must grant the unconventional Chinese with a high level of motivation, training[2] and acclimatisation. Obviously the two divisions wouldn't have attacked simultaneously. The Indian response should either have been to treat Sela as a strong delaying position or to fight to the last from properly prepared defences. The Indians were on the contrary caught in a game of self-deception. There was a conflict in their conscious and the subconscious thinking, brought about by a lack of the will to fight among the key appointments in Brigade and the battalions.

Unfortunately 62 Brigade spent much of its energy, effort and resources in preparation of defences, with dubious motivation and intentions, and yet made no preparation or plan should a withdrawal be forced upon them. It was a bad case of military hypocrisy.

The above notwithstanding, it appears that the unseemly rout at Sela had been caused by incompetence and possibly by an act of dereliction. We shall first tackle the incompetence bit. It was great folly to withdraw 4 Garhwal, the 4 Sikh LI companies at Tsogya Lakes and 2 Sikh LI simultaneously and that too at night. This is a near impossible feat to accomplish with a degree of efficiency even in peacetime, without proper rehearsals and drills. To suddenly inflict it unrehearsed and unplanned on so many troops in war was an invitation to disaster.

D company of 4 Sikh LI, as we all know, had been ordered to occupy a screen position at km 108 to cover the withdrawal of 4 Garhwal Rifles and A and C companies of its own battalion coming from Tsogiya Lakes and thereafter withdraw to Sela. 4 Garhwal withdrew at 0200 hours on 18 November. The last element of A and C companies passed through at 0450 hours. D company thereafter withdrew from the screen position after receiving instruction from Lieutenant Colonel RB Nanda, the Commanding Officer.

As D company reached km 102 just short of Sela, it found A and C companies in position astride the road. Heavy MMG and mortar fire interspersed with rifle fire was going on in the Sela area. The leading platoon of A company under Subedar Nanak Singh had managed to reach their original position but found, to their dismay, the trenches occupied by the enemy. There was a bayonet charge and casualties on both sides. The survivors, with Nanak, rejoined the company. It was now daylight.

A, C and D companies were in the open. They now came under heavy fire from the northern heights, which a few hours earlier had been the 2 Sikh LI position. These companies put in a two-pronged attack under Majors GVE Masilamani and S Rajan, to regain their old defences but it petered out in the face of stiff Chinese resistance, specially the accurate enfilade fire by enemy MMGs from the flank of the northern heights, but not before they had killed over 30 of the enemy, including an officer.

Unable to effect a link up with Battalion headquarters, Masilamani ordered the companies to withdraw southwards across the Sela ridge, through a saddle, and regroup further south.

Meanwhile Lieutenant Colonel Nanda, with B company on the forward slopes of the left shoulder of Sela, found that the Chinese had surrounded them from the east, north and west. Having withstood three Chinese attacks, after firing the last salvo from his 3-inch mortars, at about 0900 hours on 18 November, Nanda ordered his meagre force to cut across the Sela heights to the south. By this time the rest of 62 Brigade was already at Senge.

2 Sikh LI defences were the lynchpin as far as Sela defences were concerned. Any premature withdrawal from there amounted to sealing the fate of 4 Sikh LI as also offering the Chinese the most vulnerable approach on the platter. Between Kyela and the right and left shoulders of Sela, lies an extensive killing ground where the Chinese could have been simply butchered. Yes, 2 Sikh LI ought to have been withdrawn to entice the enemy into this killing ground, but after 4 Sikh LI had reoccupied its main defences, on withdrawal from Two Lakes. But by the evening of 17 November, the decision to withdraw from Sela had been taken. However, does withdrawal mean that you simply upstick and move back, unmindful of what the enemy can do to you or what you can do to the enemy ? There are instances in war when tables have been turned by trapping the enemy into a killing ground, for example in Khemkaran in 1965 Indo-Pak war. A fine battalion that was 4 Sikh LI, had been rendered useless by the premature withdrawal of 2 Sikh LI and simply sacrificed.

Now about the dereliction bit. It is reported that Brigadier Hoshiar was very angry with Lieutenant Colonel Irani, commanding officer of 2 Sikh LI, for withdrawing prematurely from Kyela. There is no doubt that had 2 Sikh LI been withdrawn after 4 Sikh LI had reestablished themselves in their main defences, the rout would have been averted. Logically therefore, 2 Sikh LI should have been ordered to withdraw during the day on 18 November or during the night of 18/19 November, as originally envisaged. Suddenly deciding to withdraw 2 Sikh LI during the night of 17/18th required clockwork precision. Cutting it too fine was asking for the impossible. 2 Sikh LI can therefore hardly be blamed. But it is sad, because this was nevertheless a serious lapse as it led to the disintegration of 4 Sikh LI, the decamping of 1 Sikh and the latter's eventual break up.

The marching column reached Senge about 9 am; by that time the vehicle column had also concentrated there. There was no information about the presence of any enemy between Senge and Dirang. Movement of some vehicles coming from the direction of Dirang seemed to reinforce the impression that the road to Dirang was open. But the Chinese were very much there, holding their breath and their fire, waiting for the main target to arrive. The smaller fish were being allowed to get away, enticing the bigger one into the net.

On reaching the lower helipad at Senge, Hoshiar summoned his commanding officer for a brief discussion. He wanted a battalion to move along the track leading to Nyukmadung village onwards to Bridge 1 area, generally keeping paralled to and above the road axis (to cover the eastern flank of the main column), and thereafter affect a link up with our forces at Dirang. The COs of both 1 Sikh and 2 Sikh LI raised their hands to object. They protested that their troops were no longer under their full control. Hoshiar then turned to Colonel Bhattacharjee, CO 4 Garhwal, and asked him if his battalion could take on this task. With two of his companies still intact, Bhattacharjee rose to the occasion and accepted the challenge. His words to his officers were: "I know we have gone through a gruelling time but let us show them that the Garhwalis can do it." An order of march was hurriedly worked out and the order given. One gets the impression that Hoshiar's long NDA tenure had made him very rusty as far as tactical concepts are concerned. He ordered the vehicle column to proceed straight to Dirang and report to Commander Artillery Brigade. For the marching column the order of march was, 4 Garhwal Rifles along the track axis, 2 Sikh LI, Brigade HQ, 1 Sikh and other minor units along the road axis. 13 Dogra less two companies was ordered to act as rearguard. This became in fact an advance operation and not a withdrawal, and that too without the benefit of tactical bounds or of artillery support, and with a highly vulnerable administrative column acting as vanguard. It was as if Hoshiar called off the war as he would have called off an exercise in peacetime (for all to go quickly back to barracks). His troops could have been on their way home, instead of having to fight their way out. The Chinese, unfortunately, did not see it as the end of a training exercise. For them the rewarding part was just beginning.

When the marching column reached Bridge 2, 4 Garhwal Rifles took the track to Nyukmadung. The rest of the column followed the main road. The vehicle column had passed Bridge 2 about two hours earlier. When the marching column turned the road bend about 800 meters beyond Bridge 2, a harrowing site came into view. Vehicles, guns and bulldozers were lying helter-skelter on the road and the area was littered with dead and dying men. This ill-fated vehicle column had been under the command of Major Brahm Sat of 6 Field Regiment. There were no known survivors.

It was now the turn of the marching column to face the sweeping Chinese fire from dominating positions on both sides of the valley. The brunt was faced by the leading elements of 2 Sikh LI. With the support of their own 2 inch mortars and 3 inch mortars of 13 Dogra deployed at Senge, they managed to clear about half a kilometer of the road. There was a strong Chinese post on a feature below Nyukmadung village which was bringing down lethal fire and holding up further advance. A platoon of 1 Sikh under second Lieutenant Surinder Dagur now swung into action and assaulted the position and managed to evict the enemy, but in this action Dagur and most of his men were killed. There was a string of ambushes further ahead. There were similar acts on smaller scale by other young officers with their small bands of daring men. It was a kind of death-wish. Hardly a young officer came out alive from these Chinese ambushes.

As darkness fell, all semblance of command and control broke down completely. The surviving troops broke out in small parties making for the mountain range south of Khouma river, hoping to make a cross-country escape to

Foothills or into Bhutan. The Chinese soon began their mopping up operation, they searched the dead bodies of Indian troops for loot. At this stage, they were in no mood to take any prisoners; such must have been their instructions. At some places they lined up Indian prisoners and shot them in cold blood[3]. A few plucky types managed to evade arrest. One of the most hair-raising feat was that of Captain PPS Bains of 4 Garhwal who spent the whole night of 18/19 November directly below a Chinese light machine gun post and because of his superb fitness, agility and fieldcraft was able to escape from the Chinese dragnet and reach Bhutan. A cross-country champion in 1958, his was a near effortless walk over those high hills. For the majority it was a hard and trying experience. This was a pity, because though the country they passed through was pretty and scenic, it was very hard going. Those who could move fast had the benefit of living off the land. Those who followed were less lucky, but for the unfit it was total misery. Without food and proper clothing, they grew weak, emaciated and sick and it took them that much longer to reach the foothills. Some were mere skeletons when they reached the foothills. Their eyes had the look of hunted animals. And, there were a few cases of frostbite and gangrene. And there were many who never made it.

Brigadier Hoshiar Singh was one of the last to withdraw from the ambush site. Greatly anguished with the day's developments, he had been trying his best to marshal his troops for counter-ambush attempts with limited success, but eventually he was left with only a handful of men and officers with him. Instead of heading for the plains, somehow he had an idea fixed in his mind that he had to reach Dirang. After a couple of day's march against the grain of the country, he found the Dirang valley crawling with Chinese. He turned back and headed towards Mandala and learnt from the locals that Bomdila too had fallen. Without food for over a week, his party, having bypassed Phudung, was resting on the bank of Phudung Chu when the Chinese overwhelmed them. Brigadier Hoshiar stood up and was directing his party to take up firing position, when he was killed by an enemy bullet. According to the Chinese version, the trigger-happy soldier who shot Hoshiar was made to face disciplinary action for a careless act because they had wanted to capture Hoshiar alive.

13 Dogra (less two companies), the rearguard battalion, was forced out of their position at Senge by the Chinese advancing down from Sela. By then they were quite aware of the fate of 62 Brigade. They crossed over to the southern range well short of the ambush site and reached Bhariabkund and Bhutan in small parties, but in reasonably good order.

4 Sikh LI, who had been cut off from the Brigade, had fought a ferocious battle to extricate themselves from Sela and had inflicted heavy casualties on the Chinese. They were able to make a clean break by making a cross-country traverse of the southern heights of Sela. They rejoined the main road halfway to Senge where they ran into a small Chinese force whom they eliminated and they also managed to capture two Chinese soldiers who were subsequently killed as Sikh LI troops ran into numerous Chinese ambushes. Throughout the day, Nanda and his officers had been leading from the front. The battalion could never join up with the Brigade and finally disintegrated in the face of vastly superior Chinese strength and firepower. In the last skirmish fought by Nanda's party at approx 10 am on 19 November near Bridge 2, this brave colonel with five officers, three JCOs and 90 other ranks fell while attacking an enemy position.

Of the others, Major Masilamani along with K M Tiwari and about forty men escaped to Bhutan. In all the battalion lost 155 officers and men in this operation, one of the highest casualty rates in this war.

The most touching case was of Captain RD Rosario who, after surviving four ambushes and having lived through a gruelling 23 days march, succumbed to frostbite and gangarene in the military hospital at Tezpur on 11 December. His body was escorted by his elder brother Lieutenant Colonel CC Rosario and flown out in an Air Force Dakota to Secunderabad to be laid to rest in the ancestral graveyard of their Catholic Church.

4 Garhwal who were on the Nyukmadung-Dirang track axis encountered relatively lighter opposition, which they were able to overcome. But they lost Vinod Goswamy and Deb, two of their very brave young officers, and quite a few men. By 3 am Colonel Bhattacharjee and Lieutenant Tandon with about hundred men reached Bridge 1, just a little after 4 Rajput had withdrawn from there. By then it was clear to them that the main column on the road axis had in all likelihood disintegrated. Bhattacharjee too could have taken to the hills at this stage but he had orders to link up with the Division headquarters at Dirang and therefore marched on towards it, unaware that there were no Indian troops there any longer. A couple of kilometres short of Dirang, in the early hours of the morning, when it was still dark, they walked into a Chinese column. For a while each mistook the other to be part of their own forces but once the identity got known, the Garhwalis knew that they had walked into Chinese captivity. The Battalion lost 3 officers, 4 JCOs and 153 other ranks during the withdrawal; five officers, 8 JCOs and 251 Jawans were captured by the Chinese.

Let us for a moment imagine that Brigadier Hoshiar Singh had refused to withdraw from Sela by hanging up his telephone, or perhaps even by faking a breakdown in radio and tele links with the Divisional HQ. General Pathania and his staff would have decamped any way. The other saving grace would have been for 4 Garhwal Rifles not to have been pulled from their covering troops position but been asked to carry on fighting for as long as possible, and for 2 Sikh LI not to have been withdrawn before 4 Sikh LI had reoccupied its original defences. It is reasonable to assume that intermittent air supply would have been possible at Sela. Let us then war game the battle with the force levels then obtaining on both sides. Would it be unrealistic to imagine that Sela would have held on for at least seven to ten days? What then would have been the fate of 419 unit bottled around Thembang and Rahung ahead of Bomdila? Could the two or three Chinese divisions be maintained at battle rates of ammunition consumption? How would it have affected the world opinion and what would have been the reaction of the USA, UK and other western powers?

As far as casualties are concerned, would the Sela brigade have incurred any more than what actually took place during their chaotic rout? On the other hand, with the heavy attrition that would have taken place on the Chinese side, the chances of a stalemate was more likely.

It was deposed by General Pathania before the Henderson Brooks Court of Inquiry and by Lieutenant Colonel Manohar Singh, Pathania's GSO 1, that the former had not given permission to commander 62 Infantry Brigade to withdraw that night and had produced the telephone log in evidence. Technically Pathania was right because as per his last conversation with Brig Hoshiar, the withdrawal was to commence only on the night 18/19 November. Brigadier Hoshiar Singh, if he had not been killed, would in all likelihood have faced some administrative or disciplinary action. That would have been a sad thing because Hoshiar was basically a brave and a noble person, who was suddenly given a very difficult job which required someone professionally more sound and who was aware of Chinese tactics. The greater anomaly is that Pathania never faced a court-martial for abandoning his post and his troops and running away from battle.

Details of Casualties of 2 Infantry Brigade in the Sela Fiasco

Details	Offrs	JCOs	OR	Total	Percentage	Remarks
Personnel present	100	132	4383	4615	-	-
Killed	38	30	862	925	20%	-
Captured	17	28	1015	1060	21%	-
Wounded	4	6	232	242	5%	including 181 captured

NOTES AND REFERENCES

1. Indeed if the Chinese met a reverse in the entire operation, it was at the hands of 4 Garhwal at Nuranong. Fittingly the battalion each year celebrates Nuranong Day to commemorate this defensive victory. 4 Garhwal is the only unit in the entire Sino-Indian war to have earned a battle honour in this war and rightly so.
2. *'The Snows of the Himalayas'.*
3. *'I was a Prisoner of War in China*, by Lt. Col. Bakshi'.

19

Headquarters Do A Bunk

As we have seen, Pathania had painted a very alarming picture to his Corps Commander on the evening of 17 November and obtained clearance for withdrawal. However, the atmosphere at Dirang Dzong was anything but warlike. A television team was expected to arrive in two days time. The General Staff's major concern during the day had been the requisitioning of commodes (toilet seats) from 65 Brigade units and the divisional troops. Life was otherwise peaceful and remained so till the morning of 18 November. The previous evening the officers had dined in the mess and had had their chhota pegs and then gone to sleep in their huts and barracks. Men huddled in blankets to cover themselves and occupied the verendahs and odd corners. No sentries were posted anywhere in the area! Even a camp-out in peacetime requires a little more circumspection.

18 November dawned peacefully, as usual. Then General Pathania learned about the premature withdrawal of 62 Infantry Brigade and a conference was called at Divisional HQ early in the morning, the agenda being to discuss the hopelessness of the situation and ways to get out of the place. Commander 65 Infantry Brigade and Commanding Officer 6 Field Regiment were also present. There was no discussion,

or planning or orders given for a formal withdrawal. It was a stark sauve *qui peut* intention uppermost in everyone's mind.

While the conference was in progress, Major Shaikh of 19 Maratha suddenly barged in, out of breath, and announced that the Chinese had attacked his company at Munna Camp and that there was an enemy road-block in area km 31. This information was enough for Pathania and others to turn tail and bunk. It was decided that two companies of 13 Dogra, which had arrived from Senge the previous night, and a troop of B Squadron 7 Cavalry would attack and clear the road block — a face saving, non-order in the midst of a frantic and chaotic stampede out of Dirang. The attack never got going. The Infantry companies had no clue about the geography of the area and could advance only up to Sagor village. The tanks found that the road was completely blocked by fleeing troops and so they abandoned their vehicles. Eventually these ineffective tanks had to be rolled down the khud to clear the road.

86 Field Battery located below Sagor village engaged the Chinese at Munna Camp which was visible from the gun position and caused numerous casualties. The Chinese retaliated by firing their mortars but, probably because they had limited ammunition, their firing was sporadic and caused little damage, though a technical assistant of the Battery was hit by shrapnel and wounded.

The GOC, with some of his staff all packed up to scoot, left in his jeep at the head of a small convoy, ostensibly to watch the progress of the battle. Actually the intention was to reach Sagor village and thence to flee up the track to Mandala. On reaching near Sagor village and finding the road blocked, with no hope of getting it cleared, the party abandoned its vehicles and took to their feet. On reaching Phudung in the valley south of the pass, they learnt that Bomdila had fallen, so they kept going along the old Udalgiri trade route eventually reaching Bhairabkund near Udalgiri, where on 22 November, after an uneventful three-day trek, General Pathania was picked up by General Kaul in a helicopter. Even the nimble-footed Chinese couldn't catch up with the fleeing general!

To go back to Dirang, Brigadier Gurbax Singh Gill, commanding 4 Division Artillery Brigade, rushed back to his basha to collect his kit and identity card and woke up Brigadier Michael Chatterjee, Commander of 67 Infantry Brigade (who had reported the previous night for briefing) still sleeping in his silk quilt. The latter, a veteran of the Burma campaign, protested that he was waiting for his morning cup of tea and was quite confounded by this sudden exodus. Eventually he had to miss his tea and the two brigadiers followed the GOC's party with their batmen.

Brigadier Cheema, Commander of 65 Infantry Brigade, on his return to his headquarters did not pause to pass any orders. He was a dark horse in a very negative sense and the chief villain in the sordid drama. With his brigade strung out in company posts, he found himself somewhat unoccupied. Specially picked to command the brigade, a responsibility he systematically shirked (by hardly ever visiting his troops), he preferred to function as the GOC's alter ego and, according to many at Divisional HQ, he was the real culprit behind the shameful abandonment of Dirang. A prisoner of war in Italy during the Second World War, he had, it is said, built up a paranoia that the Chinese too would capture him. He is reported to have been constantly urging the GOC to upsticks and bunk. He was, in fact, the head of the informal lobby formed at Divisional Headquarters whose aim it was to impress upon the GOC that the only alternative was to take to the hills. Having gone to the morning conference fully packed and ready to run away, he now left in hot pursuit of the GOC, shouting from his jeep for the benefit of his staff "Mandala Track -Mandala Track".

There was by now a kilometre-long line of vehicles abandoned on the road and an equally long line of troops on the track to Mandala. Yet many stalwart souls remained behind, in a state of disbelief, awaiting orders from their superiors. A Junior Commissioned Officer of 7 Cavalry was seen, pistol pointed forward in his hand, leading a lone Stuart tank in the midst of this melee, wanting to take the tank to the head of column; the tank got stranded and added to the congestion.

There must have been nearly a thousand troops still remaining, vastly outnumbering the hundred odd Chinese near Munna camp, who kept firing from a distance and occasionally opened up with their mortars. The intention obviously was to scare away the Indians.

There were attempts by some (Major SS Brar of the Signals who later rose to the rank of Lieutenant General and Commander of a Corps, and Major Sehgal the DAA and QMG of 65 Brigade who later wrote *The Unfought War of 62* to rally some of the troops milling around into a scratch force, but it frittered out as the troops were looking for their own officers who had either decamped or were lost in that disorganized mob. Major Brar had already dispatched his signal company, under Captain Upadhaya his second in command, with the Brigade troops earlier in the day. At 4 pm as the shadows lengthened, he and Major Sehgal thought that it was no longer prudent to remain in Dirang but before leaving they armed themselves with a 7.62 SLR each from a stack of these brand new imported rifles, just received from NATO and now abandoned — a prize cache for the Chinese.

Lieutenant Vinay Shankar too remained at his gun position with his gunners, awaiting orders, but none ever came. Presently a Lieutenant General, Commanding the School of Artillery, he recalls that there was a strange quietude in the atmosphere around him. There was no immediate threat, only a few weary Chinese lurking in the distance, at most a nuisance value. At about 4.30 pm when Dirang had acquired a near deserted look, the Battery personnel spiked the guns and followed in the wake of the divisional deserters.

Handicapped by under-moralled officer leadership and an uninspiring CO, 19 Maratha, in the absence of orders, took the benefit of the doubt and chose not to concern itself with the happenings at Dirang. They first went westward towards Lubrang and from there to Phudung and Morshing. They got away well before the Chinese could chase them, and made it safely to Bhariabkund.

History had repeated itself. Plassey had been re-enacted at Dirang. About five thousand Indians had been put to flight by a hundred odd Chinese. Who played the role of Siraj-ul-daula and who that of Mir Jafar and Seth Amin Chand? There is hardly any guesswork required.

4 Rajput's was a truly sad story. The battalion as we know was split up by companies. Two were north of Khouma river, one on the Bhutan border and another 6 kms south of Sapper Camp at Lubrang. Lieutenant Colonel Brahmanand Avasthy, the Commanding Officer, with a small element of odd bodies, was at Sapper Camp (Bridge 1 area). Known to be a brave man with spartan habits, Avasthy had joined the battalion only a week before, on promotion from the Infantry School, Mhow, where he was a senior instructor in the JC Wing. He had earlier held the coveted appointment of Adjutant of the Indian Military Academy, Dehradun. It has been said that he was among the best COs in the Indian Army at that time. Because of the wide dispersal of his sub-units, he got no chance to display his qualities. But he was surely a dismayed man. The GOC, prior to his bunk, had left instructions for 4 Rajput to be placed under 62 Brigade and cover the latter's withdrawal to Dirang. But soon after that there was no communication either with Divisional Headquarters or 62 Brigade. The Chinese, as we have seen, had by then

spread themselves in strength between Bridge 2 and Bridge 1. A and B companies of 4 Rajput, at point 3582 and Gompa Cher, were prevented from crossing the Khouma river to re-join Battalion headquarters. The company located 20 kms away at Dingpiksu-Nagakuri Remba on the Bhutan border, also ran into enemy opposition at Tirmit (near Bridge 2) and had to make it on its own. The right section of 7 Bengal Battery, however, followed the most difficult and hence the least obvious route — Morshing-Shergaon-Doimara — and in less than a week arrived at Foothills. They looked so fresh and fit, people wouldn't believe that Gosal and his men had been part of the withdrawing troops.

Avasthy with the meagre elements left behind at Sapper Camp, waited till 3 am and finally, after destroying all stores not being carried back, fell back to his company position at Lubrang. Later that the day, he began his withdrawal and reached Phudung on the 21st. En route a very large number of men from various arms and services as well as the Border Roads Organisation 'Tusker Force' joined his column and it became one of the biggest -- the approximate strength being about 500-600 officers and men. Vinay Shankar's gunners too were now part of this column, having joined up at Phudung.

In the early hours of 23 November, this force reached Priyuding, a small hamlet a few kilometres short of Morshing village, where the track bifurcated. The one to the right climbed up to Lagyala Gompa before rejoining the main track to Morshing. The other turned left before going southwards along the stream to Morshing. Someone had made an arrow sign on the track pointing towards Lagyala Gompa. One half of Avasthy's group felt that the sign had been made by our own troops or by friendly locals, but the other half, those with Vinay Shankar, felt that it could be a trap. The best of commanders at times commits an error of judgement. Having covered virtually two-thirds of the way to the plains, it wasn't really any false sense of security that made Avasthy follow the arrow mark. His Rajputs (nearly a company plus) were an intact force and he accordingly briefed his group that he was quite confident of overcoming any Chinese force he might meet, which according to him couldn't be all that big, considering the distance the Chinese would have required to come, all the way to Lagyala Gompa. In this he was greatly mistaken; but it appears that Avasthy was itching to have a showdown with the Chinese and, in his heart, hoped to gain a rare victory in this otherwise dismally one-sided war.

Lagyala Gompa, the last Buddhist monastery on the old trade route, is located on a commanding feature overlooking Morshing valley as well as the slope to the west which Avasthy's party had taken. On the latter route, the broad ridge forms into a big plateau just short of the Gompa. This was the killing ground the Chinese hoped the Indians would walk into.

After reaching Rupa on the morning of 19 November, a sizeable Chinese force had made post-haste for Morshing with the object of trapping the remnants of the Indian troops of 62 and 65 Brigades. They were in position at Lagyala Gompa on 22nd November and it was they who had planted the arrow mark at Priyuding.

At about 11 am on 23 November, Avasthy's force reached the plateau and came under Chinese fire. Avasthy in all likelihood underestimated the Chinese strength which was a good 500 strong well entrenched force occupying a commending feature. The Indians were also greatly handicapped by absence of artillery and morter support and they had limited small arms ammunition. Avasthy quickly organized a two-pronged attack on the Chinese position. The Chinese retaliated with lethal fire from their concealed dug outs. For nearly an hour a fierce battle ensued. Not a single Indian of this force survived but over 200 Chinese also lay dead.

Among the killed were suven young Indian officers in the prime of their youth, the finest specimens from NDA and IMA, who had fought fearlessly and along with 400 of their men became the unsung martyrs in one of the fiercest but tragic battles of NEFA. Lieutenant Manvir Singh was one of them. With him was his cousin Lieutenant Chattarpati Singh of 4 Rajput, son of Colonel Girdhari Singh, MC Bar and Vr C, one of the highest decorated officers of the Indian Army. The brave colonel thus made the supreme offering to the motherland. Such families ought to be treated as national heritage. It is sad when there is not even a befitting requiem and recognition both at national and army levels.

The Rimpoche (Head Lama) of Lagyala Gompa, who witnessed the battle, is still and the only one left to narrate this heroic episode. The headman of Domkho village, one kilometer from Morshing, would tell you how the Chinese stacked a few hundred of their dead bodies in the village huts before transporting them on horses/mule back to Dirang for their last rites.

The Chinese dug a mass grave for the Indians and inscribed on a flattened ration tin the names of Colonel Avasthy and other officers. They stuck this up on a bamboo stick over the grave and left. Long after the ceasefire, this grave was dug up by a party under Major Kukreti, Avasthy's erstwhile Company Commander at Dingpiksu; Avasthy's body was identified. In the left breast pocket of the jacket, was found an unposted letter to his wife and slip of paper with a prayer written on it.

For me the news of Manvir's death came as a great shock. It came as a personal grief and it was one of the few times in my life when I cried. So often threrafter have I found that it's the better and handsomer people in the real sense who depart early. May be there is a truth in the saying that those whom God loves dearly, he doesn't leave them on this earth for long as their place rightfully belongs in cleaner celestial environment.

I took the liberty of visiting Mrs Avasthy in her house at Noida in the course of my research of this book and it proved to be a pilgrimage. She gave me a couple of letters that her husband had written her a few days before he was killed and a poem she had written.

If any one deserved an award in the 1962 war, Avasthy and his brave officers and men were the ones. But such are the vagaries of war that sometimes a real warrior, a real hero, remains unsung. How many in our Army have ever heard of this great Rajput sacrifice? There is a memorial now at Lagyala Gompa in memory of Avasthy and his brave men and a statue of him. But is this all that they deserve?

An account of the Dirang episode would be incomplete without recounting the fate of A and D companies of 4 Rajput. Having been obstructed from rejoining Battalion Headquarters by effective enemy fire, and Dirang having also fallen to the Chinese, these two companies under Major Nair and Major Mullay made a long circuitous journey via Chug-Sangti-Namshu-But -Kaspi. From Kaspi they crossed over to Tenga valley but found it occupied by the Chinese. Short of Tenga they discovered a dead body of a jawan of 1 Madras which cautioned them. A little beyond, they surprised a Chinese party cooking rice, who ran away on seeing them, leaving the rice and snake pickle behind which some of them tasted. In a banana grove in the midst of Tenga river they found Major Panikar of 1 Madras, badly bitten by dimdam flies and one arm fractured and in a state of shock. He had been standing knee-deep in water for the last 48 hours and couldn't move out since the Chinese patrolled the road regularly. They took Panikar along but soon the Chinese were after them. The enemy party that had run away must have informed the garrison at Tenga. They took cover in thick jungle to the south and thus evaded the Chinese. After a gruelling journey of over two weeks, through dense jungle, they reached Bhalokpong, 50 kms north of Tezpur in the Charduar foothills, and ended their journey with a sumptuous feast when they stumbled on a hoard of rations in a deserted 'Tusker' camp. Second Lieutnant Deepak Verma (presently a Major General) of 5 Field Regiment, who narrated this story was in this party. With a half-inch growth of beard on his face, and having lost about 10 kgs of weight but otherwise looking soldierly, this handsome young officer who had nearly won the Silver Gun on our Young Officers' course, reached his Regiment at Misamari to be met with a joyous reception, and to learn that just that very day, he had been declared missing believed killed and a condolence meeting held for him! For him and the Rajputs with him, this episode will always remain the journey of their lives.

20

The Fall of Bomdila

After the setback at Poshingla on 15 November, General Pathania, the Divisonal Commander, directed that a second company of 5 Guards be sent to restore the situation. However, it could not leave till about 8 am on 16 November. Then he changed his orders, after dispatching two companies of 19 Maratha from Dirang to probe towards Sangti and Changdor; he now directed Commander 48 Brigade to send the whole of 5 Guards to Thembang. On receiving these instructions and after issuing a warning order to 5 Guards, Brigadier Gurbax hastened to km 9 in his jeep and caught up with the first company of 5 Guards, and ordered it to occupy a firm base at Thembang and await the arrival of the rest of the battalion. Back in Bomdila, Gurbax took Jai Singh, CO 5 Guards, with him and both were seen, walking sticks in their hands, rounding up porters and ponies, with Major Johri, the Political Officer, lending his full cooperation in this effort. He even made available his class III and IV employees to make up the shortage. One of these persons was Namjee Daki, Daki being the corrupted form of Dakia (postman) in Hindi.

By the evening of the 16th the battalion had been marshalled outside the barracks, with a section of 7 Bengal Battery (two 3.7 inch guns) on mule pack. Colonel Jai Singh, a mustachioed Rajput, addressed his men and poured forth some high sounding motivation. You could see that his troops respected him. 5 Guards was a spirited outfit with a lively set of officers. They were mostly tall and handsome, top-notches from the Academy, specially selected to join the Brigade of Guards. Devinder Sood, who had been an under-officer at the IMA, a course-mate of mine, was one of them. Very soon the war cry of the 'Garud Guards ka Hun Bole Pyare' and that of the Ahirs of 7 Bengal 'Krishna Bhagwan Ki Jai, Gau Mata ki Jai' rent the air. "The expeditionary force" strode out jauntily and late in the evening reached km 9 area, where it made an overnight stay before departing for Thembang in the early morning of 17 November.

PERSONAL INTERLUDE

Kapila my coursemate was the gun position officer with this force. Having nothing particular to do, I took my CO's permission to accompany the Battery to the Rahung bowl. I reached km 9 at 6 am on 17 November. At the risk of repetition, it would be pertinent to reacquaint the readers with the topography of this area. At km 9 (called mile 6 in those days) there was a well-kept camp of the Border Roads. If one walked straight down from there, one would hit the Rahung bowl in about an hour; and after a slight climb beyond that one came to the road again at km 22 (Mile 14). Directly to the east of Rahung was the Thembang feature; a track ascended steeply to it from Rahung, which 5 Guards now followed.. The Thembang feature not only dominated the track coming from Tungri and Poshingla, it also overlooked the Bomdila-Dirang road where it made a long 13 km loop, with the Rahung bowl and the fast flowing Gang river at the bottom of it.

After spending some time with Kapila and admiring the elan with which his gunners deployed their guns, I took my leave. Despite my flare for hill walking, I didn't particularly like the idea of the grinding 3000 feet climb back to km 9, I therefore made an easy 20-minute scramble to the other side,hoping to hitch-hike from there to Bomdila. While waiting at the roadside, a Mompa kept me company. He had a sly smile on his face: 'Chini Aya', he said, which made me think he was being cheeky. I shooed him away. Shortly later I was able to take a lift from a small convoy of 1 ton vehicles from Dirang. I believe this was the last column that managed to cross the road because soon thereafter the Chinese arrived and cut it off.

It was around 4 pm that the convoy arrived at km 9 amidst the first signs of warlike activity in Bomdila sector. The battle of Thembang had obviously started. I met a troop (four 25 pounder guns) of 6 Field Regiment deployed in the middle of the road. Colonel Bhupinder, my CO, was busy targeting the Chinese on the Thembang feature. It was a kind of semi-direct shoot, fed by observation from the battalion position over the wireless set, which was through on the brigade net. At an intense rate of firing the boom of the guns was impressive, though the stirring scene was rendered somewhat ludicrous by the action of the Sapper officer in charge of the 'Tusker' camp, who was frantically collecting the ejected brass cartridges to take back as souvenirs of the battle. The Brigade Commander was also there, peering through his binoculars. Himself a gunner, he was smiling happily at seeing the guns in action. The CO of 5 Guards was on the set asserting that he could deal with the Chinese. This was indeed Gurbax's brief spell of glory; he had reason to be happy because his guns were playing havoc with the Chinese.

5 Guards had reached Thembang at approx 2 pm, the earlier company having arrived there at about 6 am. The battalion was carrying limited ammunition, small arms and 3 inch mortar shells. It established itself on the open patch below the village. Reconnaissance over and having sent out a couple of patrols, they commenced digging their trenches. They couldn't have dug more than a foot when enemy activity was reported on the track coming from Poshingla. A protective patrol was sent out to sound out the enemy. Within fifteen minutes it was driven back into the battalion perimeter (it didn't yet qualify to be called a defended area, there yet being no trenches or shelters, leave alone bunkers with overhead protection). The enemy began to form up and also to spread out, to get round the flanks of the battalion. They soon opened up with mortars from north of Thembang village. Second Lieutenant SS Choudhary of the northernmost company picked up a LMG and climbed the lone tree in the area hoping to take a pot shot at the Chinese

mortarmen. This proved fatal as he was immediately shot by an enemy sniper and his dead body thudded to the ground. (Choudhary was an unlucky name in Kameng in 1962. SS was the third Choudhary to be killed within a span of one month.)

The time now was about 4 pm. 5 Guards had fought hard with whatever they had. Jai Singh had earlier assured the Brigade Commander that there were a few hundred Chinese at Thembang and he could deal with them. The mortars and the mountain guns were taking their toll of the enemy. After taking four shoots with the mountain guns, the battery commander's wireless set stopped working at this crucial juncture, but by then four 25 pounder guns had been deployed at km 9. It is estimated that there were about 1500 Chinese at Thembang, of whom at least three to four hundred were killed by Indian artillery fire. According to Namjee Daki,* who was hiding in the jungle nearby, he saw scores of Chinese being blown up as shells burst among them. Their most serious casualty was a high-ranking officer on a pony. It could well have been the commander of 419 unit. If it were indeed so, it speaks creditably of the Chinese that they carried on with their attack without even a moment's interruption. In fact they displayed a high degree of dash and initiative. When one considers that the Chinese and 5 Guards reached Thembang more or less at the same time, their attack, launched at the very moment of gaining contact, speaks very highly of their battle-drills.

By 4.30 pm his troops had run out of ammunition. Colonel Jai Singh asked his Commander for permission to withdraw from Thembang and it was granted. With darkness setting in, the Guardsmen slipped out in single file, down a deep nullah running south of Thembang. On hitting Gang River, there was a brief discussion whether to follow the Gang first eastwards and then south to the plains of Assam, or to climb up towards Bomdila. Apprehending that the enemy must have by then interjected themselves between Thembang and Bomdila, the majority followed the route down-stream. A few of the Guards officers and men however, did manage to reach Bomdila that very night, indicating that the apprehension of the main party was misplaced. It would have definitely helped the battle of Bomdila had 5 Guards managed to sneak back to their original defensive positions during the night.

Major Brij Raj Singh, the Battery Commander of 7 Bengal Mountain Battery, eager to rejoin his gun position, said good-bye to Jai Singh and took the track to Rahung. Rounding a corner, his party ran into a Chinese ambush and they were all killed. Brij Raj was into his late forties', rather old for a major to be commanding a battery. Himself an Ahir, he had risen from the ranks in the same Battery. He was a fine soldier, well liked by his men.

The Chinese now turned their attention to the two mountain guns in the Rahung bowl. The gun position officer, Second Lieutenant Akshey Kapila, returned the enemy fire using small arms and 3.7-inch howitzers. The latter with open sights effectively engaged the Chinese at 800 yards. Under cover of darkness, these guns withdrew to km 9, where Lieutenant Colonel Bhupinder Singh, CO 22 Mountain Regiment, waited for them. The Tusker camp was soon thereafter vacated, the 25 pounder guns having already fallen back to the main position at Bomdila.

5 Guards trudged over difficult terrain without food and shelter for the next ten days. They lit no fires for the first three nights and shivered in the cold of the nights but once they were fully clear of the Tenga area (which they had observed on their third day to be in Chinese hands)their journey became less fraught. They lived on wild plants and berries but by and large remained a cohesive group and reached Charduar in the plains near Tezpur. However, it

must be recorded that 5 Guards never delivered their full potential. But for that timid decision not to return to Bomdila, their unit would most surely have played a very meaningful part in the battle of Bomdila on 18 and 19 November and the eventual outcome could well have been different.

With the departure of 5 Guards, Bomdila defences (some have referred to it as a garrison, which is more appropriate) had been reduced from three to two battalions - in actual fact only six companies, because one company of 1 Madras had been sent to Dirang for the protection of Divisional headquarters and one company of 1 Sikh LI was deployed at Phudung. There was however adequate artillery, with ammunition, and enough rations.

By 9 pm on 17 November, the Rahung bowl was swarming with Chinese and their leading elements reached km 9 and established a roadblock. The locals with their women and children fled to the adjourning forest but the Chinese later coaxed them back to their homes.

> During that night while I was manning the command post as a stand-by for the adjutant, the Brigade Major called up and asked why the guns were silent. A strange question! Guns do not fire at their own initiative! It is the Infantry who must call for fire support. (Of course we had our list of unsurveyed defensive fire (DF) tasks along the likely enemy approaches of attack.) "But where were the Chinese at the moment?" I asked. I was brusquely told not to argue and to engage any DF I liked because according to the Brigade Major (who had done his staff college at Camberley) the Chinese must be made to know that we were wide-awake. I therefore, picked the DF closest to km 9 and ordered three rounds of gunfire from all guns deployed in Bomdila. Since the target had not been registered by firing earlier, the results could at best have been chancy.

It was expected that the enemy would launch his attack next morning. Given that he had no artillery, only a few manportable medium mortars with very limited ammunition and just a few hours of reconnaissance, it would be logical to argue that he was not even capable of putting in what we call a quick attack. It could only be at best a raid or a jitter-party operation. Therefore, if only the Brigade Commander had donned his thinking turban and kept his cool, and his Corps Commander had not pressurised him to carry out other senseless tasks, Bomdila defences could still have held on. With 3 J&K Rifles expected to arrive on 18 November and another battalion (6/8 GR) to follow, the situation would have been more than restored in a day or two.

However, as we know, Kaul in his message to GOC, 4 Division had committed himself; he insisted that 48 Brigade clear the road-block between Dirang and Bomdila at all cost. He now again rang up and ordered Gurbax to do so during that very night. The Brigadier was, however, able to convince him about the futility of the operation, pointing out difficulties of fog, poor visibility, the ineffectiveness of his Stuart tanks and, most pertinently, that he would in the process be uncovering and exposing his main defences. But Kaul was back at 10 am on 18 November on the telephone ordering Gurbax to send out a mobile column to Dirang Dzong (not knowing that the Division Headquarters had already fled from there without informing either Corps Headquarters or 48 Brigade and that 62 Infantry Brigade on Sela was on the verge of disintegration). Brigadier Gurbax again protested, as he had during the previous night, that his position had not changed except that a platoon of 3 J&K Rifle had arrived as advance party. To pull troops out of the defences would amount to letting the Chinese walk into Bomdila. Kaul was adamant and even threatened Gurbax with a court-martial. How one wishes that Gurbax had held his ground; in any case a court martial isn't the end of the world. A fair trial is always to be expected in our Army. Anyone else in Gurbax's place would have known that Kaul was simply flapping. A maverick in the place of the the mild and gentlemanly Gurbax would have temporarily disconnected all communication with a jittery superior. A commander on the spot must stick by his convictions and firmly ask his superior not to interfere in the local battle and to lay off. What a hero Gurbax would have been had he done that!

It was 12 noon by then. Ominously, a bank of dense fog swept over the top of the Bomdila feature. Major Maini, the lone company commander in charge of the now meagre defences, was standing above his bunker having a talk with his subedar sahib. Their attention had been drawn by the appearance of a group of soldiers (faintly visible in the fog) advancing towards them from the direction of the main Bomdila pass. The Chinese had launched their raid. Before our troops could react, a volley of bullets got Maini in the legs. Seeing him injured his troops pulled him into the bunker. He was given first aid dressing and within minutes about six of the jawans carried him down to the medical aid post, further denuding the already meagre defences. About a score of Chinese now appeared in front of the bunkers and a determined subedar, commanding an ad hoc platoon, held his ground for a while. Lieutenant Pran Pahwa of 135 Heavy Mortar Battery, the artillery observer with the platoon, engaged the enemy at very close range with artillery fire. The shells burst higher up in the branches of the thick pine trees. The effect would have been devastating on an enemy held up in the minefield and wire obstacles had any such things been laid. Instead, with numerous wide gaps in the defended position, the Chinese (about a hundred plus in strength) managed to sneak in and occupy the vacant trenches, causing confusion and forcing Pahwa and the subedar with their few men to abandon their position and escape downhill.

Gurbax's mobile column had hardly gone a couple of kilometers beyond Bomdila when it heard about the Chinese attack on the main defences of 1 Sikh LI. The column commander ordered his troops back to the battalion defences. It was too late. The Chinese caught them in the open. Taken by surprise, and in a sudden burst of panic, the Sikh LI troops just turned tail and ran. Brigadier Gurbax came out of his office on to the road and with outstretched hands shouted to the troops to stop. They paid no heed and didn't stop anywhere in Bomdila. Realizing that the Chinese had now occupied the Sikh LI position, 6 Field Regiment Battery and the mountain guns began plastering this erstwhile position, covered with a thick pine forest. For a couple of hours, with open dial sights, the guns played havoc into the pine forest. Numerous tree trunks came falling down with direct hits from the gun shells. 7 Cavalry tanks, with their main guns as also the wicker Browning MMGs, joined the deadly crescendo. That must have shaken the Chinese badly because for the next twelve hours they made no further move apart from one of their MMGs occasionally sweeping the Brigade Headquarters area with bursts of fire mixed with tracers.

Just as the guns began firing, a shaken Gurbax left in his jeep for Tenga. Some said that they heard him announcing that he was going back to fetch reinforcements. Very soon thereafter, the rest of the headquarters staff also decamped in their vehicles. Before leaving, a withdrawal order seems to have been given by word of mouth which reached only the gun positions and the troop of tanks. Many remained unaware of what was happening. The gunners, having exhausted their ammunition, withdrew.

The advance party of 3 J&K Rifles had remained back, as also Colonel Bhupinder Singh, CO 22 Mountain Regiment, and his headquarters staff. There were a few other odd bodies. Major Shashi Dang and Captain Lakhanpal, Brigade Major and Signals Officer of the incoming 67 Infantry Brigade respectively, who had fetched up that very morning for siting their headquarters in anticipation of their brigade's move, were at a loss to know what was happening. They too withdrew to Tenga valley but came back later during the night with the Brigade Major of 48 Brigade. 1 Madras, isolated from the Brigade (the Chinese had left them alone), were oblivious of this partial abandonment of Bomdila. They failed to get through to the Brigade Headquarters both on the telephone and the wireless set.

A kind of quiet descended on Bomdila, interrupted ironically by afternoon sorties of Indian Air Force Dakotas dropping ammunition boxes tied to parachutes over the DZ (dropping zone) but by then there was no one left to collect them.

> By 3 pm the battle seemed to have been over. A few stragglers passed our way. There was no communication with Brigade Headquarters, no news of our CO. The BC of the heavy mortar battery rang up for orders. I had none to give. He was a nasty chap and became indignant and called my CO names. He said that he had collected a few incriminating papers such as wireless logs and messages, to fix his superiors for their lapses in Bomdila. I went and woke up Captain KTM Pillai, our very witty and resourceful adjutant. He had had his beer and lunch and a refreshing sleep while I held the fort for him. I told him that nearly everyone had abandoned their positions including the gunners. Who gave the order? Or was it a spontaneous response on seeing the forward troops on the run? I couldn't answer that and our attempts to speak to Brigade Headquarters proved fruitless. The Adjutant and I decided that we too might as well withdraw to the School Area. As there were more stores and equipment than could be taken in one ferry, I instructed Suraj Bhan the survey Havaldar who was the seniormost N.C.O. to return for a second ferry. The Adjutant and I must have waited for over an hour but there was no sign of their return. I reckon the Adjutant did not want to be the first to suggest abandoning our position, and so it was I who suggested it to him. On our way down we bumped into a MMG gunner of the Mahar battalion. He had received a burst of small arms on the left side of his lower abdomen and was bleeding slightly in spite of the dressing, but seemed to be quite composed and on his feet. When we reached the Inspection Bungalow, we sighted

our CO with his driver, automatic fire with tracers whizzing over them. They made a dash to the Brigade HQ (a distance of about 100 yards) looking for the Brigade Commander and his staff. It was then that he heard the telephone ring; and he had his famous conversation with Brigadier Palit, the DMO, who was present at Corps HQ, who ordered him peremptorily to take over command of the Brigade (though there was sweet little left of it). At this juncture the adjutant left me to go and meet the CO. I moved off to the School Area with the wounded soldier and found Captain Kakkar, our Veterinary Officer, and about twenty odd men of the Headquarters staff, including the sheepish lot who had failed to return for a second ferry.

It was nearing dusk by then with just a few minutes of light remaining, when suddenly I heard a series of shouts which turned out to be the battle-cry of the Dogra troops of 3 J & K Rifles (Jak Rif) who were marching into Bomdila. The cheerleader was a stalwart JCO with a gold tooth, who straightaway asked me "Chinni Kahan Hai" (Where are the Chinese?). I didn't really know how to answer that, when a very sagacious Lt Col Gurdial Singh, the Commanding Officer of the unit, and a few of his officers also fetched up. He was quite disappointed on finding that the place was so completely abandoned. I told him about my own CO who I said was also around and who could brief him better. They soon met and I learnt that 3 Jak Rif would firm in the built-up area of Bomdila township and a counter-attack would be launched early in the morning, after an 8 GR battalion arrived later in the night. It never happened. Since there were no guns in situ and only a motley HQ staff of the Regiment under its orderly officer and the veterinary officer to keep company, I thought it only prudent to catch up on the sleep I had lost during the previous night. I went and informed Lt Col Gurdial Singh about our intention and indicated the two rooms where twenty odd men and we two officers would be sleeping during the night. Samunder Singh, our resourceful Regimental Havaldar Major, produced some rum and eats, but it was only halwa in ample quantity that made up the dinner. Maybe the troops had a rationale in preparing halwa because food-value-wise it is very rich. Whether it was the combination of rum and halwa or the lack of sleep for the last 48 hours, I for one was soon out like a log.

It so happened that Brigadier Gurbax had missed 3 J&K Rifles because the latter were coming up a short-cut and not following the road. He halted for the night at Tenga valley, got in touch with the Corps Headquarters and allegedly received instructions to head for Foothills. I say "allegedly" because early next morning Major Nahar Singh, a signal officer from Corps Headquarters, arrived with instructions from General Kaul to hold Rupa, about 14 kms south of Bomdila, (Rupa's importance lay in that it was located at the tri-junction of tracks from Bomdila and Tenga and Rupa valleys; it dominated the tracks that went directly to Chaku via Pirila, and to Phudung-Shergaon and onwards to Morshing-Kalakthang-Bhairab-kund.) But where were the troops to hold these defences and, more pertinently, where was the time? Would the Chinese allow us the breather? 1 Sikh LI had fled to Chaku, though their CO was with the Brigade Commander acting as always, as his alter ego. 3 J&K Rifles was at Bomdila. 1 Madras, detached and on its own, had been cut off from the Brigade for all practical purposes. The Field Battery had left its guns at Bomdila while its troops had made for Foothills. The same was the case with the troop of 135 Heavy Mortar Battery. 7 Mountain Battery less one section was at Chaku. The only troops available were 6/8 GR (who should have been at Bomdila in the first place). They were strung out between Tenga valley and Rupa and unlikely to be in a state to take on a responsibility like instant occupation of a defensive area in a strange place.

There is a mystery about the whereabouts of Brigadier Gurbax during that night. Official documents give out that he went back to Bomdila, but Colonel Gurdial, who was the main protagonist in the belated attempt to retrieve the situation, and one person whom Gurbax would definitely have contacted, does not remember the latter's return to Bomdila. What Gurdial recalls is Brigade Major Rawat's visit to retrieve some sensitive documents and to convey the Commander's instructions to withdraw from Bomdila and fall back to Rupa. Major Dang and Captain Lakhan Pal of HQ 167 Brigade accompanied him. The rear parties of 3 J&K left Bomdila at 5 am on 19 November, though All India Radio had announced the fall of Bomdila on the 18th itself.

> At about three in the morning I was woken up by Lt Col Gurdial Singh, who informed me that the anticipated counter-attack had been cancelled as 6/8 GR had not turned up and his own battalion had begun withdrawing from Bomdila. The rear parties would be gone in about on hour's time. It was kind of him to have bothered about a subaltern and his small band of men (thus saving me from an inglorious capture by the Chinese while asleep in my cosy sleeping-bag).
>
> We reacted quickly, rolled up our sleeping bags, humped them on our backs and began marching out of Bomdila at a brisk pace in the cold of the morning.
>
> We soon had enemy shells landing on the slopes around us but the road itself seemed to be safe. There were some mortar bombs too, and for all I know they were our own abandoned 4.2" mortars turned against us.
>
> By 7 am we had reached the road track junction where a track took off towards Rupa. Here we found the Brigade Commander, the CO 1 Sikh LI and a few others. They were having tea served in glass tumblers and I thought we might be offered a sip or two but that courtesy was not extended and when I found that they were interested in eliciting information from a veterinary officer two ranks my senior, who really had not much information of operational matters, I excused myself and Captain Kakkar followed suit. We were on foot, had a long distance to travel and uncertain of what the night might bring. A kilometre down the road we were pleased to meet Lt Col Gurdial Singh again and Second-Lieutenant Sinha, his Intelligence Officer, an ASC subaltern on attachment to the unit. Lt Col Gurdial Singh always had a very refreshing air about him. He was out reconnoitering a delaying position to be occupied by his battalion. It was then that we decided that it would be impossible to walk back all the 120 odd kilometers to Foothills camp, especially with the 9000 ft high Eagle's Nest Col to cross en route. We hijacked a 1 ton vehicle literally at gun point (because the driver and the co-driver felt that we

> were far too many to be carried in a mere 1-ton; but carry us it did). On reaching Tenga valley, I dismounted and let Captain Kakkar and party proceed to Chaku. There was a melee of vehicles and troops at Tenga and I went looking for my CO and Adjutant. I found my CO. There was the dog Quonde in the Jonga, which was full of odds and ends of "loot" my CO had "rescued" from the abandoned Circuit House at Bomdila. I was very fond of my CO and so I think was he of me. I was happy enough to see him and smiled at him. He asked me, 'Why are you smiling like that'? He probably had a guilty conscience. He took out couple of bottles of female cosmetics and gave them to me saying: 'With compliments of your CO', and drove off! I thereafter turned my attention to an already pillaged CSD canteen and managed to collect some tinned rations, a lucky find, as one couldn't be sure of food prospects in the immediate future. My predecessor had done a better job, having taken away a case of Scotch whisky.
>
> Suddenly the rush of vehicles increased and there were many people on the run, the Chinese were probably at their heels. I noticed a jeep come to a halt while its occupants took a pee-break. I immediately went and usurped the co-driver's seat and shared it with a very accommodating major. It was NDA training at its perverse best. There were at least a few hundred jawans trudging back in varying states of demoralization. I felt sad and guilty because most surely these troops would take a long time to reach Chaku; and it was likely that they would find the Chinese waiting for them there.

Brig Gurbax had assembled his Order Group at Rupa Bend, consisting of the Commanding Officers of 1 Sikh LI, 3 J&K Rifles (represented by its adjutant) and 6/8 GR, at about 7.30 am on 19 November. It was decided that the J&K Rifles would occupy a position on the feature immediately north of the road to Tenga. 6/8 GR was to occupy the position overlooking Rupa village. About half an hour after these instructions had been issued, with the respective commanding officers having left to brief their troops and carry out reconnaissance, a large number of Chinese suddenly appeared on the scene. They had come cross-country, literally running down the mountain from Bomdila.

They shot up the large number of troops who were on the road, which included Major Shashi Dang, who was resting on the roadside overlooking a deep nullah. Captain Lakhanpal who was sitting with him jumped down and lay doggo in the nullah during the whole day. He was lucky because the Chinese made no attempt to search the vicinity. Apparently, they were more concerned with their mission to encircle the Indian troops and foil any attempt on the latter's part to stage a rearguard action. Lakhanpal's was a classic escape, an arduous trek without food and rest. He emerged at the plains near Doimara. (Weeks later Major Dang's remains were dug up from a mass grave and identified by his brother, Capt Bal Kishan Dang of the Indian Navy.

There is a direct track from Rupa to Chaku via Pirila. The Chinese picked up a few local guides from Rupa village and followed this direct route, planning to surprise the remnants of the Indian forces at Chaku. The Chinese offensive was now on its final run. They were following Mao's maxim that when enemy is in rout, speed is of utmost importance. Greater risks can be taken. They detached a strong column from Rupa to Phudung and Morshing via Gachham following the track along the Phudung river. It was a cross-country short cut, bye-passing Shergaon. By 22 November, this force had established a strong ambush position at Lagyala Gompa above Morshing village, the fateful result of which has already been recorded.

It must be borne in mind that once 62 Brigade on Sela had disintegrated and Dirang abandoned, the whole of 18/19 November was available to the Chinese to rush troops and artillery in vehicles from Jung to Rupa. And they must have commandeered at least a few hundred Indian vehicles left abandoned on the road from Sela to Dirang. There was, therefore, no dearth of troops on the Chinese side. This would also explain the lull on the afternoon of 18 November at Bomdila. It wasn't any ruse as suspected by the Indians;

the Chinese forces were being reorganised and regrouped for the pursuit phase of the operation.

> When in the late afternoon I reached Chaku, I learnt that a halt had been ordered in the withdrawal. 1 Sikh LI was occupying the feature or rather the lower slopes just above the road. It was no defensive position; they simply sat around because they had no digging implements, only their rifles and brens, weapon scales of ammunition and two 3.7" mountain guns. Kapila had deployed one of these just above road, kept loaded. The other was in a dismantled state in one of the vehicles. Good old Hardwari Lal, who had two months earlier marched with me from Foothills to Tawang and displayed remarkable qualities, was assisting Kapila at Chaku. He had managed to nab a village chicken and had it served to Kapila for a sumptuous lunch.
>
> The atmosphere was reminiscent of what had prevailed in Jung during the retreat from Tawang. There was no order. People sat listlessly around in groups, with about 20 odd vehicles lined up on the road. Only a few enterprising persons, and I was one of them, carried some rations. Kapila and I collected some scrap wood and lit a fire and were rewarded by being eased out of it by the arrival of the Brigade Commander, CO 1 Sikh LI and a couple of others including his Sapper Company Commander. There was some futile talk about sending for digging implements and anti-personal mines. We went back to the so called gun position by the roadside. It was a starlit night and bitterly cold. There were about a half-dozen of us huddled inside a 1 ton vehicle with blankets over our heads, with Hardwari Lal keeping the vigil with his gun number 1. At about midnight he said that he could see the Chinese advancing towards us from the direction of Rupa. Indeed, there were a few hundred glowing torches lit on sticks, coming up the hill. It was surprising that no one else noticed or, if he did cared to bother about it. We thought it was our duty to inform the Brigade Commander. Kapila and Hardwari Lal went across to the Commander's basha where he was resting for the night and knocked. The CO of 1 Sikh LI, the alter ego fellow, came out and was most angry about having been woken up for such a trivial thing as the sighting of a few hundred torches. Couldn't they understand that the lights belonged to our own tribesmen who as refugees were moving towards the plains? Would the Chinese be so stupid as to use torches? He had obviously not

read Mao, who had written that when the enemy is in rout, speed in pursuit is of paramount importance and there is very little need to follow the strict rules of field-craft and tactics. Kapila and Hardwari Lal came back and we resumed the vigil.

It must have been about two hours later that a Chinese machine gun opened up from the north and sprayed our position with tracer bullets. Instantly there started a disorganised rout down the road.. Kapila and I, armed with pistols, took up lying positions on the road, looking up into the khud side. The Sikh LI troops, who were directly above us, sprang down on to the road like a horde of monkeys (some even landed on us) and took off for the plains. It was a frantic, mass exodus. We saw the Brigade Commander and our CO in the teeming crowd. We then saw a strange sight. The Sikh LI CO, sans his turban, his hair hanging down, dazed, and being supported by a couple of his jawans, as he struggled past us. Quite obviously he had been found asleep and was seized by sudden fright when the Chinese opened up. Just a few hours ago he had insulted Kapila for being too imaginative. And during the Kashmir Operation in 1948, this man had been awarded a 'mention in dispatches'!

The vehicles all started to move, with their headlights full on, inviting Chinese automatic fire. Their shooting, however, was not good and the bullets went wide off the mark. Their fire had a hollow sound, indicatng that their automatics hadn't that great a velocity.

There was little traffic discipline, each vehicle trying to overtake the next ahead. Ours were at the tail end. And then in the confusion and madness one of the vehicles in the front turned turtle and blocked the road. The logical thing under the circumstances would have been to shove the over-turned vehicle down the khud side. Just about 20 men could have done it. But as happens in a panic situation, the people simply dismounted and ran.

We must have been the very last in the lot. We, who had flung invectives at the fleeing troops, now followed suit. There was no point in surrendering to the Chinese or being killed by them.

We must have been gone on for about an hour when to our luck a jeep from our Regiment, driven by our Light Repair

> Workshop (LRW) JCO, came up from Foothills. He turned it about and, incredible as it must sound soon we were twenty in and on top of the vehicle. By the time we arrived at Foothills, it had shed its tyres and was plying only on its rims! We must have made a very gallant spectacle!
>
> It was almost first light when the staff of the reception centre met us. An officer was ordering around the troops after their ignoble flight. What amazed me again was the presence of the CO Sikh LI, totally spruced up, moving around with his reassured peace-time savoir-faire. For him the nightmare was over. Maybe there is merit in shirking bravery to go on living to fight another day. One day's coward could well turn out to be a great warrior on another day. It had already been the other way round in at least two cases in the recent past. Winners of high decorations in the Second World War and Kashmir Operations had, as we have seen, taken to athletics, and not for the best of reasons.

Over the years a false impression has been created that 48 Infantry Brigade fought a proper withdrawal operation. This is an absurd euphemism. The troops never got into any defensive position either at Rupa or Chaku. There was only the intention, or shall we say a pretension, to that effect. Unfortunately, statements made subsequently by certain senior officers and accordingly false records in war diaries have managed to confuse the issue. They have got away with it so far. Hence there is a need to examine this episode in a little more detail.

In the final analysis, the halts at Rupa and Chaku were made for rest and recuperation by demoralised fleeing troops. At Rupa bend, 3 J&K Rifles and 6/8 GR had been intact. By 7.30 am the Brigade Commander had issued brief verbal orders to the two battalions. CO Sikh LI was present but most of his troops were already on their way to Chaku, literally on the run. Lieutenant Colonel Bhupinder Singh, my CO, was also present during the orders, but all artillery elements save two guns of 7 Bengal had either been abandoned at Bomdila or had already crossed Chaku towards the Foothills. Within 15-30 minutes of the issue of these orders, the Chinese had descended upon them. The Brigade Commander, his alter ego and CO 22 Mountain were able to beat a hasty retreat in their transports. The enemy surrounded 3 J&K Rifles and 6/8 GR and both battalions suffered many casualties, with many others captured. It must be appreciated that when the Brigade 'Order Group' was receiving orders, the troops should have been in their assembly areas. One can well imagine what defences these troops could have dug while waiting for their COs. It must also be stated, in all fairness, that once the Chinese surrounded them, our troops tried to fight their way out and in the process inflicted some casualties on the Chinese.

As for Chaku, it was simply a night halt in the belief that the Chinese had been left far behind. No defences were prepared, though there was some talk of asking for defence stores from Tezpur. CO Sikh LI was throughout with the Brigade Commander and they did discuss the possibility of holding Chaku, but as we have seen, the moment the Chinese contacted Chaku and opened up with their automatic weapons, everybody just got up and ran.

There were only two commanding officers whose action at Bomdila was commendable. One was my CO, Colonel Bhupinder Singh of 22 Mountain Regiment, and the other was Colonel Gurdial Singh, CO of 3 J&K Rifles. Bhupi unfortunately was known for has couldn't-care-less flippancy and therefore never got the credit he deserved. Gurdial was as hard as nails, down to earth, crusty and professional. With a couple of more COs like them, Bomdila may never have fallen.

A word now about the fate of 1 Madras. By 8 pm on 18 November, the Commanding Officer decided that as the rest of the Brigade had withdrawn they would also have to pull out. Instructions were issued and the sub-units moved off at

11 pm. The plan was to withdraw along the ridge running east from point 3203 to Nafra and thence Kaspi but no one knew the route; it was selected off the map. They got completely lost in the jungle and finally on 20th morning emerged just above Tenga Bridge. The valley seemed deserted and it was decided to go across and head for Chaku. However, as the leading company reached the bridge it came under accurate machine gun and mortar fire from the surrounding hills. The battalion lost two officers, two junior commissioned officers and 43 other ranks killed in the brief engagement. Most of the others including their Commanding Officer were captured.

And thus ended the saddest chapter in the history of the post-Independence Indian Army. It could have been so different an outcome. If we can realize that and take some deliberate measures, especially to ensure a high quality of higher command at all times, the aim of writing this book will have been fulfilled. I must hasten to add that there were some competent senior officers too at that time, but they were just not around in NEFA.

Destiny played its part but more than that it was our rotten high command system that saw to it that all the wrong persons were sent up front, who collectively with their negative and passive efforts brought about the undoing of 4 Infantry Division, a fabled formation of Second World War fame. Must we as a nation resign ourselves to such a fate every hundred odd years? We need to ponder and look for lasting solutions.

NOTES AND REFERENCES

1. I met Daki (Namjee Ngoimu being his full name) and his wife in their hut in the old village of Rahung in the spring of 1995 and found him in his mid-seventies but as cheerful as a teenager. He was about to set off in his felt hat and riding boots for a gathering of elders at Dirang but delayed his departure

sufficiently to give me a first-hand account of the battle of Thembang. He was a trifle contemptuous of the Chinese and was particularly unhappy that they had forced a feast on the local population and fed them with dog meat. I had earlier met Daki's two sons with their beautiful wives who were living in the new Rahung village, 500 feet above the old one. The sons were doing a flourishing timber business, sported Gypsy jeeps and had TVs with dish antenna. Though quite small in 1962, they could recall most of the events. Their Hindi was near perfect.

I revisited Rahung in September 1997 and was sorry to find Daki physically in a very run down condition. I was told that he had gone to his maize fields "to see the monkeys" as they put it. He could hardly walk, but he and his wife obliged me by posing for my camera.

21

The Unilateral Ceasefire

It is evening time on 19 November. A musical performance is being held at Zhongnanhai. Mao leaves the hall alone while the music goes on. Zhou also comes out and joins Mao. Mao asks Zhou: "Have the letters already been handed over?" "Yes, all of them."

Premier Zhou has written to 20 Afro-Asian heads of States and Governments a 20-odd page letter. It explains China's principled position on the Indo-China border conflict and hopes for a peaceful solution to the dispute.

"We have fought a military war on one side and a diplomatic one on the other. We now have won both." says Mao.

Zhou: The Commander reports that the morale of (our) troops is high. Both in the East and the West, they have advanced quite rapidly. They have already reached the traditional and customary line. They have finished some 5000 (Indians) and have captured a large quantity of weapons and equipment.

Mao nodding with satisfaction: "Basically, we have finished the enemy".

Zhou: In order to create good conditions for peaceful talks we are prepared to ceasefire right there and withdraw the troops.

"I think we can. We should ceasefire, retreat as far as possible. We should yield to them a little and see how sincere they are about talks," Mao says sitting down and lighting up another cigarette.

Zhou: Our doing this will be something unprecedented in the world.

"We will have established a precedent by this. Somebody has to establish a precedent," Mao says looking at the distant Red Pagoda.

At 2400 on 21 November, 1962, the Chinese Border Guards receive an order signed by Mao Zedong. The General Staff Department sends the following urgent telegram to all formations :

"In order to seize the political initiative, the Center has decided that our government will make an announcement declaring that for the sake of promoting a peaceful resolution of the China-India border problem, our troops will unilaterally ceasefire beginning 0000 hours on 22 November. And starting 1 December they will unilaterally withdraw 20 kms from the line of actual control as it was on 7 November, 1959. Accordingly, the troops should start redeployment as follows :

22

Postscript

History often repeats itself, but it can also rebound on the present. During the 1970s, there was a distinct transformation in the equation along the 3500 km long India-Tibet border. From a position of weakness, India emerged as an equal adversary. In 1967 there was the Nathula incident when India reacted firmly and the very fact that China threatened to use air power betrayed signs of it getting somewhat unnerved. It was an indication that the worm was beginning to turn and by the early 'eighties it had turned completely. Nothing illustrates this point better than the Chinese perception of the Indian Army in 1989. It is worth quoting from the article titled "Can the Glory of the Year 1962 be Re-enacted", written by a Chinese officer.

> "Nathula may be taken as the first post in the middle sector of the Sino-Indian border. There are two eye-catching strongholds here, the northern side is held by China and the southern by India leaving a gap of 27 meters in between. Not far from there is a postal kiosk in the neutral zone where surface mail from the two sides is exchanged everyday. The border forces of the two countries provide guards for the mail exchange duty and this is the time when the guards of the two sides face each other in this neutral zone. When the relations are normal between the two countries the soldiers of the two

sides greet each other and say, "Hello: Hello:" and sometimes exchange gifts.

"During the sixties and seventies, the Indian border guards had the impression that the Chinese soldiers were poor and dirty and would offer cigarette packets to them. After the 'eighties, the Chinese soldiers discovered that a group of long bearded soldiers (implying the Sikh troops) now wore uniforms made of nylon material. The outdated Soviet model weapons carried by them had been replaced by indigenously made weapons. Again, looking deep into the distance, roads of high quality had penetrated into the front-line, making it a modern communication network. Every weekend dependants of Indian soldiers would reach the front in passenger vehicles and the Chinese guards could only console themselves with envy and false hopes.

"In 1986, there was the Wangdong incident in the Tawang sector when the Sino-Indian border had briefly flared up and although there was no exchange of fire, the Chinese soldiers suffered frostbite injuries while hastily propping up border defences, and had to be hospitalized. Indian soldiers on the contrary were safe and sound and remained unscathed.

"At that time the air situation was more perilous. The Indian forces had deployed nearly 200 fighter planes, while the Chinese side had only a few planes on duty and none for combat action. This amounts to saying that the air superiority was 200 to 0. These facts illustrate an inconceivable situation. Think for a while: if the Indian forces had launched an all out attack at that point of time, what kind of a difficult situation would it have been for the Chinese frontier guards? It goes without saying that the Chinese army has realised that the feeling of superiority cannot exist anymore".

This is a Chinese version, or rather their perception of the relative strengths on the border but not necessarily accurate. There is little doubt that the Indian Army by then had become more adaptable and experienced about operating in high altitudes. Also one cannot imagine any other army sustaining such hardships as in the operations in the Siachin (glacier) at the way the Indian Army has done for the last decade and a half. The Indian Army has travelled a long way since 1962.

If that be so, the reader may ask 'Then why this book?' The answer lies in the fact that it does not take long to unlearn. Furthermore, there has been a seachange in the last seven years in the international power equation. It will be imperative to avoid the fatal Indian penchant to relapse into apathy and neglect.

In the last decade China has left India far behind militarily and economically, but especially the latter; in overall production it has quintupled its capacity, taking a lead of 15 years in fertilizers, steel, coal and cement, and 20 years in crude oil and electricity production. This time-lag has been worked out keeping in view a 7-8 per cent growth maintained by India. In case the growth is less, the difference would be greater. Add to this India's burgeoning population, compared to China's achieved target of zero growth rate and the disparity in economic progress which is likely to widen even further. On the reforms and liberalisation front too, China remains ahead with a big margin. The agreement signed between the Presidents of China and the USA in the autumn of 1997 will cement this overall lead for years to come.

Hypothetically, a future war between India and China would be a three dimensional one, under nuclear threat. Second and third generations of aircraft, viz MIG-27, MIG-29, SU-27, Mirage 2000, J-8 and J-10, in conjunction with short-and long-range missiles, air-borne troops, rocket launchers, and heavy artillery divisions would be used with an intensity ten times than that of 1962. While the border dispute would remain potentially the main cause for a future war, it is the Tibet issue which could become the crucial factor; because for all its military and economic prowess, China's hold over Tibet remains tenuous and India could exploit that weakness.

Then there is the strategic pressure of the collusion between China and Pakistan. India is unfavourably placed. India's only viable strategy has been to maintain a military superiority over Pakistan and a defensive posture against China. But even this has been far from easy. Pakistan is trying hard to move to a position of near parity and by aiding and abetting secessionist movements and insurgencies in Jammu and Kashmir, and hoping to rekindle them in the Punjab, it is causing attrition to the morale and operational preparedness of the Indian Army. Indian politicians, caught in their own power games, couldn't care less about the mess they are creating. Clearly the Indian Army is being duped, overused, misused and even abused. On the other hand, the esteem and prestige of the Indian Armed Forces are at their lowest in the Fiftieth year of India's independence. In some ways the situation is as bad and even worse than in pre-1962. These are not good portents. It's a great challenge that the Indian higher command is faced with. They must not let down the country as their predecessors did before and during 1962. We have come full circle. The lessons of 1962 could never be more valid than they are today.

What then were the chief lessons from the "war of 1962"? We may begin with the political ones, the foremost of which are:

(a) Maintenance of the armed forces at ever-alert is the premium a nation pays for ensuring its independence and progress;

(b) There is a need to have a clear-cut national aim and policy and a closer link between political leaders and the military;

(c) Military bluff must not be resorted to without the military strength to back it up;

(d) It is a nation's interests that count. In international affairs, as someone has said, there are no permanent friends or enemies but only permanent interests; and

(e) There must be an institutionalized decision-making mechanism as the safeguarding of national security depends on it.

In India's case, despite having fought four major wars since independence and a continuous involvement in counter-insurgency operations, India's crisis management has remained ad hoc and the Army is seldom consulted. There are so many vested interests at work: the politicians, the bureaucrats and the police services have all a stake in keeping the Armed Forces isolated and denying them their say in matters of national security. And yet if India has survived, it has largely been due to the selfless service rendered by its Armed Forces. It would require a truly enlightened political leadership to correct the system and institutionalize an all-embracing decision-making mechanism; but that is unlikely to happen in the functional anarchy that today prevails in India. Basically the Army must take up the cudgels to assert its role in matters of national security, though there is bound to be a lot of noise by the politicians and a lot of machination by the bureaucrats. While their army's overt involvement in Pakistan's national affairs could be taken as one extreme, the other extreme is the subservience and down-gradation of the Army in India. There is probably no other country where an army has been treated so shabbily in the name of democracy as in India and to such detriment to national security.

It is quite obvious that many things drastically went wrong with our ad hoc system in 1962. The most serious was that of gathering intelligence and assessing it. The police-oriented Intelligence Bureau was the sole agency responsible for providing intelligence for collating and also making assessments besides being intimately involved in decision-making. For nearly a decade, B.N. Mullick, Director, Intelligence Bureau, was the de facto defense minister of India's Himalayan frontiers. India's entire framework of decision-making, based upon Mullick's assessment that the Chinese would not resort to armed conflict, went entirely wrong; so wrong and so much against our national interests that one wonders if there was some compulsion which forced him to give this advice.

Among the military lessons the most glaring and obvious is the failure of the higher command. There is something about our culture that breeds supine behaviour amongst subordinates. It is linked with the feudalistic past (common to many societies in the world) and traditions (which are wholly indigenous) such as touching the feet of elders, and abject prostration. In the Army, training and a strong sense of discipline are designed to ensure implicit and unquestionable obedience of orders. All this works well in the lower ranks, though there too, initiative, vision, and self-esteem are serious casualties. Our training and ethos need to be modified. In the senior ranks, the effect is disastrous. The majority of our senior officers are like tigers when it comes to treating their subordinates but their behaviour becomes mouse-like when facing their superiors both in uniform as well in the civvies. This split personality syndrome surely has psychological reasons. The most damaging is lack of moral courage. In the 1962 war, our senior commanders made commitments to please the political bosses. And having committed themselves, they did not have the moral courage to put forward the correct picture that the commitments made by them could not be carried through. In warfare it is disastrous to have the greater fear of the higher commander than of the enemy.

At the highest level, a Commander-in-Chief must not be exonerated for mistakes committed in war by virtue of an order of government or a minister which he considers bad, faulty or impracticable. He should give his reasons, insist the plan be changed and finally resign rather than be the instrument of the ruin of his country. In the first instance he sacks himself and is saved the ignominy that would eventually follow, with the likelihood that his successor wouldn't likewise buckle under government pressure who would thus be forced to correct its stance or decision. In the other instance he would in the wake of the debacle get sacked all the same and live in disgrace thereafter. Notwithstanding the above, the Chief of the Army is honour bound to make the best of resources available, even though he may have brought the shortcomings and deficiencies to the notice of the government. It is his patriotic duty to keep the Army motivated and trained to the maximum extent possible in relation to actual or the potential threats to national integrity.

At the lower levels, a commander has much greater space for maneuver and freedom of action, but he must know how to exercise them. He can use his initiative or even disregard senseless orders. Some may say that this is easier said than done. But a closer look at all successful operations would indicate that moral courage and audacity have been the governing features. Whom should a commander fear more, his superior or the enemy? Why should he fear either of them unless there is a weakness or weaknesses that he has failed to overcome?

In the Indian Army, the pyramidical rank structure, and lack of social and financial security, and also burning ambition are the cause of cut-throat competition, the zero error syndrome and lack of dissent, or yesmanship. Most of these foibles can be removed, which would in turn help to change the Army's ethos for the better. A little rationalization would help further understand this point. General Eric Vas, when he was Commandant, College of Combat, Mhow

(1972-74), had a theory pertaining to assessment on the courses of instruction, which he used to share with the students officers. According to him, because of the inherent subjectiveness in the best of systems, fifty percent of the students get what they actually deserve, twenty five percent more than what they deserve and twenty five percent are the unfortunate ones who get less than what they deserve. This is true in every other aspect of life including promotion to higher ranks. From this, it devolves that at least seventy five percent of our senior officers are basically deserving and competent, which by all reckoning is a good percentage; but because they are functioning in an unhealthy atmosphere, they fail when it comes to moral courage, steadfastness and fearlessness, the hallmark of true and effective higher command. Consequently, it is the undeserving 25 per cent who tend to rule the roost and cause much damage.

It is a harsh thing to say but the fact is that there is great dearth of true leaders in India in nearly every sphere. But our concern here is about military leadership. There was a brief period from about 1965 to 1975 when the Indian Army did produce top class general officers. The three wars that India fought in a span of just nine years had no doubt made the Indian Army more professional. The fact that this period coincided with the prevalence of sagacious political leadership of Shastri and later Indira Gandhi (the pre-Emergency phase) also mattered considerably. This is not to suggest that we fight another war in order to purge the higher command. What the Army needs is to constitute a reforms committee that must go into all aspects of the Army ethos. One reads so much about not many young people with merit coming to join the Army. But that amounts to barking up the wrong tree. In fact the Indian Army should be more concerned about higher leadership culture.

The second major military lesson of the '62 war was the poor or even non-existent knowledge of the enemy which, if we follow Suntzu, meant that at the very outset India had lost fifty percent chance of attaining victory before the war started. One wonders whether this deficiency in the professional knowledge of the officers has since been overcome. It would help if courses of instruction are instituted exclusively devoted to the armed forces of India's actual or potential enemies. It would also help if an additional paper in tactics in the promotion examinations and Defence Services Entrance Examination was to be introduced devoted exclusively to the knowledge of the our neighbour's military culture. After all enemy activity comprises more or less fifty percent of most wars.

The third lesson is that of physical fitness. There can be no short cuts to physical fitness and hard training. The Army needs not only physically fit and robust men, JCOs and junior officers, but equally fit colonels, brigadiers and generals. Sick and unfit officers are invariably the cause of ruin of an army. What India needs is a lean and well equipped army, given much *izzat*, and the assurance of a comfortable life after retirement; or total financial and social security to the spouse and dependents in the event of death while in service.

As regards tactical lessons, the Indian Army has imbibed them all and at present its proficiency in high altitude and mountain warfare is more than a match for the Chinese. But a reiteration of lessons learnt the hard way is never a bad thing. The most prominent lesson was violation of the principle of maintenance of aim. In the battle of Nam Ka Chu, it was changed six times over a span of one month. This situation was aggravated on occasions by disregarding the chain of command down the line. There were also instances when commanders were changed without giving them a chance to prove themselves. This was both immoral and unwise. Also, old orbats and affiliations were broken up leading to lack of cohesion and understanding. These were probably necessitated no doubt by exceptional circumstances, but the fact that they adversely affected the operations must not be lost sight of.

The concept of defence at high altitudes was faulty. In spite of holding the heights, the Indians with their road-bound mentality always reacted to enemy's outflanking moves by lifting troops from prepared defences and running back. This enabled the Chinese to occupy Indian defences and catch the troops in the open. On the contrary, in a defensive battle once the defences have been prepared, stocking done, defensive fire tasks registered, contingencies e.g. counter-attack, counter-penetration and reinforcement plans rehearsed and practised, the troops must fight from the defences and destroy the attacking enemy. The fact that the Chinese follow the teachings of Sun Tzu and Mao Tse-tung rigidly and implicitly should be exploited to the fullest to evolve our own tactics best suited to defeat the Chinese.

In defence a stage invariably comes when the situation becomes critical and the presence of a senior commander becomes essential to stem the rot. During the 1971 Indo-Pak war, in Chhamb-Jaurian sector, India's 10 Infantry Division was on the verge of being routed and was all set to abandon its defences along the Munawar Tawi. The Divisional Commander was shaky. General Sartaj Singh, the GOC 15 Corps, who arrived on the scene promptly forbade any withdrawal, and prevented the debacle. His presence in the open in spite of enemy shelling taking place all along the riverine defences gave heart to troops.

In the NEFA operations, commanders were loath to visit the front line defences. The case in point is that of Bomdila defences on the morning of 18 November, 1962. There was just one major with his artillery observer in command of the main defences. The CO was at the Brigade headquarters. When the battalion panicked and ran, the CO followed suit. A little later the Commander and his staff too ran away.

Imagine on the other hand, what the situation could have been if the Corps Commander had arrived at Bomdila or even Dirang on 17 or 18 November, and forbidden any withdrawal.

One lesson that comes out strikingly is the dominant role of artillery. Napoleon had said that the army with the longer gun wins the war. Frederick the Great had called artillery as the god of war. In the '62 war, artillery was not used to its full potential for various reasons, the most serious being failure of wireless (radio) communication. We also failed to register properly the fire-tasks and exploit the situation when the enemy was truly vulnerable. In the few situations where artillery fire was used for effect, it caused heavy casualties amongst the Chinese e.g. at Bumla, Nuranong and Thembang.

Location of divisional headquarters at Dirang was a grave mistake. That this lapse had more to do with the failure of the G.O.C. has already been pointed out. It was wrong to site the headquarters in a valley, which was not a defensible ground. Once his own headquarters was threatened, the GOC's entire tactical thinking changed and his actions from then on were dictated towards saving himself rather than commanding his formation or fighting the enemy. Had the Tactical headquarters 4 Infantry Division been sited at Senge, it is unlikely that Pathania would have ordered a withdrawal from Sela. The only way he could have run away was to have flown out by helicopter from Senge. In the event, the withdrawal of the whole Dirang garrison jeopardised the withdrawal of 62 Infantry Brigade.

The standard of minor tactics (patrolling, laying and countering ambushes) was quite dismal and it must be stated with some perturbation that there has not been even now the required improvement in this field; the high casualties in Srilanka and counter-insurgency operations, specially of officers testify to this. This is paradoxical because our young officers have always been committed, brave and honourable and now they are even worldlywise. They lead from the front. What they lack are guile and initiative; and the stumbling feature is the unimaginative and routine battle-drills aggravated by insufficient training and below-standard field craft and marksmanship. Fatigue and overuse of troops in CI operations no doubt are other factors, but these were not there during 1962, when most Indian patrols suffered heavy casualties at the hands of the Chinese.

The Indian Army has failed to exploit the leadership potential of its junior leaders, officers as well as the non-commissioned officers, mainly because of old misplaced prejudices. The British Army is run by its sergeants. In India we have Rabri Devi (a mere housewife with an illiterate rural background) as Chief Minister of India's second most populace state of Bihar. But the Army fights shy of exposing its junior leaders because of the fear that things would go wrong, which indeed is the heart of the problem.

Poor logistics have been cited as another failing responsible for the bad showing by the Indians, but this does not hold up in the light of facts. While it is true that 7 Brigade was rushed into the Nam Ka Chu area unprepared and under-equipped, and that our wireless communication was primitive with bulky and obsolete radio sets, it needs to be unambiguously stated that the remainder of 4 Division had little to complain as far as administrative support is concerned. To say otherwise is a disinformation spread by people to plead an excuse or to mislead the gullible public. At both Sela and Bomdila there were stocks of enough munitions and rations to last the defenders through 7 to 10 days of battle without replenishment. While it is agreed that the Indian Army wasn't modern by any stretch of imagination, but neither was the Chinese. The drawback was that a peacetime army had been rushed in without having been allowed to do its homework and exposed suddenly to a strange terrain and a stranger enemy.

The Indian Army has been accused of behaving like a colonial force and doing little to fraternize and win over the local population. Unpalatable, but it is true. The Army failed to fully utilize the Mompa and Sherdukpen tribes in the war effort, even though they were a motivated material. The Indian troops who continue to hail mostly from north-west India and the rest from the southern states, had no sense of belonging while fighting in these far flung frontiers. They had no stake in the region in which they fought. This is paradoxical because for over a century Indian troops had fought for the British in alien lands in different corners of the world with distinction.

General Prem Bhagat V.C., when he was the GOC-in-C Northern Command, had taken an unprecedented decision and permitted families of officers and men to come to the field areas in Jammu and Kashmir for a few months every year. Over a span of time these have now become modified family stations. The rationale is simple. Would the troops in Kamang F.D. have abandoned their defences in such haste had their families been then living in Tenga valley or the foothills of Assam as they do now? Yet for a long period it was absolutely taboo for an army wife or dependant to visit these areas, leave alone reside in the area.

These days, though numerous family stations have come up in the North-East, they remain essentially under-occupied. The reasons are many: de-induction in the wake of easing of tension with China, the CI operation against ULFA and Bodoland militants, the education problems of the children, and the general reluctance of officers' families to live so far from their homes. There are few volunteers who want to be posted to the East. Yet this part of India is very scenic and beautiful. Not many years ago a few hundred British planters had made small Englands in this part of the country, where they led contented and full lives, contributing to the consolidation of the British Raj. The position then was the reverse of today: No British planter ever visited the rest of India. They lived full lives on the Assam plains, and left them only to go straight home to Blighty, on leave or furlough. It would be a pity if Assam and NEFA were to become once again the forgotten frontiers. Let us not forget that China, Bangladesh and even Burma glance ever so covetously on these our eastern lands, so rich in natural resources and inhabited by such wonderful people.

Glossary
Abbreviations and Indian and Tibetan Terms and Words

Abbreviations

ADC	Aid-de-Camp
am	Ante meridiem
AQMG	Assistant Quarter Master General
ASC	Army Service Corps
BC	Battery Commander
BGS	Brigadier General Staff
BM	Brigade Major
Brig	Brigadier
Brig Adm	Brigadier in charge of Administration
CGS	Chief of the General Staff
CIA	Central Intelligence Agency (USA)
C-in-C	Commander-in-Chief

COAS	Chief of the Army Staff
CO	Commanding Officer
Col	Colonel
CPM	Communist Party of India (Marxist)
CSD Canteen	Canteen Stores Department Canteen
DAA & QMG	Deputy Assistant Adjutant Quarter Master General
DIB	Director of Intelligence Bureau
Div HQ	Divisional Headquarters
DGBR	Directorate General Border Roads
DMO	Director of Military Operations
DSO	Distinguished Service Order (British Military Awards)
DZ	Dropping Zone
EME	Corps of Electrical and Mechanical Engineers
FD	Frontier Division (of NEFA)
FOO	Forward Observation Officer (for artillery fire)
GOC	General Officer Commanding
GOC-in-C	General Officer Commanding-in-Chief
GR	Gorkha Rifles
GS	General Staff
GSO 1/GSO2	General Staff Officer (Grade 1 or 2 & so on)

HQ	Headquarters
IB	Intelligence Bureau
IDSA	Institute of Defence Studies and Analyses
IDSM	Indian Distinguished Service Medal (British-Indian Gallantry Award for Other Ranks)
IMA	Indian Military Academy, Dehradun
IOM	Indian Order of Merit (British-Indian Gallantry award for Viceroy's Commissioned Officers)
JCO	Junior Commissioned Officer
J&K	Jammu and Kashmir
KMT	Kuomintang
L of C	Line of Communication
Lt. Col.	Lieutenant Colonel
MC	Military Cross (British Military Award)
MMG	Medium Machine Gun
MI	Military Intelligence
MO	Military Operations
MVC	Maha Vir Chakra (Indian Gallantry Award)
NCO	Non-Commissioned Officer
NDA	National Defence Academy, Khadakvasala

NEFA	North Eastern Frontier Agency
NNRC	Neutral Nations Repatriation Commission
OBE	Order of the British Empire (award for civilians and military officers)
OPOffr	Observation Post Officer (for artillery fire)
Ops	Operations
OR	Other Rank(s)
PVC	Param Vir Chakra (India's highest gallantry award)
PLA	People's Liberation Army (of China)
pm	Post meridiem
Pt.	Point
QMG	Quarter Master General
Recce	Reconnaissance
RHQ	Regimental Headquarters
Sikh LI	Sikh Light Infantry
2IC	Second-in-Command
VC	Victoria Cross (Britain's highest gallantry award)
Vr.C	Vir Chakra (Indian gallantry award)

Indian Terms

Akhand Path & Bhog	Continuous & complete recitation of Indian religious text and its bhog (conclusion)

Ardas	A Sikh prayer to mark the end of the ceremony
Bukhari	A room/tent heater in which wood or other fuel is burnt
Gurbani	Sikh hymns
Izzat	Honour, self-esteem
Jemadar	An erstwhile JCO rank now called Naib Subedar
Laftain Sahib	Lieutenant Sahib
Meharbani	Kindness
Ragini	A folk song of Haryana and Rajasthan
Ram Ram	Greetings of Hindu troops
Rasagola	A popular Bengali sweet meat
Subedar	A senor JCO rank

Military Symbols

Tactical Position

(a) Occupied by a Platoon 

(b) Occupied by a Company 

(c) Occupied by a Battalion 

(d) Occupied by a Brigade 

Battalion HQ 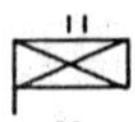

Brigade HQ 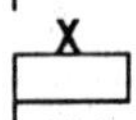

Div HQ 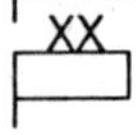

Guns	
Heavy Mortars	
MMG (generally in pairs)	

Tibetan Terms

Chorten	Stupa, cairn
Chu	River, stream
Da	Lower end of valley
Dalai Lama	The priest king of Tibet
Drukpa	Bhutanese-Bhutan
Dzong	Fort, headquarters of Dzongpon
Dzongpon	Administrator of district
Gompa	Monastery
La	Pass
Pu	Upper end of valley
Ri	Mountain
Rong	Low warm valley
Sumdo	Junction of two valleys
Tsangpo	Large river in Tibet (Brahmaputra in India)
Tse	Peak
Tso	Lake

Bibliography

Books and Publications

Bailey F.M. *No Passport to Tibet* (Hart-Davis, London, 1957)

Bakshi, Lt. Col, *I was A Prisoner of War In China*

Bhargav G.S. *The Battle of NEFA : The Undeclared War* (AlliedPublishers, Bombay, 1964)

Bhat, Sudhakar, *India and China* (Popular Book Services, New Delhi, 1967)

Brecher, Michael, *Nehru : A Political Biography* (O.U.P., London, 1959)

Bureau of Parliamentary Records, Indian China Border Problem (Congress Party in Parliament, 1960)

Chaudhari, Nirad, *The Continent of Circe* (Chhato and Windus, London, 1965)

Cohen, Stephen P, *The Indian Army* (University of California Press, Berkley and Los Angeles, 1971)

Cohen, Stephen P, and Richard Park, *India : An Emergent Power* (Crane-Russak, New York, 1978)

Dalvi, Brigadier, J S, *Himalayan Blunder : The Curtain Raiser to the Sino Indian War of 1962* (Thacker & Co. Bombay, 1969)

Galbraith, John Kenneth, *Ambassador's Journal : A Personal Account of the Kennedy Years* (Hamish Hamiltan, London, 1969)

Hasnain Maj Gen, S M, Historical Record of the Garhwal Rifles 1947 - 1987 (Garhwal Centre, Lansdown U P)

Johri, Major, Sita Ram (Retd), *Chinese Invasion of NEFA* (Himalaya Publications, Lucknow, 1968)

Kaul Lt Gen B M, *The Untold Story* (Allied Publishers, Bombay 1967)

Khera S S, *India's Defence Problem* (Orient Longmans, Bombay, 1968)

Kler, Lt Col G S, *Unsung Battles of 1962* (Lancer Publishers & Distributors, New Delhi, 1995)

Lamb Alastair, *The McMahon Line : A Study in Relations Between India, China and Tibet 1904-1914* (Routledge & Kegan Paul, London, 1966)

Letters of the Prime Minister of India, Chinese Aggression in War and Peace (Publications Division, Ministry of Information and Broadcasting, Government of India, 1962)

Mankekar D R, *The Guilty Men of 1962* (Tulsi Shah Enterprises, Bombay, 1968)

Maxwell Neville, *India's China War* (Jaico Publication House, Bombay, 1970)

Mullik B N, *My Years with Nehru 1948-64* and *The Chinese Betrayal* (Allied Publishers, New Delhi, 1971 and 1972 respectively)

Nanporia N J, *The Sino Indian Dispute* (A Times of India publication, 1963)

Noorani A G, *Our Credulity and Negligence* (Ramdy Bhatkal, Bombay, 1963)

Palit, Maj Gen D K VrC, *War in the High Himalaya* (Lancer International, New Delhi, 1992)

Palsokar, Col, R D, The Invincible Garuda of Brigade of the Guards, 1949-1990 (Brigade of the Guards Regimental Centre, Kamptee, 1990)

Panikkar K M, In *Two Chinas : Memoirs of a Diplomat* (Allan & Unwin, London, 1956)

Patterson, George, *Tibet in Revolt* (Faber and Faber, London, 1961)

Prasad, Maj Gen Niranjan, *The Fall of Tawang* (Palit & Palit, New Delhi, 1981)

Praval, Major K C, *Red Eagles : A History of Fourth Division of India* (Vision Books, New Delhi, 1982)

Proudfoot, Lt Col C L, *We Lead : 7th Light Cavalry 1784-1990* (Lancer Publications Pvt Ltd, New Delhi 1991

Richardson, H E, *Tibet and Its History* (O U P London, 1962)

Rosen Stephen Peter, *Societies & Military Power : India & its Armies* (Oxford University Press: 1996)

Ruffner Kevin C, Jawans, Sahibs & Fire-power (Field Artillery Journal Vol 52 May-June 1964)

Saigal, Lt Col J R, *The Unfought War of 62* (Allied Publications, New Delhi, 1979)

Schram, Stuart, *Mao Tse-tung* (Penguin Books, London, 1966)

Sinha, Satya Narayan, *The Chinese Aggression* (Ram Krishan & Sons)

Sohan Lal, *India China Border Dispute* (Current Events Publications Department, Dehradun, 1962)

Smith Chris, *India's Adhoc Aresnal*

S ven A, Hoffman, *India and the China Crisis* (Oxford University Press, 1990)

Sun Xia and Chen Zhibbin, *The Snows of the Himalayas : The True History of China War* (Beijiing,1991)

Tewari Maj Gen K K, *A Soldier's Voyage of Self History*

Van Eckelen, W F, *Indian Foreign Policy and the Border Dispute with China* (Martinus Nijhoff, The Hague, 1964)

Vertzberger Yaacoy Y L, *Misperceptions in Foreign Policy Making : The Sino Indian Conflict 1959-62* (Bounder, Colo., West-View Press, 1984)

Studies and Articles

1. Chinese Sources (obtained through Institute of Defence Studies and Analyses, New Delhi, and Directorate General of Military Intelligence Army HQ, New Delhi.

(a) Can The Glory of 1962 be Re-enacted

(b) White Paper on China's National Security Policy, Arms Control and Disarmament (Peoples Daily - 17 Nov.'95)

2. Extracts and war diaries of units and formations that participated in the 1962 War.

3. Presentation made in 1976 by Brigadier J Sikand and his team of officers on `NEFA Operations'.

Interviews

1. Avasthy Sushil, wife of late Lt Col B N Avasthy, CO 4 Rajput.
2. Bains Lt Col P P S (Retd) was Quartermaster 4 Garhwal.
3. Brar Lt Gen S S (Retd), Commanded the Signal Company of 65 Infantry Brigade.
4. Bhattacharjee Maj Gen S K MVC (Late), was CO of 4 Garhwal
5. Chatterjee Michael was Commander of 67 Infantry Brigade.
6. Dang Commodore B K (Retd) is brother of Late Major Shashi Dang who was Brigade Major of 67 Infantry Brigade.
7. Dubey Lt Gen K N (Retd) was Director General of Border Roads Organisation.
8. Gill Maj Gen Gurbax Singh (Retd) was Commander 4 Artillery Brigade at Dirang.
9. Gosal Brig G S (Retd), was Troop Commander of 7 Mountain Battery 22 Mountain Regiment at Bumla and Nagakuri Remba.

10. Gurbax Singh Brig, was Commander 48 Infantry Brigade.

11. Goswami Col Devinder, was BC 2 Derajal Mountain Battery at Nuranong.

12. Gurdial Singh Lt. Col (Retd.) was CO of 3 J&K Rifles.

13. Jerath Major, was a subaltern in 4 Sikh L.I. at Sela.

14. Johri Major, was Political Officer, Kameng Frontier Division at Bomdila.

15. Kapila Brig Akshey, was Gun Position Officer (GPO) of 7 Bengal Mountain Battery, 22 Mountain Regiment at Bumla and later at Bomdila.

16. Namjee Ngoimu (Daki), of village Rahung, was an eyewitness of the Battle of Thembang.

17. Netam Dorjee, is presently the Headman of Morshing village and gave an eyewitness account of evacuation of over a hundred Chinese dead from Lagyala Gompa.

18. Nawang Namja - Gaon Budha (elderman) of village Domkho near Morshing - who corroborated Netam Dorjee's account.

19. Pahwa Lt Gen Pran (Retd) was forward Observation Officer with 1 Sikh L.I.

20. Palit Maj Gen, D K, VrC (Retd), Commanded 7 Infantry Brigade from 1958-60 and was later the DMO at the Army HQ.

21. Prasad Maj Gen N (Retd) was GOC 4 Infantry Division till replaced by Gen Anant Pathania on 25 October, 1962.

22. Shankar Lt Gen Vinay, was the Forward Observation Officer and also Gun Position Officer of Field Battery at Sagor.

23. Sinha Brig A K (Retd) was the Intelligence Officer of 3 J&K Rifles.

24. Sood Maj D N (Retd), was a subaltern of 5 Guards.

25. Tandon Col, S N (Retd) was Forward Company Commander of 4 Garhwal (the covering troops at Nuranong).

26. Verma Maj Gen, Deepak, was the Forward Observation Officer with 'A' Company 4 Rajput at point 3582 north of Cher Gompa.

Index

Ahirs 84, 85

Aksai Chin 42,45, 47-50

Alexander's Cavalry 28

Alexander's Invasion 27

A-lo-na-Shun 58 Alps 161

Ancient Cultural Relations 44

Armed Forces 238

Army 29-35, 49, 52, 72, 74, 82,120, 133, 140, 150, 166, 209, 238-240, 242, 244

Army Medical Corps 152

Arunachal Pradesh 38, 41, 66

Ayub Khan (General) 30

Bailey's Trail 69, 76, 171

Barahoti and Kaurik 42

Battle of Panipat 27

Battle of Plassey 27, 41

Bhairabkund 203, 205, 222

Bhairabkund and Udal Giri 69

Bhutan 66, 196, 197

Bhutan Border 51, 136, 174, 205, 206

Bodo Land Militant 246

Bomdila 69, 71, 85, 86, 90, 118, 122-127,129-133, 137, 142 -144, 156, 163, 168, 177-180,187,188,196, 199, 202, 211-12,214-20, 223-25, 228, 243, 244, 245

Bomdila - Dirang 212

Bomdila - Dirang Road 169

Bomdila Defences 216-17

Bomdila Mandala Areas 76-77, 158

Bompu 83

Bompu And Chaku 71

Border Roads Organisation 70,88,206

Brahmaputra or Siang 67

British 29,36-38,40,41

British Army 16,245

British Imperialism 56, 57

British Indian Army 29

British Raj 82, 247

Buddha 44

Buddhism 104

Buddhist 85

Buddhist Monastery 207
Buffer Zones 37
Bumla 97, 104, 106, 111, 112, 127, 132, 161, 171, 244
Bumla and Tulungla 69
Bumla Areas 99
Bumla Tawang 168,170
Bumla Tawang Road 141
Bureaucrats 34,238
Candeth 35
Caste System 166
Central Asia 36
Chaku 225,226,228-230
Chamdo 39
Changla 163,174
Chauhan Prithvi Raj, 29
Che Dong 51
Chen Xuan Zang 58
Chen Yi 54-57, 149, 150
Chengdu Force 141
Chhamb-Jaurian Sector 243
Chiang Kai-Shek 42, 56, 61
China 16,28,30,31,36,37,39-43,69,78,140,234,236,246
China And Pakistan 237
China Border 149
China Border Guards 233
China India Border 57,146
Chindwin 161
Chinese Army 72,140,235
Chinese People Army 43
Chinese Troops 55, 56, 59, 168, 170, 179
Chou En-Lai 46, 48-50, 53, 54, 56, 63
Chug—kapsi 209
Chumbi Valley 37
CIA 30
Cinese Military 15
Clausewitz 28
Congo 33
Counter Insurgency Operations 244
Dalai Lama 37,38
Dalai Lama 48
Dalvi, J.P. 77
Decision Making Mechanism 238, 239
Defence 31, 34, 44, 76, 78, 96, 119, 120, 127, 131, 133, 143, 155, 158-61, 165, 173, 183, 184, 190, 191, 219, 239, 242, 243
Defence Planners 15
Demchok 41
Derajat 101,103,170,182
Derajat Mountain 96,118, 164
Dirang 40, 69, 86, 89, 122, 124, 125, 129, 133, 137, 138, 169, 186, 191, 193, 194, 198, 203, 205, 213, 225, 244,
Dirang Dzong 102
Ding Pksu 136
Ding Sheng 148
Dingpiksu-Nagakuri Remba 206
Dirang — Chang Dor 176

Dirang Dzong 71, 76, 128, 135, 142, 161, 162, 174, 177-80,188, 201, 217, 220

Dirang Dzong Defences 168

Dirang Episode 209

Dirang Garrison 244

Dirang Sangti 175

Dirang To Bomdila 188

Doimara 83

Duke of Marlborough 28

Dzalungla 169,170,173

Eagle's Nest 69,71,85

East Pakistan 121

Eastern Himalayas 35

Eastern Sector 57,59

Eric Vas 35

Exercise Brasstacks (Sri Lanka) 34

Forward Policy or Onkar 51,57,78

Fredrick The Great 28,244

Gandhi Indira 241

Gartok 38

Gaza 33

Geneva Convention, Violation of 182

Geyshila 117,163

Gill, Inder 35

Gompa Chu 206

Greater Himilayas 66,68

Gulab Singh Army (Maharaja) 28

Guru Nanak 157

Gyamyang 100

Han Buddhist 44

Hanniball's Crossing 161

Henderson Brooks Court of Inquiry 199

Henderson Group Committee 166,167

Henderson's Brooks Report 18

Himalaya Mountaineering Institute 72

Himmat Sinji (Maj. Gen.) 43

Hinduism 104

Holkar (Princess) 33

Human Wave Tactics 142

India 15, 29, 30-32, 36, 38, 39, 41, 42, 43 49, 50, 53, 57, 58, 59, 61, 64, 66, 68, 69, 72, 76, 80, 98, 112, 120, 140, 159, 166, 183, 234, 236, 239, 242, 245

India, Northern Borders 47

Indian Air Force 71

Indian Armed Forces 237

Indian Army 15, 17, 18, 27, 29, 30, 32, 34, 35, 72, 84, 85, 103, 106, 133, 140, 184, 205, 208, 230, 234, 235-37, 241, 242, 245, 246,

Indian Border 160

Indian Defences 130

Indian Forces 71, 127, 146, 225, 235,

Indian Media 48

Indian Military Academy 18, 114, 208

Indian Navy 225

Indian Olympic 99

Indian Troops 63,72,127,196, 246
Indian Unity 159
Indian Warrior Classes 29
India-East Pakistan Border 74
India-Tibet Border 36
India-Tibet Boundary 45,46
Indo Bhutan Border 74
Indo -Mongoloid Tribes 67
Indo Pak War 28
Indo-China 33
Indo-China Border 232
Indo-Pakistan Border 56
Ivan Chen 39
Jammu and Kashmir 237,246
Jammu and Kashmir Operations 119
Japanese Forces 40
Jia Chen of Sinkiang 54
Jie-ri Empire 58
Jung Bridge 102
Jung-Chabrala 165
Jung-Chabrala-Senge 134
Jungle Warfare School 123
Kalak Tang 69
Kameng 75,76, 92, 94, 120, 124, 127, 128, 159
Kameng Sector 17, 68, 69, 124, 132
Kashmir 29, 36, 43
ashmir Operations 29, 106
Kaul 129, 140, 150, 158
Kaul, B.M.(General) 30-32, 59, 60, 78, 79, 119, 120, 186, 187, 188, 189, 203, 204, 217, 222
Kaul, Bijji 187
Kautilaya 28
Kennedy 147
Khampa Revolt 48
Khinzamane Axis 96
Khinzamane-Samatso Tawang Track 94
Khushwant Singh (Journalist) 123
King Porous 28
Kohima 161
Kohima-Imphal Campaign 161
Korean War 147
Kulwant Singh (Lt. Gen.) 44
Kumara Mangalam 35
Kyela 165
Ladakh 35,42,47,49,50,
Ladakh and Walong Sector 17
Ladakh Sector 41,50
Lagyala Gompa 206-209
Lao 163
Lao Basti 101,104,115,154
Lhasa 37,38,39,43,149
Lhóla-Nayu-Milling 141
Lin Piao 56
Liu Bocheng 56
LOC (Line of Control) 133
Lok Sabha 49
Longju 57
Longju Area 141

Longju Incident 74
Low Caste (Mazbhi) Sikh 166
Lubrang 136,205,206
Lumla 97
Lumpu 92
Mago Chu 170,172
Mahavir Chakra 183
Manchu 38,44,130,
Mandala 69, 76, 126, 130, 132, 137, 202
Mandala Ridge 86
Mandala Track 203
Mandalisation 34
Manekshaw, Sam 35
Mongolia 37
Mao 42, 44, 45, 53, 56, 57, 59-61, 146-148, 159, 225, 232, 233
Mao Red Book 168
Mao Tse-Tung 28,243
Maurya, Chandragupta 27, 28
McMahon Line 42, 45, 49, 50, 51, 55, 56, 57, 61, 67, 68, 69, 72, 75, 94
McMahon, Sir Henry 39, 40
Media 35
Menon, V.K. Krishna 31, 35, 53, 54
Milakteng 98
Military Academy 130,205
Military Aid 54
Military Culture 242
Military Forces 15
Military History 161
Military School 33
Mir Jafar 205
Misamari 69, 81,82,83,90,122-125,162,210
Mishmi Tribals 38
Moghuls 28
Mompa Women 85
Mompas 182
Mongol Invaders 37
Mongoloid 84
Mount Kailash 46
Mughul Empire 28
Mukdang La 100, 101, 104, 105, 111, 117
Munawar Tawi 243
Munna Camp 176,202,204
Nafra 230
Nagaland 74,75,103,117,123
Nagaland And Manipur 40
Nam Ka Chu 61, 62, 65, 74, 79, 80, 93, 99, 100, 106, 131, 169, 187, 242, 245
Nam Ka Chu Area 141
Nam Ka Chu River 62
Nathu La Incident 234
National Cadet Corps 119
National Defence Academy (Khadakvasla) 33
NEFA 15, 38, 39, 40, 41, 44, 47-49, 50, 66, 67, 71, 74, 75, 77, 78, 84, 100, 120, 123, 128, 131, 141, 142, 158, 166, 167, 208, 230, 243, 247

NEFA Debacle 27

Nehru 30, 31, 35, 41-49, 50, 53-57, 59, 60, 79, 80, 120, 146, 147, 187

Nepolean 28, 92, 244

NNRC 140

Nuranong 89, 102, 118, 122, 133, 134, 142, 143, 150, 158-161, 163, 165, 184, 185, 191, 240

Nutan 33

Nyukmadung-Dirang Track 198

Operation "Leg-Horn" 59

Operation Blue Star 34

Operation Onkar 92

Opium Eaters 140

Oscar Tango Bravo Tango Procedure 115

Pakistan 30,237,238

Palit,D.K 8, 75, 77, 186,188

Panchsheel 46

Panchtantra 28

Param Vir Chakra, 98

Pass Bomdilla, 86

Karakoram 42

Kongka, 49

Pass Neti 47

Patel, Sardar Vallabhai 43

Pathania, Anant Singh 119, 128, 129, 132, 175, 176, 180, 185, 187, 188, 189, 191, 198, 199, 201-203, 211, 244

Peak Gaurichen 67

Kangto 67

Nam Che Barwa 67

Nyegi Kang Sang 67

People Republic of China 42

People's Liberation Army 30, 32, 53

Phudung Chu 196,197

Piri Range 84, 85

Plassey 205

Population Explosion 34

Poshingla 76, 123, 130, 137, 142, 161, 162, 172, 175, 178, 179, 211

Post, Dhola 51, 52, 78, 82, 92, 93, 98

Indian 50

Khinzamane 92

Longju 48

Prem Bhagat 35

Project Amar 75

Rabri Devi 245

Rahung Bowl 131, 179, 212, 215, 216

Ramayan and The Mahabharata 29

Rana Pratap 29

Rana Sanga 29

Rengza, 175

Rho and Sheo 163

Rima 38

RIMC, Dehradun 33

Rimpoche 208

River Bharaiti 67
    Dirang 71
    Gang 86, 212
    Kamang 67
    Khouma 135, 136,205,206
    Lohit 67
    Nyamjang 67
    Subansiri 67
    Tawang Chu 71, 154, 158, 159
    Tsangpo 141
Roh— Lagam 142
Royal British Military College 59
Ruduck and Gartok Garrisons 43
Rupa-Pirila-Chaku 143
Sagat Singh 35
Sangti and Changdil 211
Sapper Camp 205,206
Sartaj Singh 35
Schools Bishop Cotton 33
    Doon 33
    Lawrence 33
    Mayo 33
    Sanawar, 33
Second World War, 29, 65, 75, 81, 106, 110, 113, 119, 140, 203, 230
Sela 69,75-77,87-89,95,99,101-02,112,114-15,118,121-125, 127-134, 136,142-43,150,155,158-59,161,163-64, 166- 67, 169, 170-72, 174, 177-79, 181, 184-86, 189-91, 193, 197, 225, 244, 245
Sela Defences 169
Sela-Seng Complex 132
Seleukus 27,28
Senge 155, 165, 186, 190, 191, 193, 194, 197, 244
Senge Dzong 185, 188
Shakti-Lumla-Tawang Nexus 95
Shangri La 71
Shigatse 3
Shivaji 28
Shujden—Milling Area 141
Shukla Camp or Shangrila 88
Siachin 235
Sikh Society 166
Sikh Troops 117
Sikkim 75
Sikkim and Bhutan 44
Simla Convention 40,43,46
Singh, Zorawar 28,42
Sinkiang 42,61,72
Sino Indian Border 41, 48,56
Sino Indian War 17,27
Sino-Indian Relations 32
Siraj-ul-Daula 205
Society 29, 34
Socio-Economic Upsurge 34
South Korea 33
Soviet Model Weapons 235
Sri Lanka 244
Stuart Tank 124
Stuart Tank 204
Sulla-Samtso Track 95

Suntzu 28,243

Taimur 58

Tang Dynasty 58

Tang Taizong 58

Tawang 48, 61, 62, 69, 71, 77, 81-83, 87, 89, 90, 92, 93-97, 99- 103, 106, 108, 111, 118, 121, 124, 126-27, 132, 141, 158, 160, 161, 168, 171, 172, 226

Tawang Bomdila Jairampur 76

Tawang Chu 17, 95,96,116,118

Tawang Dropping Zone 93

Tawang Jung Sector 168

Tawang Monastery 163

Tawang Sector 235

Tawang Sela-Bomdila 15

Tawang-Chu 169,170

Tawang—Geyshe La Area 96

Tejpur 75,128,132,186, 210,215

Tejpur and Misamari 120

Teju 68

Teng Bridge 230

Tenga 215

Thagla Ridge 51,52,67-69,93

Thakurbari Planters Club 82

Themvang 76

Thimayya,K.S 30,31,32,35,140

Thorat (Gen.) 76,140

Thorat Plan 78,118,131

Tibet 37, 38, 39, 42, 43, 44, 45, 46, 48, 54, 60, 61, 66-69, 72, 129, 148, 234

Tibet and Burma 68

Tibet and China 38,39

Tibetan Labour Force 168

Tibetan Plateau 67,68,72

Timgri And Poshingla 212

Tipu Sultan 29

Tong Peng La 98

Track Chabrala Jungle 174

Trading Post Gartok 37

Gyanse 37

Yatung 37

Trap to Morsing 206

Tribal Areas 36

Tribe, Mishmi 68

Tribes, Mompa 246

Tribes, Sherdukpen 246

Tsangdhar, Artillery Base 62

Tsela Dzong Area 141

Tsogya Lakes 190

Tsona Dzong-Shao Axis 141

Tungri and Poshingla 86

Tuskar Camp 163,210

Tuskar Force 135,206

ULFA 246

Umrao Singh 78

UN 43,45

UN Troops 147

Valley, Brahmputra 38

Chaku 69

Chip Chap 49

Chumbi 38

Dirang 69, 131,170,187,196

Eagle's Nest 69
Galwan 49,62
Kaladan 81
Lohit 38
Mago 76
Nam Ka Chu 51,78
Nuranong 112,114
Rupa Tenga 143
Tawang Chu 163
Tenga 69, 71, 85, 129, 176, 187, 209, 220, 222, 246
Rupa 222
Vedas and Puranas 42
Victoria Cross 81
Vir Chakra 172,183
Walong 38, 40
Walong Sector 131,186,187
Wang Dong 235
Wango Ridge 137,178
Western Himalayas 127
Western Sector 55
World War I 40
World War II 16, 29, 56, 59, 124
Yang Cheng Wu 53
Yangyapla 175
Ye Jianying 56
Younghusband, Sir Francis 37
Zhang Guohua 54,60,62,148-151
Zhang Pengrian 53
Zhou En-Lai 146-149,151,232
Ziminthang 97

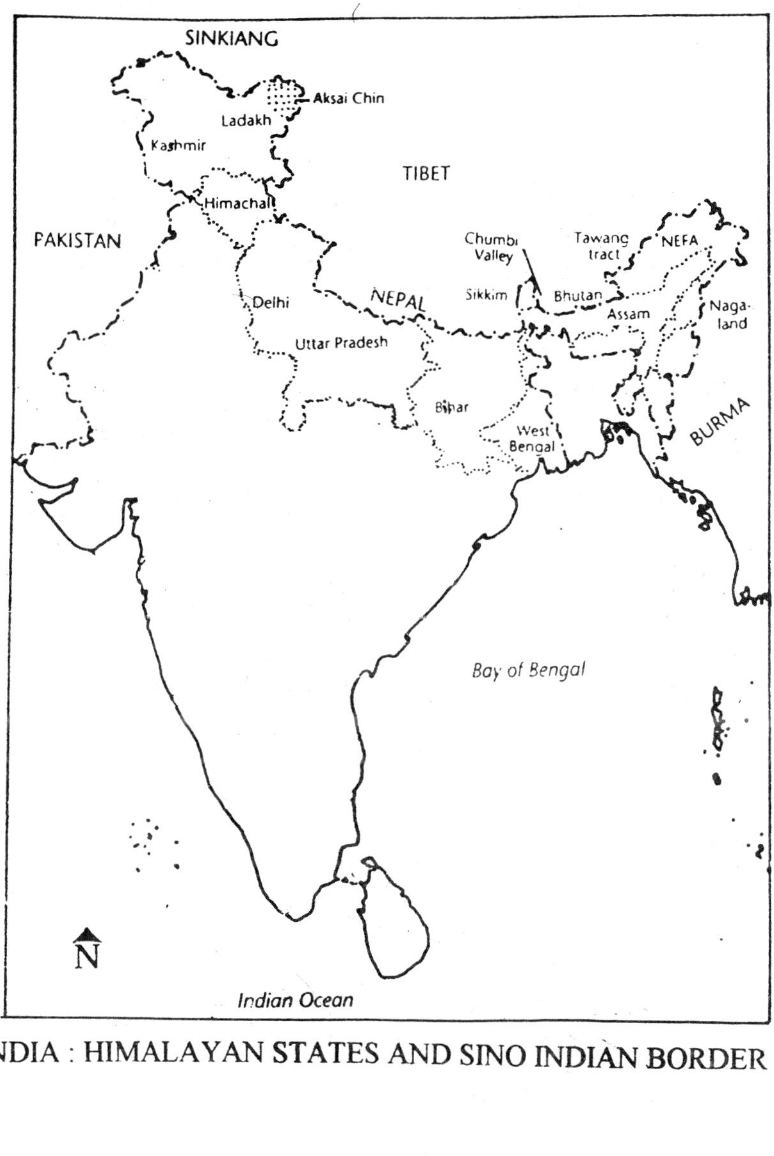

INDIA : HIMALAYAN STATES AND SINO INDIAN BORDER

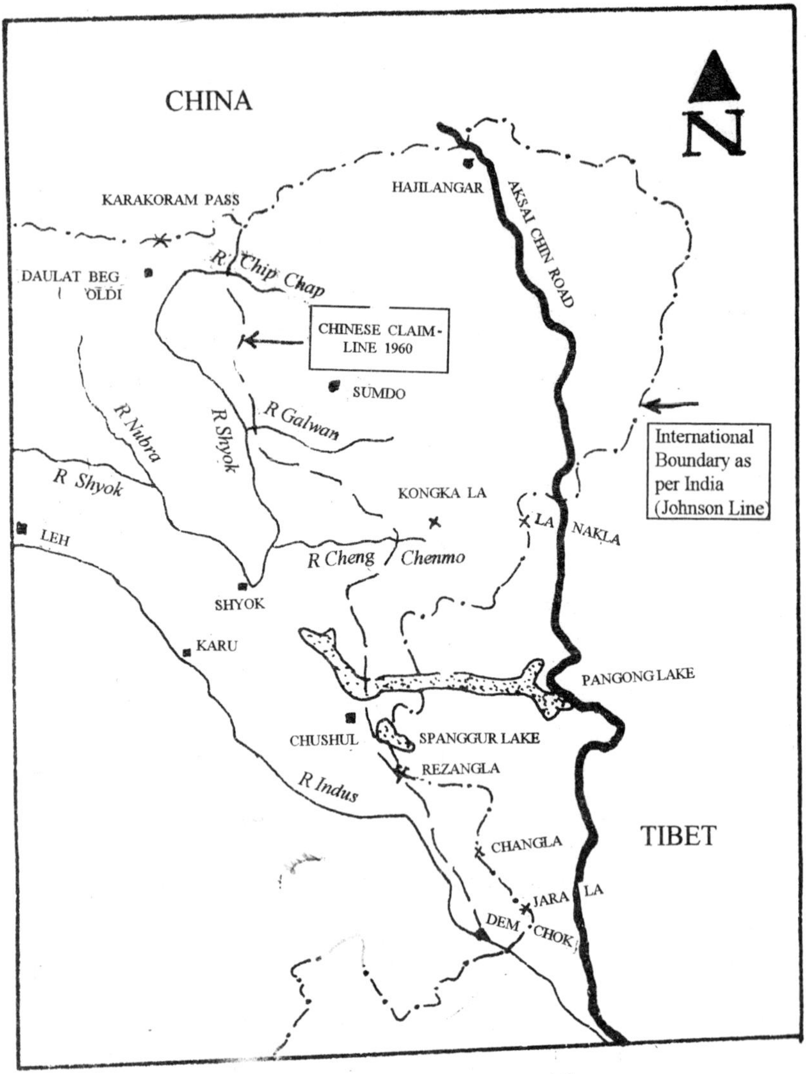

LADAKH DISPUTED AREAS

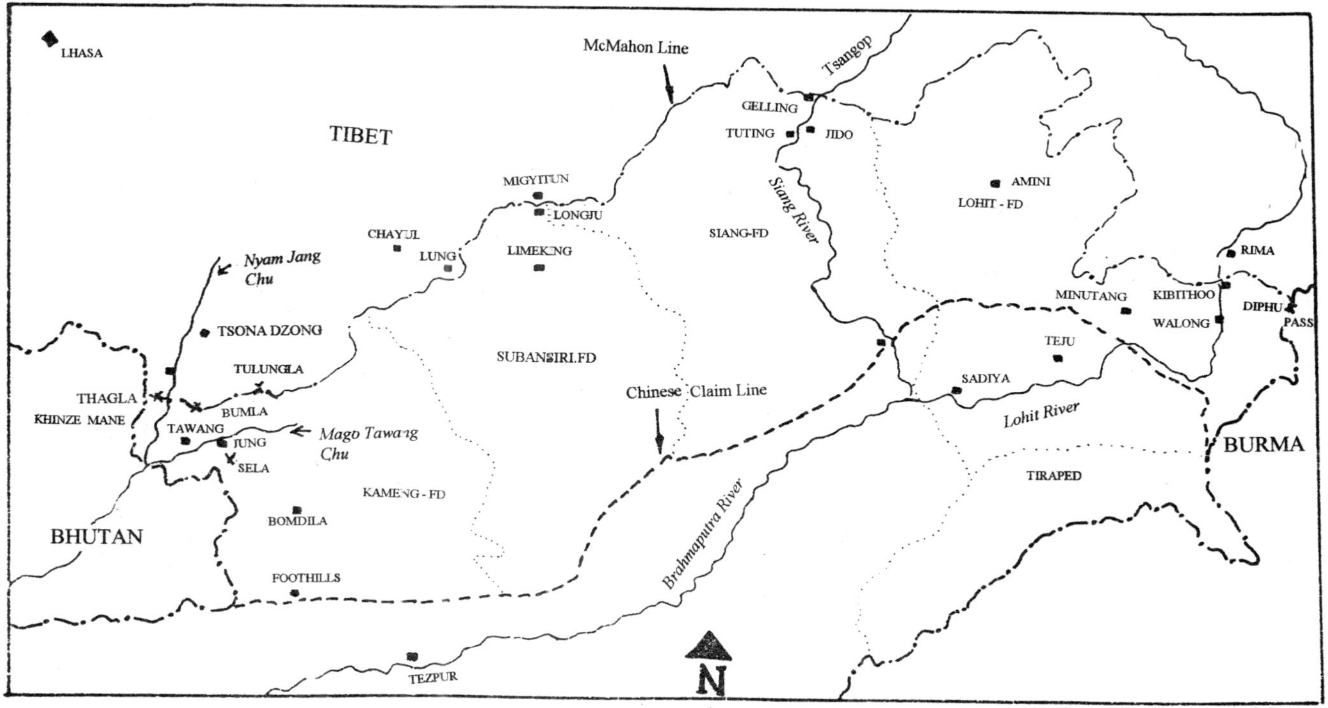

NEFA : SEPTEMBER 1962

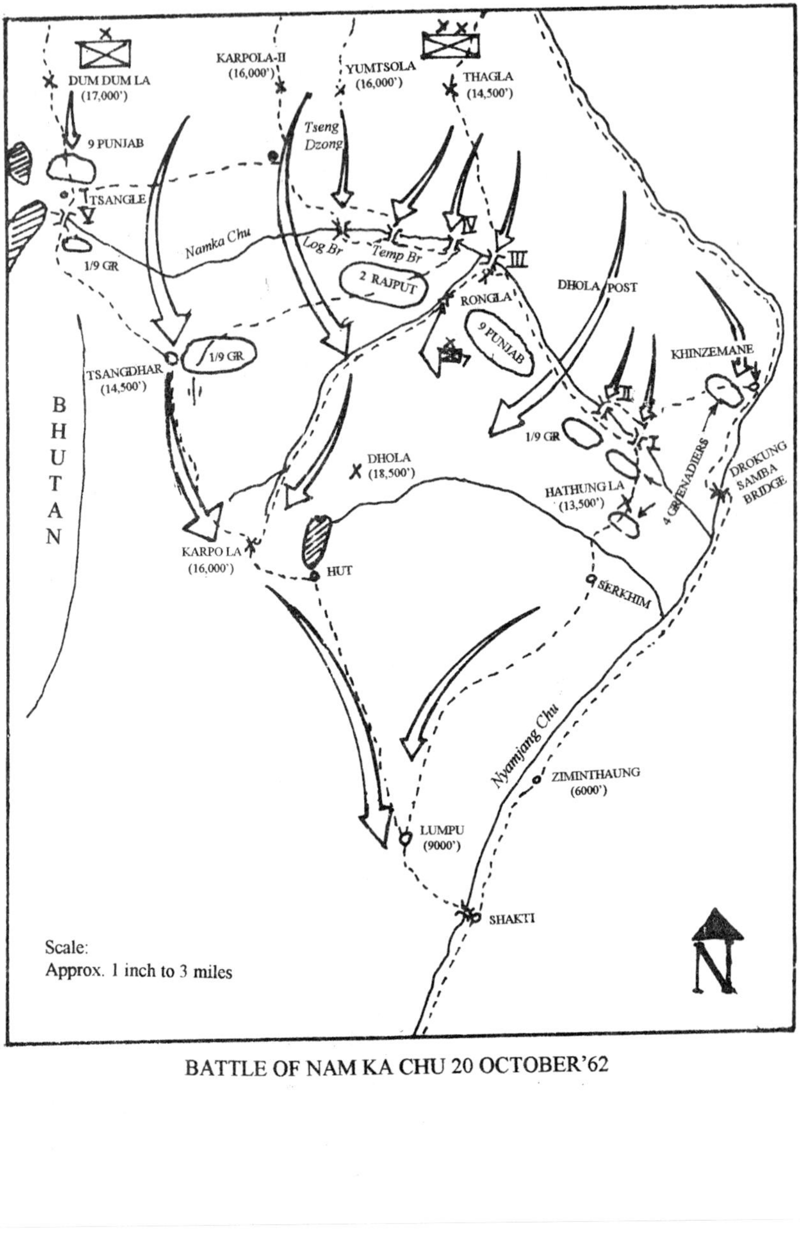

BATTLE OF NAM KA CHU 20 OCTOBER'62

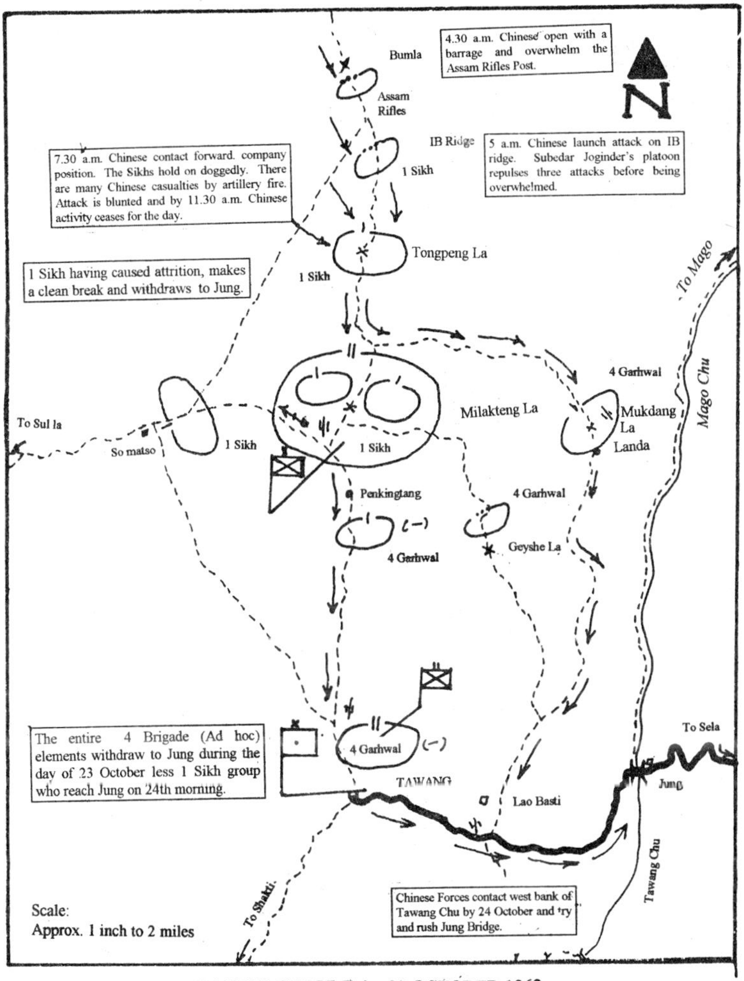

BATTLE OF BUMLA - 23 OCTOBER 1962.

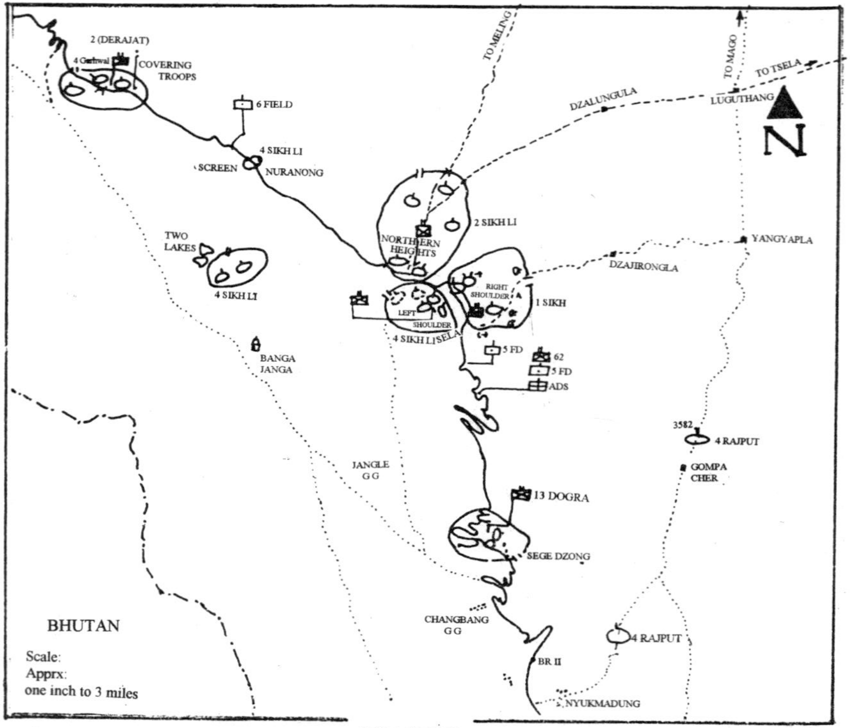

2 (DERAJAT)
4 Garhwal
COVERING TROOPS
6 FIELD
4 SIKH LI
SCREEN
NURANONG
TWO LAKES
4 SIKH LI
BANGA JANGA
TO MELING
DZALUNGULA
TO MAGO
TO TSELA
LUGUTHANG
N
2 SIKH LI
NORTHERN HEIGHTS
YANGYAPLA
DZAJIRONGLA
RIGHT SHOULDER
1 SIKH
LEFT SHOULDER
4 SIKH LI
SELA
5 FD
62
5 FD
ADS
3582
4 RAJPUT
GOMPA CHER
JANGLE GG
13 DOGRA
SEGE DZONG
BHUTAN
Scale:
Apprx:
one inch to 3 miles
CHANGBANG GG
4 RAJPUT
BR II
NYUKMADUNG

SELA SECTOR

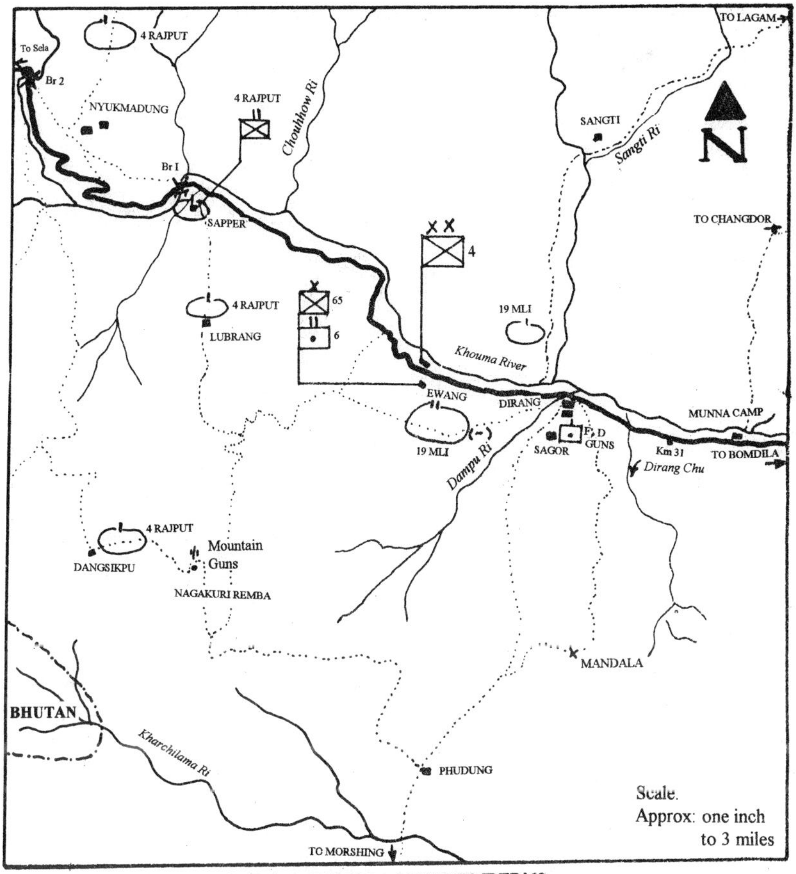

DIRANG SECTOR : 16 NOVEMBER'62

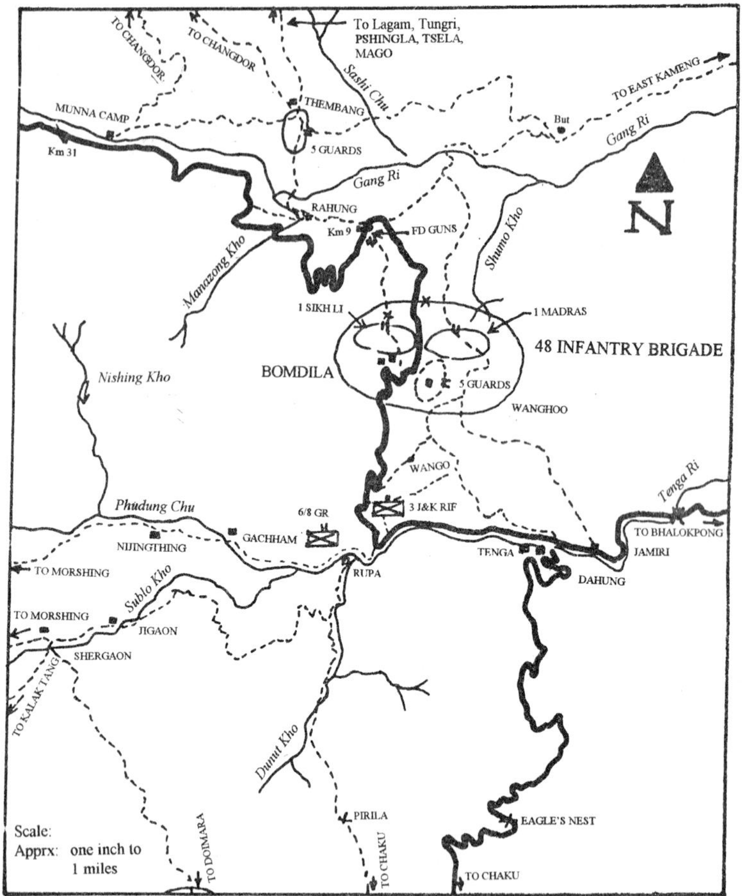

BOMDILA SECTOR : 16-19 NOVEMBER'62

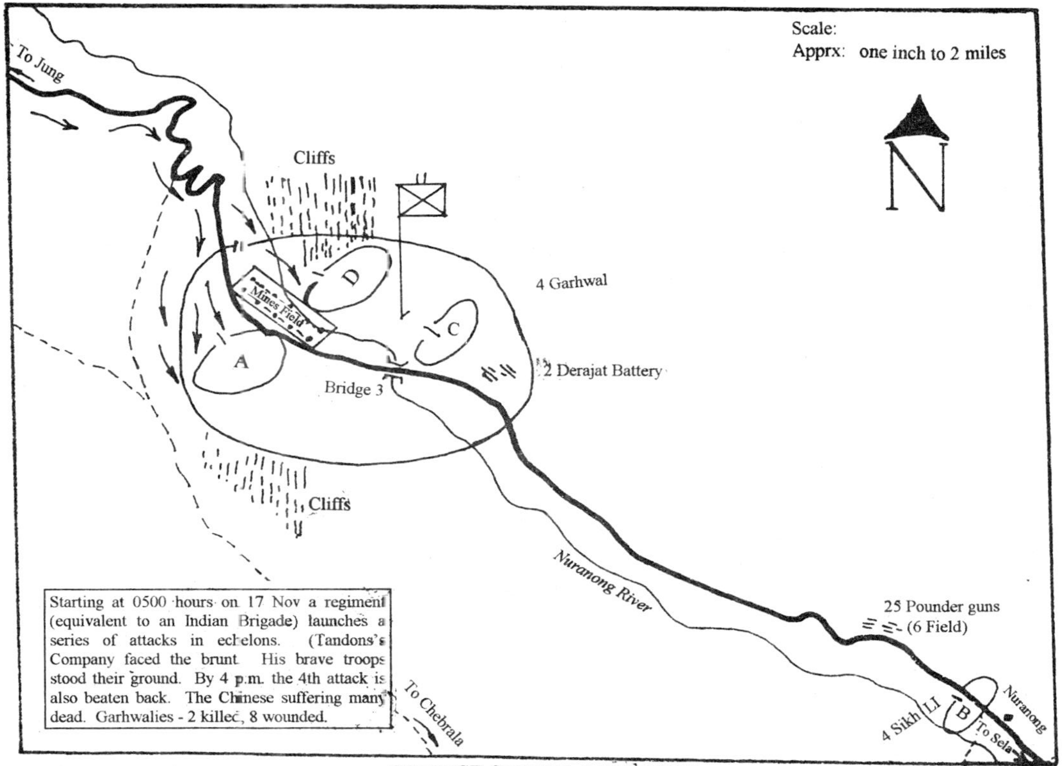

CHINESE SUFFER A REVERSE

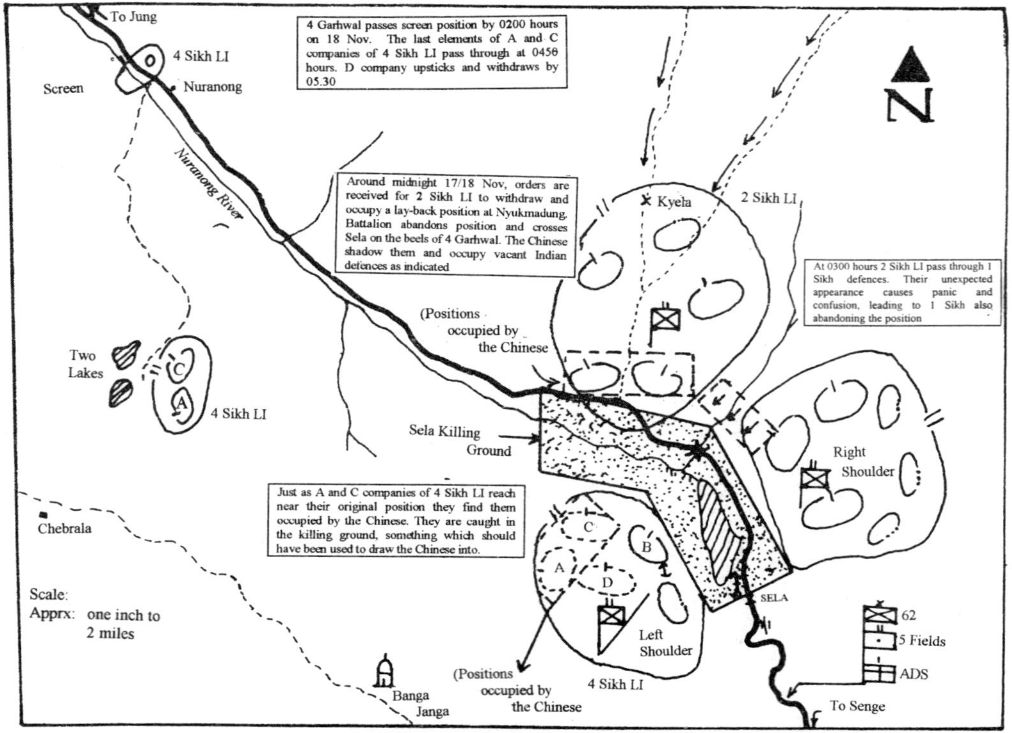

HOW THE WITHDRAWAL GOT PRECIPITATED
AT SELA - 17/18 NOV. 1962

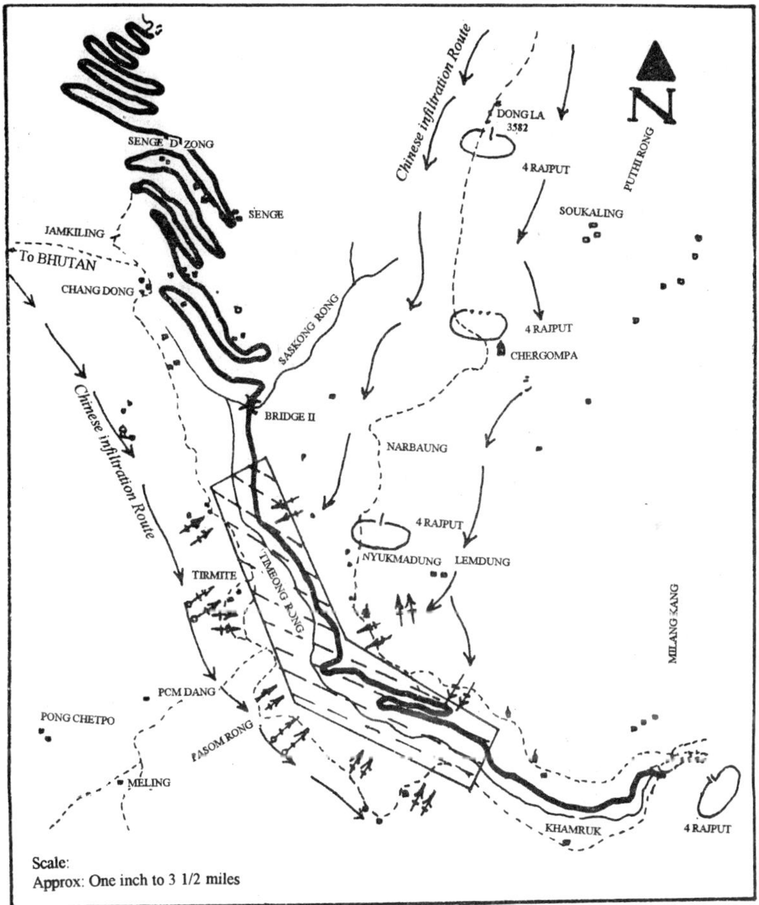

NYUKMADUNG AMBUSH - 18 NOVEMBER'62

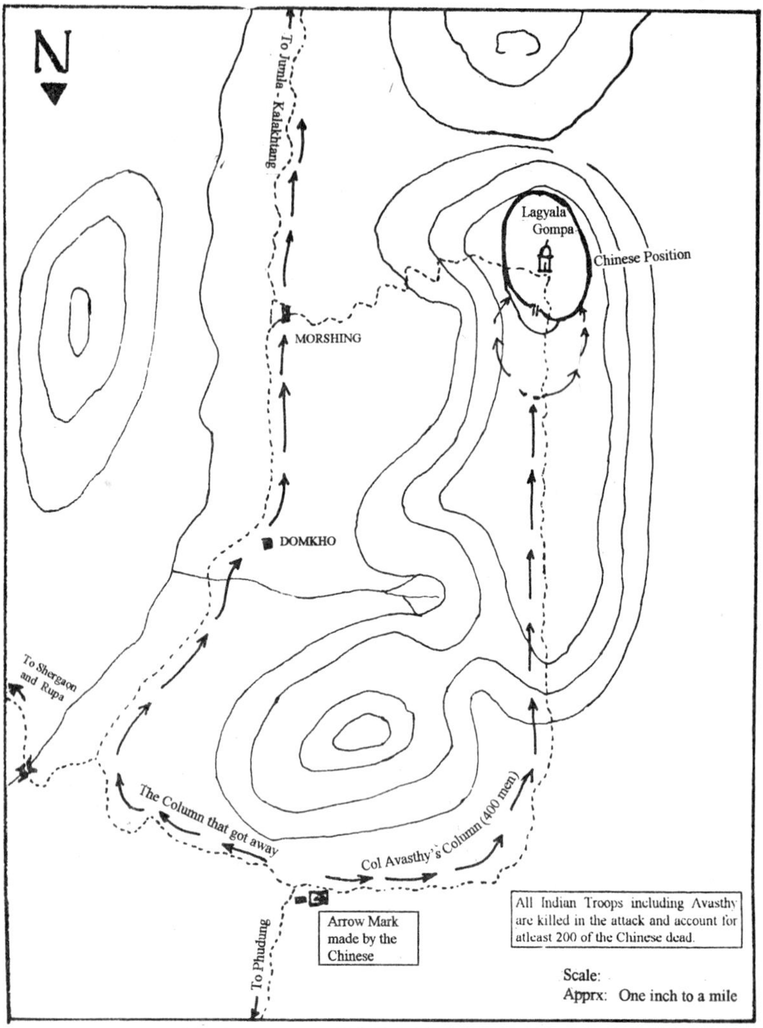

4 RAJPUT'S ACTION AT LAGIYALA GOMPA - 23 NOVEMBER 1962.

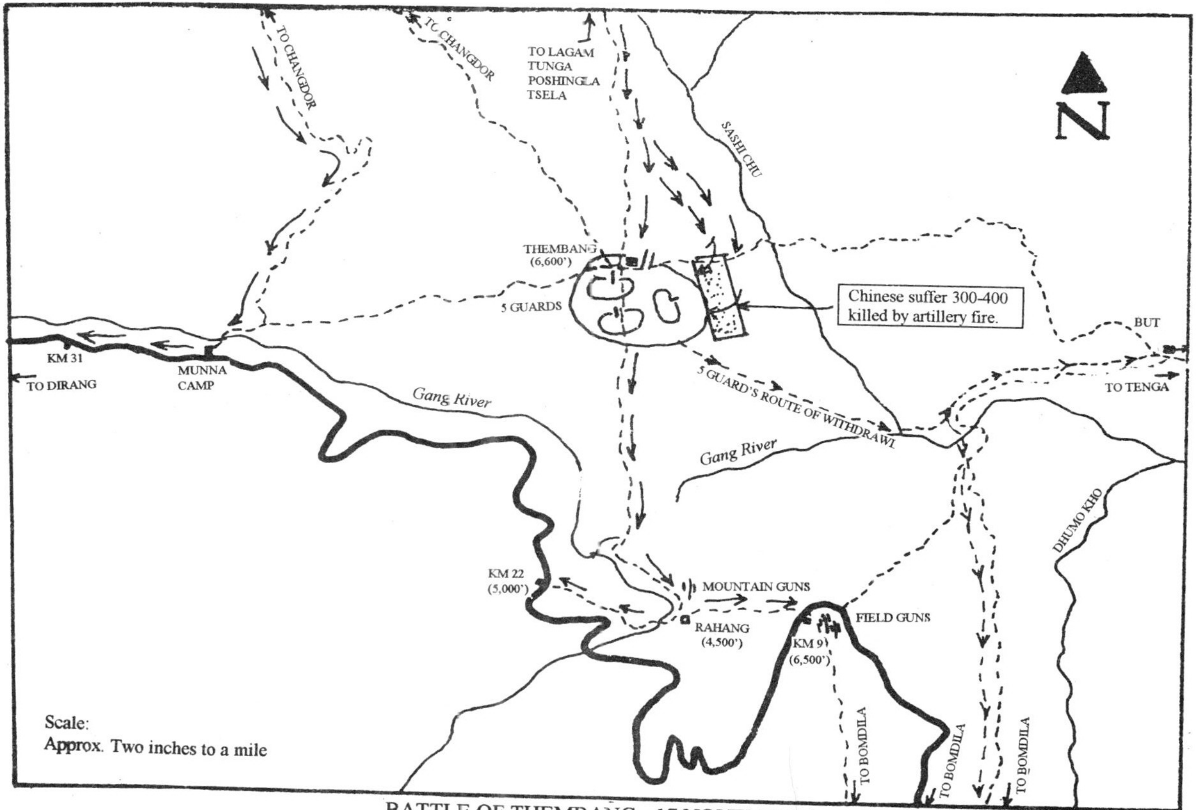

BATTLE OF THEMBANG - 17 NOVEMBER'62

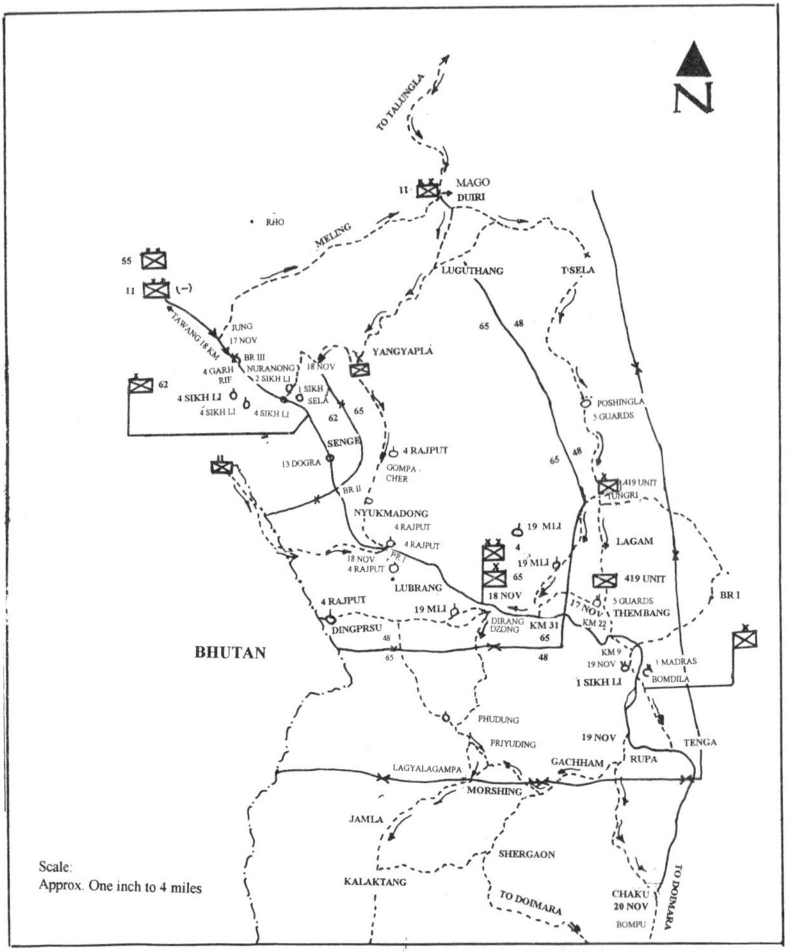

CHINESE OFFENSIVE SOUTH OF TAWANG CHU.
16 TO 20 NOVEMBER 1962.